Frances Cleaver

SECURING LAND RIGHTS IN AFRICA

Of Related Interest

DEVELOPMENT AND RIGHTS
Negotiating Justice in Changing Societies
edited by Christian Lund

ECONOMIC MOBILITY AND POVERTY DYNAMICS IN
DEVELOPING COUNTRIES
edited by Bob Baulch and John Hoddinott

LABOUR MOBILITY AND RURAL SOCIETY
edited by Arjan de Haan and Ben Rogaly

GLOBALISATION, COMPETITIVENESS AND HUMAN
SECURITY
edited by Cristóbal Kay

CORRUPTION AND DEVELOPMENT
edited by Mark Robinson

SECURING LAND
RIGHTS IN AFRICA

edited by
Tor A. Benjaminsen
and
Christian Lund

FRANK CASS
LONDON • PORTLAND, OR
in association with

EADI   European Association of Development Research
and Training Institutes, Bonn

First published in 2003 in Great Britain by
FRANK CASS
Crown House, 47 Chase Side
Southgate, London N14 5 BP

and in the United States of America by
FRANK CASS
c/o ISBS , 5824 N.E. Hassalo Street
Portland, Oregon, 97213-3644

Website: www.frankcass.com

British Library Cataloguing in Publication Data

Securing land rights in Africa. – (The European journal of
development research; v. 14/2)
1. Land tenure – Africa 2. Customary law – Africa 3. Land
titles – Registration and transfer – Africa
I. Benjaminsen, Tor A. II. Lund, Christian III. European
Association of Development Research and Training Institutes
333.3′096

ISBN 0 7146 5380 2 (cloth)
ISBN 0 7146 8315 9 (paper)

Library of Congress Cataloging-in-Publication Data

Securing land rights in Africa / edited by Tor A. Benjaminsen
and Christian Lund.
p. cm.
"[Published] in association with EADI, European Association
of Development Research and Training Institutes, Bonn."
Includes bibliographical references and index.
ISBN 0-7146-5380-2 (cloth) – ISBN 0-7146-8315-9 (pbk.)
1. Land tenure–Africa. 2. Natural resources–Africa–Management.
3. Right of property–Africa. I. Benjaminsen, Tor Arve. II. Lund,
Christian. III. European Association of Development Research
and Training Institutes.
HD966 .S43 2003
333′.0096–dc21   2002151969

This group of studies first appeared in a Special Issue on 'Securing Land Rights in
Africa' of *The European Journal of Development Research* (ISSN 0957-8811)
Vol.14/2 December 2002

Printed in Great Britain by MPG Books Ltd, Bodmin, Cornwall

Contents

Foreword

What kind of land tenure systems should African countries develop? Some observers argue that land titling is essential to free land from the web of social and cultural ties which bind its mobility and constrain its re-birth as an economic commodity. If Africa is to attract inward investment, it is argued, foreign companies must feel confident of securing firm rights over the land they need for establishing whatever enterprise they have in mind. It is as though a long queue of potential capitalists is waiting in the wings for the conductor to wave his baton, and launch the orchestra into a tune to which investors can happily dance, their bank notes showering like confetti.

This obsession held by many African and donor governments alike with bringing in capital and expertise from outside to transform their economic growth and employment prospects is, like most obsessions, constructed of misreadings and half-truths. They identify land as being too caught up in negotiation and dispute, and assume that it cannot possibly be put to productive use under such arrangements. Thus, a transparent, market-based system of land titles, using the very best in modern technology, is the obvious way forward. But, for good or ill, there is no gaggle of entrepreneurs waiting, poised to move centre-stage. African governments would do better to address the priorities of their own peoples, rather than hoping to tune their instruments to play for someone else's show.

These collected papers from across the African continent show why land titling generates more confusion than harmony. The dynamic and complex rules of the land tenure game, their continual change and re-invention are described here: flexible, contested, negotiable, bricolage, institutional shopping ... these are the terms that run through current debate on institutional change. Is this wordy self-indulgence among researchers rummaging in the bric-à-brac of a linguistic jumble sale, or are we gaining major new insights from this approach? On balance, I vote in favour of this verbal diversity and memorable metaphors, as celebration of new-found territory which brings together geographers and anthropologists, with the occasional economist and jurist who have strayed from the straight and narrow.

Many studies of institutional change walk a narrow line between, on the one hand, admitting to indeterminate and chaotic behaviour and, on the other, proposing some more systematic processes at work, albeit garnished with a good measure of 'ad-hockery'. Long gone are the days of unified theory, whether it be constrained economic optimisation, or analysis of competing interests locked in class struggle. We seem at times to be sailing out into the open seas of enquiry under cloudy heavens and having left the compass at home, on purpose. You begin to understand how people in the nineteenth century felt when the ground beneath their feet was shown through the geological record to be many millions of years old, rather than dating from 4,004 BC, as carefully calibrated from the biblical record.

We are living in a world where, it seems, nothing is certain, even the terms we use habitually. Here, we are told, customary law is no more than a colonial invention, as are tribal identities, both measures intended to maintain a tighter handle on the natives. The distinction between formal and informal is over-simplistic while the path-breaking work of Ostrom and others is criticised for its functionalist assumptions. Yet, for those interested in both the practice and policy of land issues in Africa, we have to find ways of describing situations and processes, options and consequences, in terms that can be communicated to and debated with a broad range of actors. Reasonableness needs to prevail over intellectual niceties, so that discourse can continue unhampered by too many qualifying footnotes.

Land has been, is and will remain hugely central to people's lives around the world. It provides a source of identity, income and employment, and constitutes an asset of cultural and spiritual significance as well as of increasing monetary value. Transactions in land and property are thus particularly fraught, laden down with baggage and uncertainties of many kinds. Having recently been involved in selling and buying a house in Britain, I know too well the trials of negotiation, contest and brinkmanship, and have felt the sinking feeling in the stomach pit when what looked to be a firm deal starts to fray at the edges, prior to the fabric of the agreement being rent apart through duplicity and greed. How much more so must rural people feel as they face the shifting sands of rapid political and institutional restructuring under way in much of Africa? How to hedge bets by playing parallel games and make friends with influential people, while watching your back for counter-claims on your own assets? The approach followed by the papers here helps illustrate for us the lives and choices faced by individuals as they juggle their assets and desires. Reliance on case studies of named individuals opens up a window on another's world and helps bring home their struggle in the face of machinations by kin, neighbours and bureaucrats.

Yet this focus on individuals makes it harder to draw broader lessons. Are we doomed to relativistic statements of 'well, it all depends'? Or can we discern nevertheless some general trends about land relations? Some boldness is needed to stick one's head over the parapet, and take the risk of sniping.

There is a consistent trend towards privatisation and individualisation of land rights, accompanied by increasing exclusion of weaker groups, as might be expected given the growing scarcity and value of land. Such privatisation receives succour from the broader global paradigm which vaunts the superiority of private, as opposed to collective, ownership. Formalisation of land rights is seen as necessary to support such a continuous shift, which implies a growing role for governments to exercise mastery over land rights management, whether at local or national level. This formalisation is not alien to many rural dwellers, who themselves see the benefit of tying down in more tangible form the detail of agreements made over land. Increasingly, this involves a shift from reliance on oral witness to signatures and stamps on pieces of paper. Such written contracts, while often drawn up outside the statutory system, have adopted the language, form and expression of the latter approach. Governments could usefully find means to recognise the validity of such paper-based transactions, so long as they conform to certain general principles.

So what kinds of tenure system for African countries? Policy and law need to be seen more as a means to accompany and legitimise evolving practice, rather than a series of tools designed to engineer a different kind of society. This would mean greater decentralisation of decision-making and effective local governance able to respond to local needs. Yet the power implications of this shift in approach are unlikely to gain it adherents among governments, except in rhetorical terms. As many a revolutionary has asserted, power is never willingly handed down from above, but must be seized from below. Reaffirmation of the strength, diversity and flexibility of local practice, as shown in this volume, provides one step in the argument for bringing about such a shift in power.

Camilla Toulmin,
IIED, October 2002

Abstracts

Reinventing Institutions: Bricolage and the Social Embeddedness of Natural Resource Management
FRANCES CLEAVER

This study challenges the oversimplified way in which abstract and bureaucratic 'design principles' derived from resource management literature are translated into development policy and practice, in pursuit of robust and enduring institutions. Drawing on research in the Usangu Basin, Tanzania, it explores the socially embedded nature of institutions for common property resource management and collective action. The concept of 'institutional bricolage' is outlined; a process by which people consciously and unconsciously draw on existing social and cultural arrangements to shape institutions in response to changing situations. Contrary to much theory, this study shows that institutions formed through bricolage are a dynamic mixture of the 'modern' and 'traditional', 'formal' and 'informal'.

Neither Tragedy Nor Enclosure: Are There Inherent Human Rights in Water Management in Zimbabwe's Communal Lands?
BILL DERMAN and ANNE HELLUM

Zimbabwe, like other Southern African countries, is undergoing legislative, political and administrative change in its water sector. This reform process is responding to international concerns of growing water scarcity and the needs for sustainable development. Among the national concerns are inequalities in water distribution, growing water needs for development and reductions in government spending for water management. In this analysis we examine the relationship between commercial and primary water use in the light of the interplay between international, national and local systems of water control and distribution. In Zimbabwean colonial and post-colonial water law, and in local customs and practices, there is the clear recognition that all Zimbabweans have free 'legal' access to water for primary uses. We argue that there is potential for building water reform on this concordance with the emerging principles of primary water as a human right.

The Interplay Between Formal and Informal Systems of Managing Resource Conflicts: Some Evidence from South-Western Tanzania
FAUSTIN P. MAGANGA

Measures to establish formal legal systems and to formalise informal arrangements have ignored the overlaps and interactions between formal and informal systems, and have increased tensions and conflicts between different resource users, as well as between government and villagers. Conflicts occur at different levels, with some of them embedded in marital and familial relations. The different levels and types of conflicts call for the coexistence of a variety of institutions to manage them. However, many villagers prefer to settle their conflicts through informal channels, although some may prefer the 'formal' channels whereby a favourable judgement is hoped for, with the principle of Court Assessors facilitating the interplay between formal and informal systems. Principles of conflict management are discussed, including systems of punishment, co-operation and conflict mitigation.

Scrambling for Land in Tanzania: Processes of Formalisation and Legitimisation of Land Rights
RIE ODGAARD

Access to land is usually not seen as a problem in Tanzania. However, based on empirical evidence from South-West Tanzania, this study shows that increasing competition for land and pastures gives rise to a new tendency of double safeguarding of land rights: formalisation of customary rights and legitimisation of 'modern' rights. Looking at land rights from the perspective of social relations and processes of negotiation, it is argued that all social groups are still actively involved in land negotiation processes, even if they are differently positioned and therefore have different types of land rights, depending on whether they are indigenous or guests/immigrants, men or women. However, the double safeguarding process implies more formalisation, individualisation and *de facto* privatisation and complicates negotiation processes. This results in a gradual exclusion of vulnerable groups such as the poor, pastoralists, due to their land use patterns, and women, due to gender inequalities.

When Farmers Use 'Pieces of Paper' to Record Their Land Transactions in Francophone Rural Africa: Insights into the Dynamics of Institutional Innovation
PHILIPPE LAVIGNE DELVILLE

In various parts of francophone Africa, farmers use 'pieces of paper' to record transactions such as the 'sale' (with all the inherent ambiguity of the term) of land or delegation of cultivation rights. The aim of these local institutional innovations is to certify that the transaction has taken place. The parties often try to get these contracts validated by a local government authority. Although the procedures may be incomplete and not legal, such 'informal formalisation' of transactions does help to reduce uncertainty and provide greater security within the complex web of tenure relations. New insights can now be gained into local dynamic processes and the role of the state in making tenure rights more secure.

Monetary Land Transactions in Western Burkina Faso: Commoditisation, Papers and Ambiguities
PAUL MATHIEU, MAHAMADOU ZONGO and LACINAN PARÉ

In western Burkina Faso, new land transactions based on money are on the rise, and the actors of these transactions try to make them visible through formal and informal means. The diversity of the practices of formalisation reflects the variety of resources and expectations actors have as far as securing rights is concerned. In an institutional context marked by uncertainty and a plurality of norms, the practices of formalisation play a key role in the strategies by which the actors try to make their claims and rights legitimate, visible, and more likely to be enforced and not challenged in the future. In order to bridge the gaps and ideological tensions between 'customary' and modern perceptions of land (as a commodity), the actors of the transactions combine discourses and practices which carry meanings and refer both to the images of custom and to the logic of commercial exchange.

Race for the Prize: Land Transactions and Rent Appropriation in the Malian Cotton Zone
TOR A. BENJAMINSEN and ESPEN SJAASTAD

Since the late 1950s, southern Mali has experienced a rapid rise in cotton production and exports. More recently, cultivation of grains has also increased, and the cotton zone is now a net exporter of grains to other parts of Mali as well as neighbouring countries. Considerable population growth has also attended this boom in the agricultural sector, and urban centres in the cotton zone are now undergoing rapid expansion. This has in turn led to vast and rapid increases in the value of land surrounding these centres. Although this land is attractive as agricultural investment objects, the main rent formation is due to the values realisable through development of residential plots. This analysis describes how customary land on the periphery of two of the major towns in the cotton zone has become part of a race, where the winners, rather than those ending up with legal possession, are those that have managed to extract the maximum portion of the land's rent. Through a study of roughly 40 land transactions in the area, as well as interviews with key actors, it is shown how regional and urban commune officials are able to use the tools of expropriation and title registration to secure almost the entire rent for themselves and their employers. Customary holders, on the other hand, who are often forced to sell their land despite traditional prohibitions, are generally left worse off than if urban expansion and the associated rent formation had not occurred. Fundamental changes in both the expropriation and titling processes are required to remedy the situation.

Custom, Contracts and Cadastres *in North-West Rwanda*
CATHERINE ANDRÉ

The study is based on two surveys of land transactions in north-west Rwanda carried out in 1988 and 1993. This is a densely populated region, located near commercial and administrative centres. Here, the land 'market' is very active and land purchases and sales multiplied from the 1950s to 1993. Land appropriation and management is conducted according to 'custom', which is evolving under pressure from individualistic and exclusive tensions as well as that from the market. While a statutory order prohibits the sale and purchase of land, this regulation is not respected in rural areas. This has occasioned the emergence of written contracts and local *cadastres* as endogenous practices which are not supervised or controlled by the state. Most of the sellers were forced to sell for economic reasons. This has led to an increase in the proportion of landless and a concentration of land in fewer hands.

Formalisation and Informalisation of Land and Water Rights in Africa: An Introduction

TOR A. BEJAMINSEN and CHRISTIAN LUND

People's efforts to secure land and water rights in Africa follow many different paths, and the literature on African land tenure documents varied and shifting strategies. The centrality of land, water and other natural resources in peoples' livelihoods has also meant that such resources have enjoyed the keen attention of the state – whether colonial or independent, central or local. Rights to land and other natural resources not only determine control over economic sources of livelihood but, for states and governments, have also meant political control over African populations [*Berry, 1993; Chanock, 1985; Mamdani, 1996; Merry, 1986; Moore, 1986*]. Moreover, in many African communities, land is charged with historical and contextual signifiers, and the symbols by which people and government deal with land are ripe with meaning and values. Therefore, whenever people or institutions deal with land issues many agendas are affected at the same time, resulting in social and political friction and negotiation [*Benjaminsen and Lund, 2001; Juul and Lund, 2002*]. Access to land still remains a central preoccupation in most African societies, and while issues such as 'globalisation' and 'hegemonic discourses' demand much scholarly attention, this should not steer us away from the mundane everyday politics of institutionalisation of rights and exclusion. On the contrary, it becomes all the more important to investigate empirically how local-level competition, conflict and power reshape social institutions and move with a distinct dynamic that does not necessarily fit dominant discourses [*Adger et al., 2001*].

Tor A. Benjaminsen (t.a.benjaminsen@noragric.nlh.no) is a senior researcher at Noragric at the Agricultural University of Norway. Christian Lund (clu@cdr.dk) is an associate professor at International Development Studies, Roskilde University and currently guest researcher at the Centre for Development Research, Copenhagen. Most of the studies in this collection were presented as papers at a seminar organised by the 'Custom and Conflict in Land and Water Management in Africa' network on 6–7 September 2001, directed by Rie Odgaard from the Centre for Development Research in Copenhagen (rie@cdr.dk), and generously funded by the Danish Council for Social Science Research. The editors wish to thank the anonymous referees of all the contributions for collegial and vital assistance.

Legal pluralism is a concept that is central to ongoing tenure debates in Africa. This is a perspective on the legal order, which stems from late nineteenth and early twentieth-century research on tribal peoples in colonised societies. Here, the central question was how the social order was to be maintained in the absence of European law. Studies uncovered a host of complex indigenous forms of social control and procedures for mediation and adjudication. Early writings on this referred to a distinction between law and custom, law being the metropolitan written rules, while custom referred to the mostly unwritten pre-colonial rules. The dichotomous perception of law and custom ascribed civilising qualities and state power to law; and persistence, tradition and unequivocal popular recognition to custom [*Merry, 1988: 875–9*]. However, customary law did not consist of indigenous rules *per se* but was a product of colonisation, whereby the colonial power accepted certain versions of the recorded indigenous traditions as customary law pertaining to native matters [*Berry, 1993; Bruce, 1986: 14–17; Chanock, 1985; Moore, 1986; Ranger, 1983; Le Roy et al., 1995: 109*]. Indigenous rules were rationalised into customary law to fit the format of metropolitan state law. Hence, while the colonial administration inculcated the dichotomy of modern versus customary, the coexistence of a written formal general law, state-sanctioned selected customary law, and local indigenous rules often prevailed and mutually influenced each other.

In this volume, Frances Cleaver points out that the distinction between formal and informal may be seen as a false dichotomy. She suggests that 'local resource use practices and management arrangements are likely to be a complex blend of formal and informal, traditional and modern'. Rejecting the simplistic classification of institutions as either 'formal' or 'informal', 'modern' or 'traditional'/'customary', Cleaver instead proposes using the terms 'bureaucratic' and 'socially embedded'. Indeed, when suggesting it is rewarding to investigate formalisation and informalisation, it is less as absolutes than as competing social, economic and political processes with institutional ramifications. As for institutionalisation, in the introduction to her seminal book, *Law as Process*, Moore simply states, '[t]he making of rules and social and symbolic order is a human industry matched only by the manipulation, circumvention, remaking, replacing, and unmaking of rules and symbols in which people seem almost equally engaged' [*Moore, 1978: 1*]. Hence what we are witnessing is competing forms of institutionalisation: one backed by state law and the bureaucracy, encoded in official language and often exercised with the props of modern statehood; the other the institutionalisation of informal practices more or less grounded in ideas and values embedded in institutions seen as distinct from the colonial and post-colonial state. The competition often unfolds as one form of practice undercuts the other and offers ways of circumventing and replacing the other. The challenge is to identify these countervailing processes empirically.

As most of the essays in this collection show, such empirical investigations indicate that while reality obviously does not fall into neat dichotomies but is a blend of coexisting mutually influencing forms of power, discourse and rationality, people and institutions occasionally manoeuvre as if the world could be divided into compartments. Often the state will attempt formalisation, but there is, in fact, no neat dichotomy of formal/state on the one hand, and informal/non-state on the other. Reality is messier.

First, in most societies the state is a multi-institutional conglomeration rife with competition that may undo formalisation. Thus, while formalisation is often propelled by states, governments and reform, formal rules and regulations are also negotiated and undone by corruption, political networks and powerful alliances with, and indeed within, the state. Such informalisation tends to undermine and dissolve formal rights and serve the interests of those with privileged access to political power and strategic information. Second, formalisation processes are not the state's exclusive preserve; people may in fact create new practices and institutions to take care of what the state could or should have done. They may use the language of the state as well as its props in terms of contracts, deeds, attestations, etc. The irony of such informal formalisation [*Mathieu, 2001*] is that distinctions at one and the same time get increasingly blurred (who is exercising state authority?) and become increasingly important (who can produce formal proof of rights?). The central theme in the following analyses is how various processes of formalisation and informalisation of tenure rights interact and produce land tenure systems which are neither regulated by predictable rules and structures nor characterised by sheer anarchy.

FORMALISATION AND INFORMALISATION

States are drawn typically towards standardisation and one-size-fits-all solutions. In the area of land use and access to land and natural resources, states attempt to standardise and formalise local tenure systems and to make them 'legible' [*Scott, 1998*]. This is not only a modern or colonial phenomenon. In pre-colonial Africa, governments also tried to impose one mind-set on people and to organise societies according to their aspirations. A well-known example is the Macina Caliphate in Mali, which established a state based on *shari'a* in the mid-nineteenth century. The Caliphate gained political and administrative control both at central and local levels. It controlled the courts and the legal system and introduced the Dina Code in the inland delta of the Niger River to regulate access to the rich dry season pastures [*Vedeld, 2001*]. Today, the Dina Code is labelled 'customary', and is contrasted with Roman law introduced through the French colonial system.

The colonial state, whether British, French, Portuguese, Belgian or German, introduced legislation at an early stage to regulate the use of and access to forests, pastures, wildlife and water in Africa. It ranged from expropriation and eviction of local people through various forms of nationalisation and exclusion, systems of permits and concessions, and the introduction of taxes, to the delegation of control to local chiefs and other authorities who acted as custodians of the amorphous entity known as the 'natives' [*Berry, 1993; Bruce, 1986; Chanock, 1985; Mamdani, 1996; Mann and Roberts, 1991; McAusland, 2000; Merry, 1986; Moore, 1986*]. In practical terms, a tremendous variation continued to characterise the various tenure systems, partly because the states' capacity to enforce their various laws had often been modest to say the least. It would seem that a common feature of African land tenure is the accidental and somewhat capricious local outcomes of state interventions whenever the state, in an uneven and haphazard way and with varying degrees of permanence, had asserted its power to rule.

Today, formalisation of land and water rights in Africa continues under various labels: decentralisation, *gestion de terroir*, community-based natural resources management, user pays principle, land or water reform, tenure reform and privatisation. Not all attempts at formalisation will lead necessarily to standardised packages lacking flexibility. In South Africa, the Draft Land Rights Bill, which was shelved by a new minister coming into office in mid-1999, was an ambitious and innovative attempt at allowing people to choose the tenure system that would be appropriate to their circumstances [*Claassens, 2000, Cousins, 2002*]. The proposed Bill was open both to vesting titles in individuals and groups. However, when the Bill was ready to be presented to parliament, it was decided by the government that the content was too controversial and politically sensitive [*Turner and Ibsen, 2000*]; it was also said to be too complex and expensive to implement.

The first contribution in this volume, dealing with processes of formalisation and informalisation, is by Frances Cleaver. She explores the socially embedded nature of institutions for natural resources management in the Usangu basin in Tanzania. This case study is used as a stepping-stone to challenge the idea that better institutions can be 'crafted' by resource users and policy-makers. Cleaver emphasises that such formalisation processes tend to bestow privileges to just a single aspect of people's identities. Hence, complex social and livelihood identities and multiple motivations are neglected. In large parts of Africa, there are people who farm, keep livestock, take on paid labour, and sell fruits, vegetables and handicrafts. They may be Muslims or Christians, but they may also identify with a local culture implying other moral pressures. People therefore have multiple identities which change over time. By overlooking this dynamic character of rural life and people's identities, formalisation processes may fuel rather than dampen conflicts through an emphasis of differences.

In contrast to institutional theory and its proposed crafting of single-purpose institutions, Cleaver proposes a concept of institutional bricolage. This implies that people may assemble and adapt norms, values and arrangements from various backgrounds and identities to suit a new purpose. Many institutions formed by the processes of bricolage are multi-purpose, and they may not therefore be labelled 'formal' or 'informal', as this distinction becomes blurred in the processes of borrowing and adaptation. Cleaver suggests rather that an understanding of the processes of bricolage may enable development efforts to recognise and build on such institutions and eventually help to deflate conflicts and improve the management of natural resources.

Bill Derman and Anne Hellum analyse an ongoing attempt at formalising water use and management in Zimbabwe through a new water reform. Internationally, there is a general push towards making rural water use more productive and efficient, which involves looking at water as an economic good including the introduction of the 'user pays principle'. However, as the authors demonstrate, the attempts at formalising this principle are undercut by local practices of sharing water freely. Changes meet resistance in the form of social values and local systems of control. The principle of no-cost access to water was, moreover, once bolstered by bureaucratic sanction, and it would seem particularly difficult to change peoples' behaviour through formalisation of certain new principles if it is to replace law as well as practices that enjoy some concordance.

Faustin Maganga's contribution is also based on fieldwork in Usangu in Tanzania. It describes how the introduction of new formal institutions altered litigation strategies. The new formal court system relies on an adversarial principle in contrast to a reconciliatory principle of the informal institutions. This situation has, contrary to the declared intentions of the legislators, led to uncertainty among many small-scale producers and opened up avenues for land-grabbing for the wealthy who may thrive in a 'winner-takes-all' system. The question remains whether poorer people will also seek the formal settings or whether two segregated institutional arenas will eventually emerge.

Rie Odgaard also investigates tenure systems in Tanzania. Her article describes how formalisation and informalisation need not necessarily clash. People attempt to institutionalise their land rights through formalisation of customary rights while at the same time attempting to legitimate formal or 'modern' rights according to custom. On the one hand, people with customary rights to land attempt to have such rights recorded by the village administration and the like. On the other hand, people who have been granted land administratively by the state but are strangers to the area attempt to solidify their claims by performing various customary rites like burials in the area. The official German colonial policy of interment of the dead provided the opportunity of establishing physical markers of property on the landscape in the form of graves. However, in recent years, ever more elaborate graves appeared on the landscape as new, originally administratively provoked, customary signifiers of property. Hence, formal and informal practices intertwine, but to the exclusion of those – mainly pastoralists and women – for whom this particular custom as well as administrative allocation of land are beyond reach.

INFORMAL FORMALISATION

In most African countries, the only possible formal landowners are still the state and individuals with title deeds. However, to obtain a title is a cumbersome and costly process, beyond the reach of most rural poor. This has in many places with emerging land scarcity opened up a process of what one might call informal formalisation. Thus the informal recording of property transactions on paper, or other formalised ways of registration and transaction, seem to develop in parallel to the states' generally less than successful efforts at formally recording the land tenure situation [*Mathieu, 2001*]. Such informal practices are produced and invented through local institutional innovation using whatever means are available. They are composite practices combining, with more or less ambiguity, operations issuing from the repertoire of contract, documents and market exchange with operations stemming from customs and interpersonal relationships as they are dynamically lived in local society.

In his contribution, Philippe Lavigne-Delville draws on cases studied in various countries in francophone Africa (Ivory Coast, Burkina Faso, Benin, Rwanda and the Comoros) to discuss how farmers use various forms of signed documents to record land transactions. These written documents are found mainly in cases of definitive transactions involving the transfer of money. Only when sales are unusual and illegitimate are they accompanied by written contracts. These documents, which are attempts to formalise informal transactions, are diverse and vary from region to region. However, Lavigne-Delville has identified three common features:

• Contracts are incomplete and vague when it comes to the content of a transaction itself. A higher degree of precision may be perceived as unnecessary in some local contexts when people know each other, while in other cases a certain ambiguity may be in the interest of one of the parties.
• Witnesses generally sign contracts to strengthen transactions. In addition, an official validation of a transaction is sought by approaching an authority which could be customary or religious but is usually the locally-based administrative one, which is requested to sign and stamp documents.
• Registers are often kept locally by lineage chiefs or other leaders to keep track of land tenure changes in the area. These records may then be used in

the event of a dispute; on the other hand, such registers are often missing within local government offices.

In the following contribution, Paul Mathieu, Mahamadou Zongo and Lacinan Paré analyse new types of land transactions in the cotton zone of western Burkina Faso. These are new practices involving the transfer of money through selling or renting land – a process associated with emerging land scarcity, again leading to an increasing level of tension and tenure conflicts. The authors have identified five different ways people attempt to formalise land transactions in the study area. These are, with an increasing degree of formalisation:

- an exaggeration of the customary relationship between grantor and receiver of rights through gifts, sacrifices, and public displays of gratitude, etc. This can be interpreted as a way of concealing a transaction that goes against tradition;
- land investments, which are public displays of ownership, often used to validate a transaction. If the former owner does not question these investments, it implies a public acceptance that the new holder is the rightful owner;
- handwritten documents testifying the transactions are used in many cases. These documents are deliberately left incomplete and they usually avoid mentioning terms such as 'sell', 'buy' or 'allocate';
- in some cases, typewritten documents which are used; the format of these documents replicates an administrative style with the local police or administration being asked to sign and stamp them;
- ambitious documents aimed at formalising an informal transaction in what the authors call a record of palaver (*procès-verbal de palabre*). The seller, buyer, the customary authority and the local administration must all sign this document, which is required in order to continue the process towards obtaining a legal title.

The empirical setting of the following study, authored by Tor A. Benjaminsen and Espen Sjaastad, is just across the border from western Burkina Faso in the cotton zone in Mali. These two regions are similar in many respects, but with a national legal framework that differs to a certain extent. Both regions are economically relatively dynamic with agricultural development driven by a cash-crop cotton sector, leading to an influx of people and increasing pressure on agricultural land. Benjaminsen and Sjaastad describe how agricultural land around the two main towns in the Malian cotton zone is being converted rapidly from what is perceived as inalienable customary tenure to private property. The authors call this ongoing competition for land rent a 'race', because of its speed. The actors involved compete both against time and each other. Farmers must sell their land before it is swallowed by town expansion through expropriation, which implies minimal compensation, while urban buyers must obtain titles before being expropriated; the state and the commune must expropriate before titles are obtained, and speculators must buy rapidly and obtain titles before land is expropriated. The prize in this race is not so much the land itself as its value, and the winner is not necessarily the one who acquires the title to the land but, instead, the individual who has managed to appropriate the land rent. The findings in this analysis support an adage: it is mostly the wealthy, the powerful and the informed who manage to appropriate the lion's share of the cake that rent formation represents.

Catherine André's study is based on two surveys of land transactions carried out in 1988 and 1993 in north-west Rwanda. Both surveys were undertaken of the same hill in a densely populated region situated close to commercial and administrative centres and with high population growth. Land is scarce in the area, and this situation has led to the development of an active land market. Contracts from land sales consulted in the two surveys also show that the frequency of sales increased from the 1950s to 1993. In the 1950s, money gradually replaced livestock in land transactions, and from the 1960s money was the means of payment in all the transactions recorded in the surveys. Even though this process may have led to increased tenure security for disadvantaged groups such as tenants and women (at least for those able to afford to purchase land), it also caused increased inequality. Of the total number of sales, 67 per cent were distress sales. This led to an increase in the proportion of the landless and a concentration of land in fewer hands.

CONCLUDING REMARKS

Formalisation lends itself easily to an evolutionary perspective. Indeed, the widespread concern with written documents, recording and registration of rights has an element of irreversibility to it. Moreover, most governments and donor agencies, their reforms and policies and a good number of theories on property either work to that end, or envisage an 'in-the-long-run-inevitable-development' [*Platteau, 1996*]. It is difficult to confirm or dismiss evolutionary perspectives outright; it very much depends on the time frame and institutional opportunities. None the less, the present crop of essays demonstrates that various developments occur at different paces. However, there is little indication of a linear development towards general state-sanctioned and guaranteed private property [*Benjaminsen and Lund, 2001*].

Increasing pressure on land through the combined effect of population growth and increasing commercialisation of land-based activities causes land values to rise. As expressed in the Evolutionary Theory of Land Rights [*Platteau, 1996*], this process leads to individualisation of land tenure, which also implies more independence enjoyed by farmers regarding land management, including the possibility of transferring the land to other individuals. Customary constraints on the sales of so-called 'inalienable' land are gradually relaxed as land scarcity increases. The first land transactions would emerge and be supported by written documents to provide some sort of security for the buyer [*Platteau, 2000*].

So far, the four contributions on informal formalisation in this volume conform to this evolutionary perspective. However, when it comes to the tail-end of the theory – the titling process – reality is more complex and varied than envisaged. According to the theory, in the crucial and enabling stage of this endogenous individualisation process, the state will intervene and legally sanction the new tenure situation. However, the state's formal land titling process tends to be too bureaucratic and costly and, hence, beyond the means of most small-scale farmers. Instead, formalisation does indeed take place, not necessarily by the direct intervention of the state, but rather in terms of its expression. The state's forms of expression, such as language and format, appear increasingly important, but these are not necessarily accompanied by the state's mastery of its domain. It would seem that since formal titling is out of reach of most farmers, the second best option is informal formalisation, which provides some measure of certainty and security. Whether this will eventually lead to formal registration is, on the other hand, uncertain. Idioms of tradition are equally significant in the justification of rights to resources. Those who master current and characteristic modes of expression, who know when to observe tradition and institutionalise rights in informal settings and when to substantiate them through the formal institutions of the state, thrive in these conditions. Exclusion is the result, it appears, in many cases, but even here, making predictions may be hazardous in light of the perseverance of local politics and the logic of inclusion.

REFERENCES

Adger, Neil, Benjaminsen, Tor A., Brown, Katrina and Hanne Svarstad, 2001, 'Advancing a Political Ecology of Global Environmental Discourses', *Development and Change*, Vol.32, No.4, pp. 681–715.
Basset, T.J. and D.E. Crummey (eds.), 1993, *Land in African Agrarian Systems*, Madison, WI: University of Wisconsin Press.
Benjaminsen, Tor A. and Christian Lund (eds.), 2001, *Politics, Property and Production in the West African Sahel: Understanding Natural Resources Management*, Uppsala: Nordic Africa Institute.
Berry, Sara, 1993, *No Condition is Permanent – The Social Dynamics of Agrarian Change in Sub-Saharan Africa*, Madison, WI: University of Wisconsin Press.
Bruce, John W., 1986, *Land Tenure Issues in Project Design and Strategies for Agricultural Development in Sub-Saharan Africa*, Madison, WI: Land Tenure Centre.

Chanock, Martin, 1985, *Law, Custom and Social Order: The Colonial Experience in Malawi and Zambia*, Cambridge: Cambridge University Press.

Chanock, Martin, 1991a, 'A Peculiar Sharpness: An Essay on Property in the History of Customary Law in Colonial Africa', *Journal of African History*, Vol.32, No.1, pp.65–88.

Chanock, Martin, 1991b, 'Paradigms, Policies and Property: A Review of the Customary Law of Land Tenure', in K. Mann and R. Roberts (eds.), *Law in Colonial Africa*, Portsmouth, NH/ London: Heinemann/James Currey, pp.61–84.

Claassens, Aninka, 2000, 'South African Proposals for Tenure Reform: The Draft Land Rights Bill', in Toulmin and Quan [*2000: 247–66*].

Comaroff, John L. and Simon Roberts, 1981, *Rules and Processes – The Cultural Logic of Dispute in an African Context*, Chicago, IL: University of Chicago Press.

Cousins, Ben, 2002, 'Legislating Negotiability: Tenure Reform in Post-Apartheid South Africa', in Juul and Lund [*2002*].

Hansen, Thomas B. and Finn Stepputat (eds.), 2001, *States of Imagination: Ethnographic Explorations of the Postcolonial State*, Durham, NC: Duke University Press.

Juul, Kristine and Christian Lund (eds.), 2002, *Negotiating Property in Africa*, Portsmouth, NH: Heinemann.

Lavigne Delville, Philippe (ed.), 1998, *Quelles politiques foncières pour l'Afrique rurale? Réconcilier pratiques, légitimité et légalité*, Paris: Karthala/Coopération Française.

Le Roy, Étienne, Karsenty, Alain and Alain Bertrand, 1995, *La sécurisation foncière en Afrique. Pour une gestion viable des ressources renouvelables*, Paris: Karthala.

McAuslan, Patrick, 2000, 'Only the Name of the Country Changes: The Diaspora of "European" Land Law in Commonwealth Africa', in Toulmin and Quan [*2000: 75–95*].

Mamdani, Mahmood, 1996, *Citizen and Subject. Contemporary Africa and the Legacy of Late Colonialism*, Princeton, NJ: Princeton University Press.

Mann, Kristin and Richard Roberts (eds.), 1991, *Law in Colonial Africa*, Portsmouth, NH: Heinemann.

Mathieu, P., 2001, 'Transactions informelles et marchés fonciers émergents en Afrique', in Benjaminsen and Lund [*2000: 22–39*].

Merry, Sally Engle, 1988, 'Legal Pluralism', *Law & Society Review*, Vol.22, No.5, pp.869–96.

Moore, Sally Falk, 1978, *Law as Process*, London: Routledge & Kegan Paul.

Moore, Sally Falk, 1986, *Social Facts and Fabrications – 'Customary' Law on Kilimanjaro 1880–1980*, Cambridge: Cambridge University Press.

Platteau, J.-P., 1996, 'The Evolutionary Theory of Land Rights as Applied to Sub-Saharan Africa: A Critical Assessment', *Development and Change*, Vol.27, No.1, pp.29–86.

Platteau, J.-P., 2000, 'Does Africa Need Land Reform?', in Toulmin and Quan [*2000: 51–73*].

Ranger, Terence, 1983, The Invention of Tradition in Colonial Africa', in E. Hobsbawn and T. Ranger (eds.), *The Invention of Tradition*, Cambridge: Cambridge University Press, pp.211–62.

Scott, James, 1998, *Seeing Like a State. How Certain Schemes to Improve the Human Condition Have Failed*, New Haven, CT: Yale University Press.

Shipton, Parker and Mitzi Goheen, 1992, 'Understanding African Land-Holding: Power, Wealth and Meaning', *Africa*, Vol.63, No.3, pp.307–25.

Toulmin, Camilla and Julian Quan (eds.), 2000, *Evolving Land Rights, Policy and Tenure in Africa*, London: IIED/Natural Resources Institute.

Turner, Stephen and Hilde Ibsen, 2000, *Land and Agrarian Reform in South Africa: A Status Report*, Cape Town: School of Government, University of Western Cape, Research Report No.6.

Vedeld, Trond, 2001, 'History, Continuity and Change in Fulani Resource Regimes', in Benjaminsen and Lund [*2001: 117–43*].

Reinventing Institutions: Bricolage and the Social Embeddedness of Natural Resource Management

FRANCES CLEAVER

I. INTRODUCTION

This study questions the idea that appropriate mechanisms can be designed to ensure optimum resource use, beneficial collective action and hence to build social capital. I argue here that the school of 'institutional crafting' in natural resource management is based on concepts which are inadequately socially informed and which ill-reflect the complexity, diversity and *ad hoc* nature of institutional formation.

Three aspects of institutional bricolage are illustrated here: the multiple identities of the bricoleurs; the frequency of cross-cultural borrowing and of multi-purpose institutions; and the prevalence of arrangements and norms which foster co-operation, respect and non-direct reciprocity over lifecourses.

In elaborating the concept of bricolage, I raise questions about whether local institutions are amenable to design, the scope for negotiating the norms which underlie institutional arrangements and the extent to which different institutions may be emancipatory or exclusionary. I conclude that development interventions aimed at institution building should be based on a socially informed analysis of the content and effects of institutional arrangements, rather than on their form alone.

II. CONFLICTS OVER RESOURCES IN THE USANGU BASIN

Planners and policy-makers perceive the Usangu Basin as facing problems of degradation and depletion of its grazing land and water resources, due to multi-user competition, and an institutional deficit resulting in open access resource use. Competition over natural resources is a critical concern because the severe drying up of the Ruaha river has potentially deleterious effects on the perennial swamp (the *ihefu* – an area of precious biodiversity), on hydro-electric power

Frances Cleaver is Senior Lecturer at the University of Bradford, UK; email: f.d.cleaver@bradford.ac.uk.

generation, on irrigated agriculture and on the wildlife tourism potential of the downstream Ruaha National Park. A DfID funded project (Sustainable Management of the Usangu Wetland and its Catchment – or SMUWC) has been investigating the causes of resource depletion in Usangu and developing local capacity to collectively manage the natural environment.

The Usangu basin is characterised by a long history of in-migration (of Baluchis from Iran, Masaai and Sukuma pastoralists from the north of Tanzania and agriculturalists from neighbouring areas). Whilst potentially competing groups of users in the Usangu basin are various, the most common characterisation of this competition is as one between ethnically based groups of sedentary agriculturalists (the 'indigenous' Sangu and in-migrants such as Nyakusa and Hehe) and itinerant pastoralists (predominantly Il Parakuyu Masaai and Sukuma). Notably, 'ethnic' agriculturalists predominate in local political and administrative structures. Often implied in policy discussions is a developmental struggle between entrepreneurial 'modernising' agriculturalists and intransigently 'backward' pastoralists.

In project and policy documents and in the discourse of development at district and regional level natural resources are frequently characterised as 'fragile' and 'depleted' by conflict ridden over-use, the cause of degradation being their open access status caused by the erosion of traditional authorities and ever-increasing population pressures [*SMUWC, 2001a*].

Local bureaucratic village institutions are characterised at best as ineffectual (through poor communication, high turnover of officers and lack of resources), at worst as corrupt and rent seeking. Village councils are seen as badly organised, informed and equipped, lacking transparency and often dominated by a few powerful people [*SMUWC, 1999, 2001a*]. Indigenous or traditional resource management arrangements are largely unrecognised or thought to be non-existent. There is then a perceived management deficit in terms of the organisation of collective action and the control of natural resources.

Crafting Institutional Solutions

Despite the 'conflict and corruption' analysis of existing institutions, policy and project documents assert the 'natural' basis of co-operation latent in village life and put great faith in the efficacy of *new* formal institutional arrangements to support collective resource management [*SMUWC, 2001b*]. The Village Land and Natural Resource Management Committees proposed in original project documents (subsequently implemented as Environment Committees) epitomise ideas commonly expressed in institutional theory. They are intended to operate 'in a formal and transparent way if they are to work effectively and to win public confidence'. Their purpose is to assess land and water use trends, introduce land registration, formulate village land use plans, allocate land and water rights, draft by-laws, identify and resolve conflicts. The committees are intended to be representative, consisting of 'a reasonably small group' to facilitate consensus on complex issues and to make it easier to provide training. The village committees are to be linked with other layers of resource management arrangements, in particular through interaction with district level natural resource management teams [*SMUWC 1999*].

Such prescriptions clearly derive from theories about the type of 'robust' institution suited to resolving common property resource management dilemmas. A focus on formal public structures with clear boundaries, transparency, representativeness and the codification of rules through written bye-laws, contracts and the specification of property rights is common to the literature on ' design principles' for institutional development. Ideas about the benefits of small and relatively homogeneous groups of decision-makers (usually representing 'a community') neatly linked or 'nested' within layers of structures (for example, at district national or regional level) and the possibility of such groups identifying and implementing an optimum level of resource use are also prevalent [*Bromley and Cernea, 1989; Ostrom, 1990, 1992, Wade, 1988, Agarwal, 1997*].

How likely are such new institutions, established with a strong focus on formalisation, transparency, representation, regulation and rights, to provide 'the answer' to collective resource management in Usangu?

III. INTERROGATING INSTITUTIONAL THEORY

There are a number of grounds on which the faith placed in such prospective arrangements can be criticised [*Cleaver, 2000*]. These include simplified and unilinear models of institutional evolution, the assumed primacy of narrow productive concerns amongst resource users and a purely instrumental view of culture and social structure as a 'resource bank' from which social capital is drawn to facilitate the implementation of good resource management decisions.

A short digression on the terminology of institutions is appropriate here. In rejecting dichotomous classifications of institutions as either formal or informal, traditional or modern, it is difficult to find alternative labels without reproducing false polarisations. In this analysis I generally use the terms 'bureaucratic' and 'socially embedded' to distinguish between institutions. Bureaucratic institutions are those formalised arrangements based on explicit organisational structures, contracts and legal rights, often introduced by governments or development agencies. Socially embedded institutions are those based on culture, social organisation and daily practice, commonly but erroneously referred to as 'informal'. It should be clear from my argument in this study that the two are not necessarily easily distinguishable; 'bureaucratic' institutions may be 'socially embedded', but are not inevitably so, while processes of bricolage may result in the bureaucratisation of 'traditional' cultural or social arrangements.

Institutional theory and much policy tend to favour an analysis of institutions as either 'weak' or 'robust' and to attribute normative value to bureaucratic arrangements, partly because of their visibility and legibility to development agencies. Weak institutions can be transformed into strong ones by resource users and policy-makers through an active process of institutional design and crafting [Ostrom, 1992: 60]. Ostrom sees crafting as a continuous evolutionary process of developing the optimal institution for the job in hand. Culture and social structure then becomes another raw material, part of the institutional resource bank from which arrangements (especially distributional norms and relations of trust) can be drawn which reduce the 'social overhead costs' of co-operation. Increasingly such resources are referred to as 'social capital' but as Ostrom herself admits there is generally a lack of understanding about how to 'create, maintain and use social capital' [Ostrom, 1992: 23].

Ideas about the strategic use of social capital are not confined to institutional theory, but have become widespread in development thinking. For example, in common with institutional theory, sustainable rural livelihoods (SRL) literature conceptualises social relations as a potential store of assets upon which people can draw to construct effective livelihood strategies. SRL literature broadly defines social capital as resources of reciprocity and trust, which can be drawn upon by households in the composition of sustainable livelihoods. Social relations, institutions and organisations are seen as critical mediating mechanisms as they enable and constrain the actions of individuals and households [Scoones, 1998; Ellis, 2000]. Substantial stocks of social capital are seen as necessary in generating wealth both for households and communities, in ensuring beneficial collective action and common property resource management and the proper working of local administrative and political structures [Narayan, 1997; Uphoff and Wijayaratna, 2000].

Such instrumentalist views assume individual actors are political and social entrepreneurs who rationally utilise social capital to craft institutions in pursuit of optimal resource management. Interactions over resource management then become modelled as transactions about which the individuals make the appropriate calculations of cost and benefit, based on single preferences. Because of the emphasis on tangible and identifiable behaviours and incentives, there is a tendency towards attributing greater value to formalised modes of interaction and codified norms.

However, it is often claimed that in order to properly utilise social capital, institutions must be appropriately 'embedded' in the social milieu from which the norms to support purposive decision making can be drawn [Ostrom, 1990]. Such concepts of embeddedness imply a state of solidity and fixedness; the firm location of institutions in the social environment. Rather than seeing dynamic social relations and the changing cultural milieu as the very stuff of people's lives, they are seen as a social cement which can be consciously utilised to strengthen institutions. These rather mechanical views of social embeddedness clearly link with the formalised arrangements preferred by institutionalists. However, they throw little light on processes of institutional evolution, which I suggest are more ad hoc, approximate and shaped by social life and culture than is implied by concepts of design and crafting. In much institutional theory, social capital is viewed as an undoubted good and institutional change as occurring along unilinear trajectories of evolution towards a robust state, or deterioration, dysfunction and collapse. These assumptions, reinforced by the terminology of the market (investment, capital, costs, transactions), obscure rather than elucidate the relational nature of collective action, the ebb and flow in social life of relations of trust and association across lifecourses, and the mix between conscious and unconscious motivation and action on the part of agents.

In this study I outline an alternative approach to conceptualising institutions through understanding processes of bricolage. I show how a variety of socially embedded institutions for collective action exist in Usangu in addition to the newly introduced bureaucratic resource management structures. Institutions of co-operation are embedded in everyday relations, networks of reciprocity and the negotiation of cultural norms. Through processes of bricolage these may combine with or replace contracts, legal rights and formal sanctions; without such bricolage and the social embedding of new arrangements, bureaucratic institutions are unlikely to be effective.

IV. INSTITUTIONAL BRICOLAGE

An alternative approach to institutions is needed, which allows us to look beyond the formal organisations and to conceptualise social relations as more central than simply context or assets. Drawing on the work of Douglas [*1973, 1987*] Peters [*1994*] and Giddens [*1984*] as well as my own previous work on resource management in Zimbabwe [*Cleaver, 2000*], I suggest that the concept of institutional bricolage enables us to do this.

Douglas elaborates Levi-Strauss's concept of 'intellectual bricolage' [*Douglas, 1987: 66*] and extends it to institutional thinking to illustrate how the construction of institutions and decisions to act are rarely made on the basis of individual rational choice. Instead 'institutions do the thinking' on behalf of people and institutions are constructed through a process of bricolage – gathering and applying analogies and styles of thought already part of existing institutions. Symbolic formulae are used repeatedly in the construction of institutions, thereby economising on cognitive energy by offering easy classification and legitimacy [*1984: 76*]. She emphasises the sameness and constraint of this form of institutional development; 'The bricoleur uses everything there is to make transformations within a stock repertoire of furnishings' [*1987: 66*]. In earlier work Douglas considers the concept of institutional leakage: 'Sets of rules are metaphorically connected with one another, allow meaning to leak from one context to another along the formal similarities that they show' [*Douglas, 1973: 13*]. This suggests a less conscious and less rational/functional formation of institutions than that proposed by many authors writing of the institutions of common property resource management.

Adapting Douglas and Levi-Strauss I use the term 'institutional bricolage' to suggest how mechanisms for resource management and collective action are borrowed or constructed from existing institutions, styles of thinking and sanctioned social relationships. This raises the question of the critical role of human agency in shaping and reshaping institutions; how far do individuals act as institutional engineers? Douglas suggests that the constraining aspects of socially embedded institutions seriously circumscribe the scope for individual thought and action: 'Institutions systematically direct individual memory and channel our perceptions into forms compatible with the relations they authorise' [*Douglas, 1987: 92*]. A less constrained view of the individual's role in institutional formation is put by Giddens [*1984*] who sees the individual as a possessor of agency as well as specific and often multiple social identities which may change over lifecourses. Different *bricoleurs* are thus likely to apply their knowledge, power and agency in respect to social relations, collective action and resource management in differing ways. The result is a rich diversity of pliable, if approximate, institutional arrangements.

Building on both Douglas and Giddens, I reject a view of individuals as rational and essentially economic resource appropriators, and attempt to reconceptualise them as conscious and unconscious social agents, deeply embedded in their cultural milieu but nonetheless capable of analysing and acting upon the circumstances that confront them. Individual action is characterised both by agency and structural constraint. For example I have previously illustrated in an examination of water management in Zimbabwe [*Cleaver, 2000*] how people consciously reduce the cognitive effort of responding to change by drawing on and adapting existing norms and mechanisms to new purposes. Less consciously, the use and adaptation of pre-existing customs and practices confer new arrangements with the legitimacy of 'tradition'; they become part of the 'right way of doing things'. Many institutional arrangements are forged in practice through daily interactions, the necessary improvisation involved in social life [*Bourdieu, 1977*] and the constant use of resources.

I suggest that it is a false dichotomy to pose a realm of 'traditional' informal, culturally and socially embedded institutions against a 'modern' domain of rationally designed committees and formal structures, and to suggest that one is likely to be better than the other at resolving conflicts or managing natural resource use. Local resource management arrangements are a complex blend of formal and informal, traditional and modern. The evolution of collective decision-making institutions may not be the process of conscious selection of mechanisms fit for the collective action task (as in Ostrom's model) but rather a messier process of piecing together shaped by individuals acting within the bounds of circumstantial constraint. Institutions so derived may survive partly due to the legitimacy bestowed by 'tradition', the moral command of what went before over the present [*Giddens, 1984*]. Institutions are formed through processes of bricolage in which similar arrangements are adapted for multiple purposes, are embedded in networks of social relations, norms and practices and in which maintaining social consensus and solidarity may be equally as important as optimum resource management outcomes.

The concept of bricolage helps us to examine the complex and dynamic nature of natural resource management and the 'fit' between institutions and the web of livelihood networks and practices in which they are embedded. I will proceed to elaborate processes of institutional bricolage by illustrating three aspects of bricolage with selected data from Tanzania; the complex identities and norms of the bricoleurs, the practice of cultural borrowing and adaptation of institutions to multiple purposes and the prevalence of common social principles which foster co-operation (as well as conflict) between different groups of stakeholders.

V. AGENTS, IDENTITIES AND THE ARTICULATION OF NORMS

Rejecting the idea of narrowly rational 'institutional engineers' in favour of the socially embedded 'do-it yourself' bricoleurs, we then need to socially locate such agents. Indeed Granovetter suggests that the social and historical embeddedness of institutions manifests through networks of personal relations [*Granovetter, 1992: 62*]. Institutional theory is often deficient in investing resource users with any meaningful social identity. It generally emphasises productive identities (such as 'irrigators', 'pastoralists') and a very limited number of social roles ('leaders', 'women'). People participating or represented in formal institutions are commonly assumed to have overriding productive incentives and/or clear social roles which render them fit for the task. In this model there is a key role for community representatives in shaping the institutions, mediating the social and cultural norms, producing and interpreting rules and enforcing sanctions. The emphasis on such participators is problematic as formal institutions often reproduce existing patterns of inequity (in Usangu inequalities of wealth, ethnicity and gender) and may serve to shape and reinforce other differences.

Livelihood Flexibility and Lifecourses

The privileging of single aspects of people's identities for institutional purposes is problematic as it ill reflects complex social and livelihood identities and multiple motivations. Nor does it reflect the importance of temporality in the formation of identity-people's relationships, their productive and reproductive concerns change dramatically during their lifecourse with neither economic activities nor ethnic identities alone adequately reflecting their interests. For example, in Usangu people's interests rarely fit easily into the agriculturalist/pastoralist divide; many pastoralists are semi-sedentarised and engaged in cultivation, whilst young pastoralist men migrate or mine gold in order to establish themselves economically. Similarly, as agriculturalists generate surplus they may invest in cattle, and use these to marry, support extended families, diversify into business. If people's identities are dynamic then the social materials and norms which shape institutions are likely to be equally difficult to categorise. An example of overlapping identities generating complex norms and networks is provided by one interviewee, Karim, a farmer of rainfed maize and groundnuts. He also engages in business; buying and selling charcoal and buying rice when the price is low, storing and selling when it is high. He is chairman of his hamlet and chairman of the water committee. He is a Sangu by ethnic origin and a traditional healer (herbalist). He follows Sangu traditions and ceremonies, particularly emphasising the worship of ancestors, in order to ensure the well-being of the family and productivity of natural resources. He is also a Muslim and he and Islamic leaders gather at his home for prayers and the appropriate Islamic traditions and festivals.

In emphasising particular identities and roles, formal institutionalism may not just reproduce but reinforce or amplify social divisions. This is particularly so when a static interpretation of 'culture' is adopted and incorporated into bureaucratic institutions as illustrated by Maganga who shows how the codification of customary law in Primary Magistrates courts and Ward Tribunals, may emphasise ethnic differences in Usangu [*Maganga, 1999; Maganga and Juma, 1999*].

Representation, Articulation and Exclusion

Institutional theory and policy implies that representatives on committees and in associations directly represent the resource users by translating community norms into more regularised institutional arrangements [*SMUWC, 2001a, 2001b*]. However, norms and practices, and the relationships of trust and co-operation which underlie them, are often generated and negotiated outside the formal institutions. Institutional bricolage then, takes place in a wider arena than that defined by the visible structures of bureaucratic resource management institutions. Evidence from Usangu illustrates the diverse location of decision-making, the importance of households and wider social networks in the generation of norms and practices of resource use. For example, children and young people play a major role in resource use and management through practice in Usangu, although they have no place in bureaucratic institutions. Children as young as three herd small livestock whilst older children and 'youth' make decisions about where water or feed herds and are explicitly consulted by their families over matters of livestock welfare, grazing and the implications for cattle condition. In the dry season children and young people may stay away from home in the grazing camps at the *ihefu* for months at a time, managing their animals and their use of pasture and water, and participating in a form of collective cattle protection militia. The key role of children in resource use and their complete lack of inclusion in bureaucratic management structures raise questions about the mediating processes between the creation of rules-in-use and their development into collective arrangements. The concept of institutional bricolage more adequately allows us to reflect the diverse location of the generation of institutional arrangements.

Bricolage is an authoritative process and some 'bricoleurs' are likely to possess more authoritative resources than others. Overlapping social identities mean that people may call on a variety of attributes to justify institutional position or influence. These vary from economic wealth, specialist knowledge or official position, to kinship and marriage, or personal characteristics such as eloquence, strength and honesty – a point well illustrated by Dikito-Wachtmeister [*2000*] in relation to women's participation in water resource management in Zimbabwe. Multiple sources of authority mean inevitable negotiation about who has the right to form the rules.

An example of the complexity of authority, articulation and participation in processes of bricolage is found in the role of women in resource management in Usangu. Women interviewed often stated that they felt able to participate fully in meetings to discuss resource management at hamlet level, but only to observe at wider village meetings, where they felt they 'did not have the language' to contribute. None the less women were significant managers of resources in practice, even in areas presented to us as 'traditionally' the concern of men, like cattle production. Women in fact played major roles in cattle breeding, in caring for sick cattle, preparing medicines, breeding and in decisions about milk production and cattle sales [*King and Ole-Lengisugi, 1999*]. Evidence from household interviews suggests that in the majority of cases, both men and women regarded decisions over natural resource use as properly made by all adult members of the family. However, both traditional cultural mechanisms for managing grazing and formal bureaucratic organisations of cattle keepers exclusively involved adult men. How far the decisions made in households and the resulting practices coincide with or contradict the rules and norms being produced in more formalised institutional settings is a moot point and illustrates the diverse location of processes of bricolage.

Bureaucratic institutions created through design and socially embedded arrangements formed through bricolage may both reinforce and perpetuate social divisions. Despite the possibility that new bureaucratic institutions could be emancipatory in including people previously excluded, in Usangu the poorest people rarely participate in such fora (even if formally eligible to do so) due to extreme time and labour constraints. Moreover, the poorest families are characterised by social isolation and very weak networks, so impeding their ability to contribute to processes of bricolage through daily social interaction. The poorest families in our study received little or no support from their neighbours who characterised them as 'unlucky' or 'lazy'. If they had been unfortunate enough to have suffered a number of family bereavements, particularly of children, surviving members were often suspected of witchcraft and treated with suspicion [*SMUWC, 2001c*].

A recognition of differences in social power amongst resource users necessitates a focus on the daily interactions and beliefs upon which such inequities are based, if we are to avoid reproducing these in new bureaucratic institutions.

Norms and the Limits to Negotiation

The concept of bricolage implies an active assembly of parts, the adaptation of norms, values and arrangements to suit a new purpose. It implies both a conscious scrutiny of some beliefs, and an unconscious acceptance of others in the formation of institutions. The simultaneous acceptance and questioning of traditions can be illustrated by the case of Rahel, a Maasai woman who is also a born again Christian (Pentecostalist) and an elder of the church. She belongs to a Maasai women's choir which functions as a women's support group and all members of the household take part in a collective labour group of ethnically mixed neighbours for agricultural work. Her husband has not converted to Christianity and is the hamlet leader and a leading member of local and national Maasai cultural and political structures. Rahel sees both advantages and disadvantages to the household of their diverse cultural and social networks. Her strong Christian beliefs lead her to question certain manifestations of Maasai culture such as consumption of alcohol, bad language used at ceremonies and the worshipping of spirits. She approves, however, of the links which her husband has forged through his Maasai leadership activities and the social support provided through marriage arrangements and extended kin networks. It was evident from interviews that cultural norms were heavily debated in this household and that some accommodation between potentially conflicting positions was arrived at.

Varying claims on tradition and modernity are common in the construction of institutions through bricolage, a point well illustrated by Upperman's study of traditional irrigation in Tanzania where he shows how concepts of tradition and modernity are used in gendered contestations over access to resources in an irrigation system [*Upperman, 2000*]. But there *are* limits to negotiation, some norms being so deeply embedded that people would find it almost impossible to be discursively critical of them [*Odgaard and Bentzon, 2001; Cleaver, 2000*] Indeed Douglas suggests that institutional arrangements are often so deeply embedded that it is almost impossible for people to subject them to conscious scrutiny: 'The high triumph of institutional thinking is to make the institutions completely invisible' [*Douglas, 1987: 98*]. Understanding institutional formation then requires us to try and uncover the deeply embedded principles which underlie people's choices and shape conscious decisionmaking, to identify the scope for flexibility in negotiating norms and practices.

VI. IMPROVISATION AND THE REINVENTION OF INSTITUTIONS

The concept of the crafting of institutions suggests that specific institutions are deliberately developed for particular functions. Thus an Irrigation Committee regulates the distribution of water and maintenance of furrows and a Grazing Association co-ordinates the use of grasslands. However, single purpose institutions are not favoured through processes of institutional bricolage. In the multiple processes of institutional evolution through bricolage, existing decision-making arrangements and relations of co-operation may be co-opted for new purposes. Such adapted, multi-purpose institutions abound in Usangu. For example, in study villages evangelical church choirs seem to be some of the most vibrant forms of associational life, with membership crossing ethnic, gender and livelihood divides. Members not only sing in church but may also function together as rotating credit groups, collective labour groups (also working as hired labour gangs on village works) and singers at 'traditional' social ceremonies and functions. Such embedded institutions combine productive and social functions, draw on both traditional and modern forms of interaction.

'Informal' institutions and decision-making about natural resource management are deeply culturally embedded. Livelihoods are not simply technically and economically rational sets of survival strategies but are clearly linked to ideas about a desirable way of life, to practices in relation to resources, to other people and to aspirations that are heavily loaded with symbolic meaning [*Mehta et al., 1999*]. This has been elaborated in regard to water use [*Mosse, 1997; Adams, 1997; Cleaver 2000*]. However, cosmologies are not merely inherited as a static part of culture but are learnt and adapted in the business of everyday life [*Bourdieu, 1977*]. Institutions formed as a result of bricolage in the multi-ethnic Usangu basin may be multi-cultural in origin, intersecting formal and informal, traditional and modern domains.

Mixing Traditional and Modern Arrangements

An example illustrates the mixed origins of institutions formed through bricolage. Farmers in Usangu commonly refer to 'traditional' smallholder rice irrigation systems (differentiating these from government run large schemes) However, this 'tradition' has a mixed and partly exotic provenance. Rice growing probably started in the mid nineteenth century, introduced by members of Arab trading caravans, whilst the irrigated gardens of the indigenous Sangu were observed by early explorers (personal communication: Rie Odgaard). 'Modern' rice irrigation was introduced into Usangu by Baluchi immigrants from Iran in the 1940s. 'Traditional' smallholder irrigation management draws on adapted committee structures introduced under government and NGO development projects (now mostly defunct) and on 'indigenous' collective labour arrangements. Whilst water co-operatives and associations were in some cases established in the past in order to formally claim water rights, many of these are non- functional, farmers perceiving them as unnecessarily bureaucratic [*Gillingham, 1999*]. However, roles, such as 'chairman' established under such projects, often remain. Conflicts over irrigation water are generally resolved between irrigators themselves, by reference to 'traditional' elders and (Sangu) customs, only if unresolvable are they referred to the Village Government and to Ward tribunals. Baluchis resolve disputes through reference to Islamic law or statutory rights [*Maganga and Juma, 1999*].

The evolutionary ebb and flow of irrigation management institutions, their mixed origins and the preference for socially embedded arrangements rather than bureaucratic ones all illustrate processes of institutional formation through bricolage.

Improvisation

The improvisatory, *ad hoc* and often intermittent nature of institutional arrangements formed through borrowing and adaptation are further illustrated by the example of the management of the water pump at Ukwaheri village. The example also illustrates how quickly formal institutional arrangements become adapted to social relationships and divisions.

Prior to the building of the 'SMUWC pump' in 1999 at Ukwaheri hamlet, severe water shortages were experienced here, sometimes resulting in the night-time stealing of water from other villages by Ukwaheri women. The water pump is managed under the village authorities and there is a six-member waterpoint committee and two specially trained mechanics. The committee has three duties which were 'given' to them in their training: to maintain the pump in working order, to regulate water use and opening hours, to collect payments for use of the pump.

They have tried different forms of charging for water use. They tried charging a flat rate of 20 sh. per bucket, paid at the point of use, but this was problematic to enforce as it meant supervising water collection at all times. They also tried charging all adult users over 22 years old 1,000 sh. for the duration of the water-scarce season. However, people proved reluctant to pay these charges and expressed doubts over what happened to their money once collected. While Sukuma residents were willing payers, Sangu residents often refused to pay, expressing little trust in the (largely Sangu) committee and leadership. Nevertheless, by the middle of 2000, 170,000 sh. had been collected and deposited at the bank.

At the time of the research the committee were planning to introduce a different system of payment whereby houses are charged differentially according to their actual water use. Therefore a Sukuma household who may collect 30 buckets every two days will be charged more than a Sangu household who only collect five or six buckets a day. The committee claimed to have a good idea of approximate water use by household and therefore to be able to set such charges. They intended to charge for the dry season only – at other times of the year people collect from other sources and demand on the pump is reduced.

Potentially people can be fined for breaking water pump by-laws which relate to taking turns in water collection, keeping the surroundings clean and a prohibition on allowing animals to drink at the pump. No-one has, as yet, been fined for breach of these. However, the improvisatory nature of institution building, illustrated by this example, does not mean that any arrangement is possible or acceptable, new arrangements generally have to be awarded some social legitimacy, even if this involves inventing tradition.

Leakage of Meaning

Deeply embedded understandings of the 'right way of doing things' mean that people discursively draw on legitimising symbols (derived from the state, from culture and tradition, from the natural world), to cognitively anchor new institutional and social arrangements. In Douglas's words 'there needs to be an analogy by which the formal structure of a crucial set of social relations is found in the physical world, or in the supernatural world, or in eternity, anywhere so long as it is not seen as a socially contrived arrangement' [*Douglas, 1987: 48*].

Although claims on tradition can be seen as legitimising devices, tradition is not automatically accepted by all actors, nor is it necessarily sacrosanct. Paradoxically, in Usangu, the potential for questioning tradition on the one hand and the general legitimacy of tradition on the other, means that cultural institutions may be 'borrowed' between ethnic groups, a key aspect of bricolage. The leakage of cultural rules and meanings across ethnic divides is well illustrated by the case of Mama N'Giriama, the caretaker of an important Sangu shrine, who conducts the rituals concerning the fertility and well-being of the *ihefu* and the people who live there. In her interpretation of the wishes of the ancestral spirit she emphasises incorporation and accommodation. She claims that there is a place for all on the *ihefu,* as long as people show proper respect and ask permission of the spirit to use it. The rituals she conducts appear to have become a multi-ethnic institution. For example, Sukuma and Masaai pastoralists (whose own ancestral spirits are based in distant lands of origin) may come and seek the blessing of the N'Giriama spirit so that their cattle do not get lost or stuck in the *ihefu.* Similarly people of different ethnic origins consult Mama N'Giriama for help in solving personal or health problems.

The Sungusungu – An Example of Bricolage

In processes of borrowing and adaptation the distinction between what is modern and what is traditional becomes blurred, tradition becomes reinvented. Additionally the line between formal organisation and socially and culturally embedded networks through which co-operation is forged become blurred. In Usangu we found an adaptation of traditional Sukuma militias of young men, to replace or supplement official Village Defence Committees. In several villages fear of cattle theft, the need to resolve potential competition over grazing and lack of confidence in government institutions led to the local establishment of a *Sungusungu* or cattle militia, borrowed from Sukuma customary defence organisations. Such institutions have become cross-ethnic, with ethnic Sangu and Masaai as well as Sukuma operating as 'commanders'.

The *Sungusungu* is made responsible by village consensus for cattle security and keeping order in the seasonal grazing lands. It operates on a basis of demarcation of roles between elders and youth, a practice common to all ethnic groups, with the youth acting as the foot soldiers and the elders acting as advisers on tactics, bestowers of charms and medicines, and dispensers of justice. This unofficial militia is considered by members to be formally accountable to (modern) village government, while the practices of its operation are largely based on socially embedded principles of reconciliation and conflict minimisation.

The *Sungusungu,* like many institutions formed through processes of bricolage, is multi-purpose. Villagers reported how they call on *Sungusungu* when facing problems requiring collective action, such as searching for a lost child, and use Sungusungu communication channels to disseminate messages around the village. One of the *Sungusungu* operating among seasonal grazing camps at the *ihefu*, organises the disparate camps of young men (from widely dispersed villages) into units, the commander collects from them a seasonal subscription of cash and this is used as a common welfare fund to pay for a bus or bicycle to transfer a sick herder to his home area.

The benign nature of the *Sungusungu* that we find in Usangu is in contrast to more violent *Sungusungu* vigilante groups documented elsewhere in Tanzania. The diversity of insitutional forms and purposes all going under the name *Sungusungu* [*Abrahams, 1998*] further illustrates processes of bricolage and the adaptation of 'traditional' arrangements to new purposes.

The Transaction Costs of Bricolage

It is often claimed in institutional theory that socially and culturally embeddeding institutions economises on transaction costs as people can quickly draw on common norms in formulating collective arrangements [*Mehta et al., 1999*]. However, whilst calling on familiar symbols and devices offers a sort of cognitive efficiency, it does not necessarily constitute a short cut to formulating legitimate institutions. In processes of institutional bricolage 'the categories of political discourse, the cognitive base of the social order are being constantly negotiated' [*Douglas, 1987: 29*]. Collective consensus, decision-making, forging and renegotiating norms, maintaining social networks, reputations and relations of trust are not easy processes, and require inputs of considerable time and energy. Community meetings are often lengthy, with an emphasis on achieving consensus rather than voting, and issues may only be resolved over weeks and months as some social consensus is gradually formed and the acquiescence of dissenters secured [*Cleaver, 2000*]. The time and effort involved in institutional bricolage are a particular burden to the poorest people who may be partially excluded as a result. Many interviewees from the poorest households in Usangu specified time constraints as their reason for non-participation in village decision-making.

An example of the effortful creation and maintenance of norms is seen in the priority given to avoiding or resolving conflicts, in constructing institutional mechanisms which emphasise reconciliation, forgiveness and an expectation of future co-operation.

VII. CONFLICT AVOIDANCE AND CO-OPERATION

The solidarity that makes collective action possible is something that has to be constantly worked at and neither socially embedded nor bureaucratic institutional structures obviate this. Here I use the example of the commonly held desire to avoid, minimise or peacefully resolve conflicts to illustrate how certain deeply embedded social values shape preferred institutional arrangements.

Project and policy approaches tend to see conflict as undesirable, as a breakdown in normal relations, something to be avoided or resolved as quickly as possible and optimistically insistent on perceiving co-operation as the norm and as 'the basis of village life' [*Devitt, 1999; SMUWC, 2001a*]. Perversely, though, bureaucratic institutional arrangements often emphasise the open confrontation of difference and the strict penalisation of non-conformers [*Ostrom, 1990; SMUWC, 2001a, 2001b*]. However, evidence of conflict and co-operation suggests a more complex picture than this. Conflict is both an integral part of normal life and something to be avoided or underplayed whenever possible.

A basic psychological dislike of conflict is illustrated by interviewees who identify the occasional conflicts with neighbours and kin as a major (if intermittent) source of stress in their lives, especially when associated with witchcraft. Additionally, where relations of reciprocity and institutions help to channel access to resources [*Berry, 1989*] then conflict must be avoided to ensure secure access to material livelihood assets. In Usangu, agricultural and pastoral families are networked through labour exchange, the use of draught power and by intermarriage as well as by church and club membership. But an over-emphasis on direct and instrumental reciprocity is misplaced. Relations of co-operation may be indirect and function across lifecourses and even generations as well as across localities. Additionally, many interviewees, when asked to identify the benefits of belonging to specific groups and associations, emphasised the opportunity for enjoyable social interaction, of social and psychological support, in addition to functional and productive benefits.

I suggest that values of social respect and conflict avoidance are deeply embedded and that these link moral behaviour to individual and community well-being (a form of moral-ecological rationality is explained further in Cleaver [*2000*]). The role of the supernatural (spirits, the ancestors and God) in securing the well-being of both humans and natural resources is strongly linked in cultural codes to people's behaviour, principles of respect and the desirability of peaceful coexistence.

Norms of conflict avoidance are common to all types of resource users in Usangu. Despite the rhetoric of high levels of conflict in Usangu and supposed irreconcilability of different cultures, Maganga [*SMUWC, 2001d*] found very few cases of conflicts over resources reaching court, reflecting a strong desire among people to resolve these at the lowest possible level. Values emphasising social respect and deference to elders are common to all social groups (if not always adhered to), but interviewees suggested that people do not merely inherit positions as leaders but also earn them through their ability to resolve conflicts and encourage harmonious relations with communities. Several interviewees had moved from their home area in order to avoid conflicts with neighbours and kin.

Celebrating Reconciliation, Reinforcing Co-operation

If collective action is to work, positive co-operation has to be reinforced, social capital built. The practice of actively embedding relations of co-operation in cultural and social life and of emphasising inclusive relations is common to the institutions formed through bricolage in Usangu. In direct contrast, literature on institutional design principles emphasises the need for impartial, rigorously enforced sanctions against non-co-operators [*Ostrom, 1990, 1992*]. Such principles, reproduced in policy documents [*SMUWC, 2001b*] emphasise confrontation and punishment rather than compromise and reconciliation and may erode rather than reinforce the social trust on which institutions depend.

The imperative towards emphasising co-operation even where conflict exists is strong. Evidence of potential conflict being minimised and turned towards co-operation instead is illustrated in accounts from Usangu and elsewhere in Tanzania [*Mnzava, 2000; Maseruli, 2000*]. These illustrate how communities (often hamlets and villages) may impose fines or penalties on those repeatedly offending against communal rules or failing to co-operate in communal work. Such penalties are only imposed when the social situation and extenuating circumstances of the offender are taken into account, a certain amount of 'social riding' being permitted. When extenuating circumstances are not taken into account, fines may be contested. In the relatively uncommon event of fines actually being levied, then the proceeds (money, livestock, household goods) are used to fund a celebration (a beer drink or feast) for those who did participate in the communal activity as well as the offender. According to informants, one of the purposes of this occasion is to 'celebrate forgiveness'.

It would be naive, of course, to present too rosy a picture of conflict avoidance and reconciliation. We have plenty of examples of mistrust between people (particularly over the management of funds), and norms of reconciliation may not benefit all. Maganga [*SMUWC, 2001d*] cites several cases of women filing for divorce through Ward Tribunals, possibly because they did not want to accept the reconciliatory mediation of local (male) elders at hamlet and village level. Moreover, certain people may be identified at village level as lazy, drunken or even witches and therefore unworthy of reconciliatory efforts. Despite undoubted limitations, however, I suggest that values prioritising conflict avoidance and reconciliation are deeply socially embedded and shape people's preferred arrangements for collective action and use of natural resources.

VIII. CONCLUSIONS

In this study I have outlined the concept of institutional bricolage in an attempt to strengthen our understanding of processes of resource management and collective action. The introduction of new bureaucratic institutions or organisational arrangements are not necessarily robust and enduring, nor do they automatically ensure beneficial collective action and optimum resource use. Arrangements which rely on a blueprint derived from abstract and universalised 'design principles' may result in inadequate institutional solutions as they fail to recognise the depth of social and cultural embeddedness of decision-making and co-operative relations. Bureaucratic arrangements may be based on principles which bypass or contradict those inherent to local decision-making and co-operation, such as the minimisation of conflict. New bureaucratic institutions are unlikely to have evolved through a process of institutional bricolage and may be perceived by local people as costly, lacking in legitimacy and cumbersome. It is possible that such new institutions will gradually be subjected to a process of evolution, that over time processes of bricolage will ensure their redundancy or their adaptation to create more socially embedded arrangements.

In recognising the plurality of institutional arrangements and avoiding sterile dichotomies of traditional and modern, formal and informal, economic and social, we should beware of normatively attributing value to particular types of arrangement. There are indeed questions of how far bureaucratic institutions based on individual rights and the principles of modernity undermine social trust, relationships based on the ethics of care and mutual interdependence as suggested by Upperman's study [*2000*] of the formalisation of water rights in Tanzania. While bureaucratic arrangements are not necessarily inclusive, fair and emancipatory, socially embedded institutions may reproduce social divisions or gloss over inequality. Indeed it is possible that different kinds of institutions contribute to the same exclusionary processes.

However, plurality also creates opportunity, processes of bricolage, of borrowing, of institutional improvisation which may also create spaces for negotiation, contestation, and for different voices to be heard. Rather than seeing plural and *ad hoc* institutional arrangements as dysfunctional (as does much development policy [*Berry, 1994*]), we could see their very plasticity as providing scope for shaping social distribution and relationships in more equal and emancipatory directions.

If there is a solution to the problem of managing natural resources through institutions of collective action, I see it in finding ways in which newly introduced bureaucratic arrangements can complement or reinforce the positive aspects of socially embedded arrangements. Where natural resource management requires strengthening, we need interventions based on an understanding of the content, underlying principles and social effects of institutions, not merely their visible form. I see great potential for effective development interventions which recognise the importance of processes of bricolage, rather than simply emphasising their manifestation as structures and outcomes, deliberately crafted. The knowledge gained through an archaeology of institutions should not delude us into thinking that institutions are wholly amenable to design. We cannot predict exactly how newly introduced arrangements will become revised, adapted and socially embedded over time, or abandoned and forgotten, through processes of institutional bricolage.

REFERENCES

Abrahams, R., 1998, *Vigilant Citizens. Vigilantism and the State*, Cambridge: Polity Press.
Adams W.M.,. Watson, E.E, and S.K.Mutiso, 1997, 'Water, Rules and Gender: Water Rights in an Indigenous Irrigation System, Marakwet, Kenya', *Development and Change*, Vol.28, pp.707–30.
Agarwal, A., 1997, *Community in Conservation: Beyond Enchantment and Disenchantment*, CDF Discussion Paper, Conservation and Development Forum, Gainesville, Florida.
Berry, S., 1989, 'Social Institutions and Access to Resources', *Africa*, Vol.59, No.1, pp.41–55.
Berry, S., 1994, 'Resource Access and Management as Historical Processes: Conceptual and Methodological Issues', in C. Lund and H. Marcussen (eds), *Access, Control and Management of Natural Resources in Sub-Saharan Africa* – Methodological considerations, Occasional Paper 13, International Development Studies, Roskilde University, Roskilde, pp.24–45.
Bourdieu, P., 1977, *Outline of a Theory of Practice*, Cambridge: Cambridge University Press.
Bromley, D.W. and M.M. Cernea, 1989, *The Management of Common Property Natural Resources, Some Conceptual and Operational Fallacies* ,World Bank Discussion Papers No.57, World Bank, Washington DC.
Cleaver, F., 1999, 'Paradoxes of Participation: Questioning Participatory Approaches to Development', *Journal of International Development Studies*, 11, pp.597–612.
Cleaver, F., 2000, 'Moral Ecological Rationality, Institutions and the Management of Common Property Resources', *Development and Change*, Vol.31, No.2, pp.361–83.
Devitt, P., 1999, *Community Engagement Programme Report*, SMUWC, Rujewa, Tanzania.
Dikito-Wachtmeister, M., 2000, 'Women's Participation in Decision Making Processes in Rural Water Projects: Makoni District, Zimbabwe', PhD thesis, University of Bradford, Bradford.
Douglas, M., 1973, *Rules and Meanings*, Harmondsworth: Penguin.
Douglas, M., 1987, *How Institutions Think*, London: Routledge & Kegan Paul.
Ellis, F., 2000, *Rural Livelihoods and Diversity in Developing Countries*, Oxford: Oxford University Press.
Giddens, A., 1984, *The Constitution of Society: Outline of the Theory of Structuration*, Cambridge: Polity Press.
Gillingham, P., 1999, *Community Management of Irrigation in the Usangu Wetlands and Their Catchment*, SMUWC, Rujewa, Tanzania, Dec.
Granovetter, M., 1992, 'Economic Action and Social Structure: The Problem of Embeddedness', in M. Granovetter and R. Swedburg (eds.), *The Sociology of Economic Life*, Oxford: Westview Press, pp.53–81.
King, A. and N. Ole-Lengisugi, 1999, *Livestock Consultancy*, Interim Report, SMUWC, Rujewa.
Maganga, F., 1999, *Resource Conflicts and Conflict Management: Fieldwork Findings from Iringa and Mbarali District*, Copenhagen: SASA.
Maganga, F. and I. Juma, 1999, 'From Customary to Statutory Systems: Changes in Land and Water Management In Irrigated Areas of Tanzania: A Study of Local Resource Management Systems in Usangu Plains', A Report Submitted to ENRECA, Dar es Salaam, Sept.
Maseruli, B., 2000, 'Local Institutions and the Management of Natural Resources', unpublished Field Notes, College of African Wildlife Management, Mweka, Tanzania.
Mehta, L., Leach, M., P .Newell, Scoones, I., Sivaramakrishnan, K. and S. Wray, 1999, *Exploring Understandings of Institutions and Uncertainty: New Directions in Natural Resource*

Management, IDS Discussion Paper 372, IDS, Brighton, Nov.

Mosse, D., 1995, 'Social Analysis in Participatory Rural Development' in *PLA Notes No. 24. Critical Reflections from Practice*, IIED, Sustainable Agriculture Programme, London.

Mosse, D., 1997, 'The Symbolic Making of a Common Property Resource: History, Ecology and Locality in a Tank-Irrigated Landscape in South India', *Development and Change*, Vol.28, No.3, pp.505–30.

Mnzava, D., 2000, 'How Modern Water Resources Management Conflicts with Traditional/Indigenous Management; The Case of Arusha Water Project', unpublished paper, University of Bradford, June.

Narayan, D., 1997, *Voices of the Poor: Poverty and Social Capital in Tanzania*, Environmentally and Socially Sustainable Development Studies and Monographs Series 20, Washington, DC: World Bank.

Odgaard, R. and A. Weis Bentzon, 2001, 'Rural Women's Access to Property in Patrilineal Communities in East Africa – In a Web of Norms', paper presented at a seminar on 'Formalisation and Informalisation of Land and Water Rights in Africa', Skodsborg, Denmark, 6–7 Sept.

Ostrom, E., 1990, *Governing the Commons: The Evolution of Institutions for Collective Action*, New York: Cambridge University Press.

Ostrom, E., 1992, *Crafting Institutions for Self Governing Irrigation Systems*, San Francisco, CA: ICS Press.

Peters, P., 1994, *Dividing the Commons: Politics, Policy and Culture in Botswana*, London: The University Press of Virginia.

Scoones, I., 1998, *Sustainable Rural Livelihoods: A Framework for Analysis*, IDS Working Paper No.72, IDS, Brighton.

SMUWC, 1999, *Management of Village Land and Natural Resources Document*, SMUWC, Rujewa, Tanzania, Oct.

SMUWC, 2001a, *SMUWC Final Report: Community Engagement Programme*, http://www. usangu.org/reports/cep.pdf

SMUWC, 2001b, *SMUWC Final Report: Sub-catchment Resource Management Programme*, http:// www.usangu.org/reports/srmp.pdf

SMUWC, 2001c, *SMUWC Final Report: Rural Livelihoods*, http://www.usangu.org/reports/rural.pdf

SMUWC, 2001d, *SMUWC Final Report: Conflicts*, http://www.usangu.org/reports/conflicts.pdf

Uphoff, N. and C. M. Wijayaratna, 2000, 'Demonstrated Benefits from Social Capital: The Productivity of Farmer Organisations in Gal Oya, Sri Lanka', *World Development*, Vol.28, No.11, pp.1875–90.

Upperman, E., 2000, 'Gender Relations in a Traditional Irrigation Scheme in Northern Tanzania', in C. Creighton and C.K. Omari (eds.), *Gender, Family and Work in Tanzania*, Aldershot: Ashgate, pp.357–79.

Wade, R., 1988, *Village Republics: Economic Conditions for Collective Action in South India*, Cambridge: Cambridge University Press.

Neither Tragedy Nor Enclosure: Are There Inherent Human Rights in Water Management in Zimbabwe's Communal Lands?

BILL DERMAN and ANNE HELLUM

I. INTRODUCTION

Access to fundamental resources, such as water, has moved centre-stage in development and human rights discourses. Proponents of a rights-based development approach argue that access to basic water should be seen as a human right.[1] Apart from the Convention on the Rights of the Child (CRC), which gives the child a right to clean drinking water, the right to water is not directly expressed in any binding human rights instrument.[2] The satisfaction of basic water needs can be interpreted as an implicit part of the bundle of human rights that make up the right to livelihood as embedded in Article 11 of the Covenant on Social, Economic and Cultural Rights.[3] From this perspective a right to water derives from the right to life, the right to health and the right to food.[4]

International and national actors have generated the water reform process that is taking place in Zimbabwe. Internationally they respond to hypotheses of growing water scarcity and the needs for sustainable development. Nationally they respond to growing water needs for development.[5] The most important principles that so far have been agreed on at international conferences on water management are embodied in the Rio Declaration on

Bill Derman is Professor of Anthropology and African Studies, Michigan State University and Anne Hellum is Professor of Women's Law and Human Rights at the Department of Public and International Law, University of Oslo. They would like to thank Stanley Vombo and Andrew Magwaza for their assistance during fieldwork. Stanley Vombo, a CASS research fellow, had been carrying out research in this area for three years but his focus has been the new institutions. Bill Derman has been supported in related research by a Fulbright- Hays Research Grant, a Wenner-Gren Foundation grant for Anthropological Research and the BASIS CRSP for Water and Land Research in Southern Africa. Anne Hellum has been supported by the Ministry of Foreign Affairs/Norwegian Research Council Program Development Related Women's Law Research taking place at the Institute of Women's Law at the Faculty of Law, University of Oslo and the NORAD funded co-operation between the Institute of Women's Law in Oslo and the Women's Law Centre at the University of Zimbabwe. They also wish to thank the Centre for Development and the Environment, University of Oslo for facilitating this research co-operation about land and water reform in Zimbabwe.

Environment and Development of 1992, Agenda 21 of 1992 and the Dublin Statement on Water and Sustainable Development of 1992.[6] The four principles agreed on in Dublin are:

*   fresh water is a finite and vulnerable resource, essential to sustain life, development and the environment;

*   water development and management should be based on a participatory approach, involving users, planners and policy-makers at all levels;

*   women play a central part in the provision, management, and safeguarding of water;

*   water has an economic value in all its competing uses, and should be recognised as an economic good.

These principles reflect an attempt to balance liberal economic thinking on international development policy voiced by international actors such as the IMF and the World Bank, participatory natural resource management with broader concerns for the environment and women.[7] A critical issue in relation to international and national water policy is how the concerns of the poor will be balanced against an increased market orientation.

The Dublin principles, like many other international policy documents, do not provide an exhaustive notion of water as an economic good. In the Dublin Report 'economic' refers to using water beneficially while ensuring its renewal, its ecological health and its productive use. Economic uses may refer to balancing multiple concerns while employing different policy options to use and protect water resources in relation to different groups. There is a recognition that not all groups may afford the full economic costs of water and there are limits to having water users pay the full costs of water supply. This is often termed the 'user pay' principle. In Zimbabwe where the 'user pay' principle has been adopted, it is limited by the category of 'primary water', water used for domestic purposes in rural areas, which does not have a price.[8] In this study we draw attention to the challenges that new innovative forms of commercial cropping emerging within the common property regimes in communal lands, such as women's gardens, represent, with a view to drawing a dividing line between commercial and primary water uses.

Overall, there is the importance of taking historical, social, economic and cultural contexts into consideration as far as the application of the Dublin principles is concerned. In Zimbabwe, as in many other nations, water reform has taken place as though there were no water management systems other than those of the nation-state. In this study we show how access to water, like most other natural resources, is regulated by both statutory and unwritten customary norms. We explore whether, and to what extent, colonial and post-colonial water law and local customs and practices recognise everyone's free access to water for primary uses.

In understanding how water management systems change, we seek to question whether or not there is an uni-directional movement towards the privatisation and commodification of water. On the one hand, authors such as Vandana Shiva have criticised the idea that nature should be commodified and, on the other, there are more empirically based concerns as to whether water privatisation serves broader public interests, especially those of women and the poor.[9] The legal pluralist literature suggests that water reform has to take into account at least two or more legal 'systems' at work with respect to allocating water and water rights. Hence, how customary rights of existing water users are acknowledged, and whether new allocation patterns are imposed or negotiated with users will have a major bearing on rural livelihoods as well as food security.[10]

With a view to these broader questions, we examine the interplay between international, national and local systems of water management. We compare discourses and practices in different time periods to show how the strength of local ideas and the management of water continue to prevail, despite colonial rule and new national laws. The study is organised in four sections. First, we briefly discuss water law and the division between primary and commercial water in colonial Southern Rhodesia and then in Zimbabwe. In colonial Southern Rhodesia the right to primary water was embedded in the earliest legislation concerning water and this right has been maintained until the present.

Secondly, we focus on the interrelationships between local water regulation in communal lands and national laws and policies. Of major concern is the relationship between Zimbabwe's new water policies based on balancing free access to water for primary purposes and the user pay principle for commercial waters. We ask whether and to what extent local principles and practices have influenced national legislation and policy? In turn, we enquire how and whether national legislation and policy have influenced local practices and principles?

In the third section, we explore water management and allocation patterns in three villages in Mhondoro Communal Land, linking national water policies to the norms and principles underlying local beliefs and practices about sharing water for domestic purposes. Finally, we link national and local norms to international discussions on whether or not water should be considered a human right and the implications of doing so. Placing the discourse about human rights to water in a broader historical and cross-cultural context, we suggest these rights should be approached as a process deriving from a multiplicity of international, national and local norms and practices.

II. WATERS DIVIDED

Zimbabwe's waters have been divided into categories of commercial and primary use since the beginning of the twentieth century. This division of water seems to reflect the core land tenure division between commercial (formerly European) lands and communal (formerly Tribal Trust Lands) lands. It also reflects the dual legal system where imported Roman Dutch law and British common law applied to white settlers, while relations between black Zimbabweans were regulated by customary law. In the Water Act of 1998, not substantially different from earlier ones, primary water was defined as water used for: (1) domestic human needs in or about the area of residential premises; (2) animal life; (3) the making of bricks for private use; and (4) dip tanks.[11] Commercial water use was an economic concept encompassing agriculture, mining, livestock, hydroelectric power, etc. Water used for commercial purposes must now be permitted, while water for primary use was not.[12] To access primary water, no permission was required.

Commercial agriculture is by far the largest consumer of Zimbabwe's water using 75 per cent of all water, while the urban industrial mining sector consumes 20 per cent, and the communal lands only about five per cent.[13] Water management for commercial purposes is centred around thousands of small, medium and large-scale dams, while water use in communal areas centres on boreholes, open and closed wells, streams, rivers and small dams. Apart from dry season vegetable gardens located along streams, rivers, seasonally flooded grasslands (*vleis*) and, increasingly, boreholes, agriculture is primarily rain-fed.

At first glance it would appear that the notion of primary water should be linked to the indigenous idea that no one will be denied access to water. However, this seems not to be the case. Primary water, in the sense of the Water Act, is not a recognised category among African peoples in Zimbabwe. It was a concept introduced and stemming from a residual, non-reflective category embodied in the earliest Southern African water laws. In discussions with the drafters of Zimbabwe's new water law, it was assumed the concept came from Roman Dutch law, remained there unchanged, and was then incorporated into the new Water Act without further reflection.[14] There was no explicit concern with customary law and customary water rights, unlike other areas of colonial regulation such as land, marriage, inheritance and even political leadership.

In our reading of the Shona literature and our own research, water cannot be denied to anyone, for good rains or poor rains were understood as indicators of social well-being or social conflict [*Bourdillon, 1987; Lan, 1985; Maxwell, 1999* and others]. Droughts were said to be caused by serious breaches of conduct both in general and people's dealing with water. Good communication with ancestors needed to be maintained to ensure rainfall and a good water supply. In general it was believed that water could not be individually owned, and that everyone had a right to use it as they saw fit within the norms and practices of the different cultural groups. It is difficult to ascertain how water management actually took place in Shona, Ndebele, Tonga and other societies in nineteenth-century Zimbabwe, so this will not be pursued any further.

Primary water appears to recognise everyone's right to use water as a necessity of life. The first regulation of water was by the Order in Council, 1898, Section 81 pertaining to the British South Africa Company. It required the company to ensure that natives or tribes had a fair and equitable portion of springs or permanent water. This was in the areas assigned to tribes for their agricultural and pastoral pursuits. However, a not very subtle change in language occurred in 1927. The positive requirement of 'fair and equitable' was changed to 'any decision that substantially affects the requirements for primary use of water by Tribal Trust Land (TTL) residents should be approved by the Board of Trustees for Tribal Trust Land'. This is now a recognisable negative obligation in contrast to the Order in Council which contained a positive one. The last time that primary rights are mentioned is in the only book on the subject, *Water Law in Southern Rhodesia*, by Judge H.J. Hoffman [*1964*].

Throughout the colonial period Water Acts required the colonial authorities to respect the primary use rights of Tribal Trust Land inhabitants. This principle was embedded in the Water Acts of 1927, 1964, 1976 and 1998. For many years it was the Chief Native Commissioner who examined the effects on the water supply of a native reserve of appropriations by private individuals or the Rhodesian state. This resembled the reasonable use doctrine as developed in English water law.[15] Later it became the government engineer who certified that the interests of the tribesman were not affected [*Hoffman,1964: 88*]. In 1964 it was at the discretion of the governor to select someone to represent the interests of occupants of TTLs when cases involving their water supply were discussed. The Water Court was required to seek the approval of the Board of Trustees of Tribal Trust Land if their requirements for primary water were to be altered by any decision or award of the Water Court.

It is significant that natives were not to be represented by themselves. In discussions with a Water Court technical expert and a chief engineer from the Department of Water Development they could not recall any water right being altered because it affected TTL residents.[16] In debates on the Water Laws during the colonial period, there is no participation by either 'natives' or representatives of groups with other notions of water management. There is no record in Hansard (the preparatory works of the legislation) of recognition of alternative systems of water management and allocation. In short, a single uniform colonial system was put in place over multiple ideas and concepts of water management. Our tentative conclusion is that the primary water concept, originating in Roman Dutch law, was influenced by the reasonable use doctrine that evolved at the turn of the nineteenth century in English law. Moreover, it was the British South Africa Company which brought it into Southern Rhodesia/Zimbabwe without examination via the Cape Colony Water Law, thus remaining unchanged throughout the twentieth century.

In general, development or progress during this period is believed to lie with the European or white sector. The development of water, as with most other economic developments, was associated with the colonialists, while the colonised were seen as passive and mainly responsible for themselves through subsistence agriculture. The colonial state did not take much responsibility for the TTLs until the 1950s and certainly not for the TTL water supply. The dynamic was in commercial water, not primary water.

III. INTERRELATIONS BETWEEN LOCAL WATER REGULATION IN COMMUNAL LAND AND NATIONAL LAWS AND POLICIES IN WATER REFORM

The Water Act of 1998 and its companion, the Zimbabwe National Water Authority Act, were to remedy past legal and institutional inadequacies.[17] In the following we focus on the policy framework that has guided the reform and the dimensions of that reform that have direct applicability to communal areas. The policy framework has been articulated in *Towards Integrated Water Resources Management: Water Resources Management Strategy for Zimbabwe* [*GOZ, 2001*]. Water was considered a critical national resource to be vested solely in the state. Unlike other water acts, water could no longer be owned by any private individuals or corporations. All Zimbabweans would have equal access to water and stakeholders should be involved in decision-making in the development and management of the resource. Further, all development in water resources should be economically viable and environmentally sustainable [*GOZ, 2001: 11*]. What is both significant and interesting is that most of the reform processes involved commercial water, not primary water. In order to use water for commercial purposes, permits were now required. It is the obtaining of a permit that legitimises the use of Zimbabwe's waters for commercial purposes be it for agriculture, mining, industry or waterworks by towns and municipalities. Turning to the key provisions of the acts, the aim of greater equality of access is achieved by the following measures:

(1) Ending the priority date system of first in last out. This is to be replaced by a 20-year permit system.[18] The new allocation system remains undefined but we presume it will be some form of proportional allocation so that in drought years all users will lose an equal proportion of their water.

(2) Broadening the scope of who may apply for a permit to use water. Communal area residents may now apply for permits on their own without having the District Administrator do so on their behalf. For water to be used for agricultural purposes, it still needs to be tied to land. What this means for communal area residents who do not have individual title deeds is unclear since permits have not been issued yet.

(3) Democratising water management by increasing the participation of stakeholders, especially black communal farmers. Under the previous Act, waters were managed by either government or River Boards whose membership was restricted to water rights holders, typically white commercial farmers. It was up to the discretion of the government to represent the interests of communal area residents. Under the new Water Act, waters are to be managed through Catchment Councils and the Subcatchment Council, which are composed of different stakeholder groups, including communal area residents and Rural District Councilors. They are to carry out their work in coordination with the new Zimbabwe National Water Authority (ZINWA).

(4) Retaining the wide definition of primary water, although Catchment Councils are empowered to limit it. In concert with global water policies, water is to be considered an economic good. In Zimbabwe this has been captured in the phrase 'user pays'. This refers only to commercial water since primary water cannot, by a matter of law, be priced. The main concern of water policy is to promote the use of commercial water through encouraging business activities. Although the strategy emphasises a uniform policy for all Zimbabwe, the development of water in communal areas still takes place under District Development Fund's and Rural District Councils' water and sanitation programmes. These remain, overwhelmingly, for primary water.

A broader study of the water reform carried out by the Centre for Applied Social Sciences at the University of Zimbabwe (CASS) shows that primary water supplies, while central to communal areas, are in practice peripheral to the Catchment Councils' interests because they claim this is the domain of 'development institutions'.[19] From the water development perspective that still dominates Zimbabwean water policy, communal areas are regarded as underdeveloped due to the lack of water rights/permits, low use of commercial water, low use of water for irrigation and lack of storage capacity for water to enable the carrying out of agricultural and other activities.

However, there are important new commercial initiatives in the communal areas which require irrigation. These include the growing of a wide range of horticultural crops such as flowers, vegetables, tobacco (both cured and air dried), fruit orchards, etc. There has also been an increase in mining (including gold-panning and rock excavation). None of these activities to our knowledge have received a right to water. In sum, there would appear to be differences in the acceptance of ideas of the user pay principle. In the water reform policy a key future concern is how would a water management system respond to these trends in communal area commercialisation? It is possible to ignore these commercial uses when they only account for a very small percentage of water consumption. However, we would anticipate that these uses will increasingly render problematic the deep historical division between commercial and primary water.

The planning for the water management of a catchment now rests in the hands of Catchment Councils.[20] In order for Catchment Councils to issue permits they must have approved Catchment Plans which require a fairly detailed accounting of actual water use. This is where primary water needs to be conceptualised and accounted for initially. The implementation of the user pay principle requires a clear separation of what is primary and what is commercial since this is not specified in the definition of primary water in the Water Act. While rural water supply has been provided by government free of charge, the maintenance and repair of boreholes has become the responsibility of users. In addition, consultants looking into the implications of the user pay principle have now started a discussion on whether borehole users should pay for their water, since they are being encouraged to use water for productive purposes (that is, more commercial ones).[21] The Mazowe Catchment Council's debate as to what constitutes commercial water illustrates issues that the increasingly market-driven water discourse is giving rise to. When drawing a dividing line between commercial and primary use, they have relied upon a technological answer. If water is moved by hand, it is, according to this view, not commercial; if it is moved by some of form of machinery, it will be considered commercial.[22]

There is, in practice, the general push to make rural water use more productive, which is leading towards a greater formalisation of water use. This process of formalising water use has been the result of several trends, both internal and external, including the making of all water subject to government control, increasing stakeholder involvement in the management of water, increasing commercial production particularly in communal areas with small-scale irrigation, treating water as an economic good and quantifying the water necessary to sustain specified environments. In addition to the language of water reform, there are the emergent human rights discourses on a right to water. Human rights discourse has not entered the water reform process in Zimbabwe but, among those involved, there is a sense that the basic need for water must be met for all people and the environment.[23]

The new water policy maintains a single uniform water management system that has been put in place over other ideas and concepts of water management during the colonial era. In communal areas and resettlement schemes, both men and women's access to water still relies heavily on customary use rights. Access to water is, like most other natural resources, regulated by both statutory and customary norms. The regulations framing the new water management system are moulded on a large-scale commercial farming model without much thought given to the needs of the new and innovative forms of commercial cropping which are gradually emerging within the common property regimes in the communal lands.

IV. HOW WATER IS MANAGED IN MHONDORO COMMUNAL LAND

Because the water reform process has ignored local norms and practices among communal land populations, we have decided to explore how, under increasing commercialisation and water reform, residents of a communal land near Harare manage their waters.

We chose the communal land of Mhondoro 100 kilometres to the south and west of Harare to examine how primary water is managed, and focus on the three villages of Bangira, Murombedzi and Kaondera in the chieftainship of Mashamayombe. The area is high plateau and located within the drainage of the Mupfure River, which is part of the Sanyati Catchment. We selected this area due to a rapid and recent increase in tobacco-growing, a relatively high number of private wells and the existence of a dam project. Commercial farms surround Mhondoro with a significant number of dams for irrigation and water management in general. This study was undertaken during a time when rainfall was plentiful. Furthermore, there was adequate water for cattle, which reduced the human–cattle competition for water found in much drier areas of Zimbabwe. Lastly, it appeared that population growth had greatly slowed due to labour migration and HIV/Aids.

Tragedy and Enclosure?

As part of a broader study of water management in selected communal lands in three catchments, a survey of water use and awareness had already been carried out in two of the three villages, Kaondera and Bangira in Mhondoro.[24] The results showed that 20 per cent of households were growing tobacco, all in one village; 70 per cent of households had invested in water, and 90 per cent of households had some form of dry season garden which required hand irrigation.[25] We made the assumption that because deep and open wells were located on homesteads, they were 'private'. This seemed reasonable given the growing of tobacco and other cash crops. We assumed that these trends in the commercialisation of agriculture would be reflected in the management of water, and expected to find decreasing open access to the water resources of the area. We were curious to see if there was an emerging informal market in water as there had been in land, and to know if there was an increasing neglect of common water resources such as boreholes, wells and dams. Bev Sithole, in her thesis about use and access to wetlands (dambos) in communal lands in Zimbabwe, concluded that water that had been open access was now subject to enclosures and restrictions in the Mutoko area located in the Mazowe Catchment [*Sithole, 1999*]. Pius Nyambara's study of land acquisition in Gokwe demonstrated the various kinds of transactions that the commercialisation of agriculture is giving rise to in the communal lands and how this determines patterns of differentiation [*Nyambara, 1999*]. In recent years, the ways in which common property regimes concerning land and water are being transformed through transactions between local actors, who are unequal in wealth and power, have been described and analysed within the anthropology of law [*Moore, 1998*].

In analysing preliminary findings in terms of a broader survey, observations through visits to the area, and discussion of water management in Mhondoro, we expected to find weak indigenous institutions for managing water, the reason being that water resources are dispersed and not linked to a central authority. When villagers were asked who was the most important person in the allocation of water sources, 73 per cent responded either the chief or spirit medium. This is consistent with their view on what they do to maintain water supplies. Eighty-four per cent said they observed rules and/or perform rituals to do so. Hence, the link between rainfall, ancestors, social relations and the land remains strong despite other changes.

The colonial period saw little or no public investment in water, water supply or water management institutions. In the early post-independence period there had been a focus on improving rural water supply and sanitation. This was done initially through the construction of new boreholes funded by a wide range of international donors and the Department of Water Development (DWD), District Development Fund (DDF), Rural District Councils (RDC) and private organisations. Local institutions were created to manage these new water sources, the most important being Borehole Committees. In reflecting on this history, we assumed that the institutions for managing common water sources, both indigenous and recent, would be weak, and speculated that these weak institutions might create the space for successful commercial actors to privatise or dominate water resources.

As the Zimbabwean government withdrew from rural areas during the 1990s under the combined policies of structural adjustment and decentralisation, local communities were left to find alternative economic sources for expanding the water supply. In 1997 the Mupfure Pilot Catchment Project began the process of creating the structures for stakeholder management of water which included Mhondoro Communal Land. Recently, Africa 2000, a UNDP-sponsored NGO, constructed a dam for cattle and gardens in Mhondoro. Heifer International provided cattle for a livestock project in Bangira. The Zimbabwe Tobacco Association (ZTA) built a borehole in Bangira Village for irrigating tobacco seedlings and their transplantation, and also provided seeds and fertiliser in the first year. The government provided cement and personnel to construct individual wells on homestead property in Kaondera. These efforts are based upon increasing opportunities for rural residents to increase their incomes through commercial activity. It appeared to us that the development of what appeared to be private wells on individual homesteads were part of this process.

In sum, there was been increasing investment both public and private in water in the three villages. New institutions have been created to respond to these initiatives and developments. These included: a dam committee, garden committee, a Ward Water Association, a Heifer Committee, the continuation of the borehole committee, and a local Tobacco Growers' Association. In addition, the chief, headmen and spirit mediums remained active in water management in the area. This activity led us to suspect that more powerful or wealthy individuals would act to enclose the new water resources for themselves and their interest groups.

In August 2001 we interviewed chiefs, headmen, politicians and villagers in the three villages with Stanley Vombo, who was a research fellow for CASS. On the basis of our observations a local research assistant carried out a more systematic investigation of water use in the area. These interviews and observations modified our initial assumptions regarding the effect of commercialisation on local water use. Despite the closeness of the villages, they each present significant differences in water management. We will briefly treat them in turn.

Bangira

In Bangira, the site of tobacco growing and the dam, we found that the borehole constructed by the ZTA primarily for tobacco growers had become a common source of drinking water for the whole village. It was open to anyone who needed water. The borehole dug for the Chiyedza Cooperative by the European Union in 1996 had also become a community borehole. The dam was used for watering livestock for people from six villages. In Bangira all the people had been allocated land in an area close to the water, and everyone in Bangira village was given access to land and water. This does not mean that benefits are equal. Villagers without livestock do not benefit nearly as much as those that have.

There is one privately dug well in a homestead at the opposite end of the village. This well is the drinking source for a number of households close to the well. At times the well dries up; none the less the water is, according to the owner who is a widow, not restricted but shared to the last drop; she could not deny anyone access to safe drinking water. There is also a private borehole built by one of the most successful tobacco growers whose waters are shared if the nearby borehole pump breaks down.

Murombedzi

In Murombedzi there is only one borehole that properly belongs to the nearby primary school. In principle, a borehole is open to everyone. The borehole, which is considered safe, has a cover but this is now old, rusty and falling apart. This borehole frequently breaks down and Murombedzi residents have to find alternative sources of drinking water. The most used source of drinking water is an open well that belongs to a widow. The well, which her husband had paid for to be dug, is in her *vlei*-fenced garden on the outskirts of the village, and is used to provide water for approximately 36 families (approximately 150 people) on a daily basis. This well has never gone dry, not even in the severe drought of 1992. The widow did not feel that she could or should deny anyone access to the well, despite some damage to her garden from livestock due to well users leaving the gate open.

There was a second well located on the property of a recently arrived family. According to the owner, anyone was free to use it, although most villagers chose not to, or thought it was not open to them; however, three families did use this well. A fairly wealthy woman owned the last well which was not used by other villagers. She claimed she did not stop anyone from using it, none the less it was not used by other villagers. A number of villagers used boreholes in neighbouring villages, with one group regularly using the pump well which had been privately dug in Kaondera but not properly covered. Another group of villagers would use other boreholes if the school borehole broke down rather than other wells in the village.

Kaondera

In Kaondera, a village of 20 homesteads, there was one private well that was turned into a common well, enclosed and with a pump installed. Almost all the villagers who did not have their own well used this source, as well as several families from Murombedzi. Ten private wells were dug in the 1990s on residents' homesteads; these are closed, usually with a substantial cement structure and a pulley system to lift water. These wells are used for drinking water and for irrigating home gardens. Two households without wells used a relative's well on a neighbouring property.

Cross-cutting the Individual/Communal and Domestic/Commercial Domains

We now turn to a discussion of the legal status of the norms and principles underlying the local beliefs and practices about sharing water.

Despite our expectation of increasing privatisation, we found no evidence of this taking place. Rather, there was a trend of private wells or boreholes being funded for specific economic purposes and made available to all for drinking and cooking. In a relatively small area with multiple sources of water, these were the ones which were perceived as safe or good for drinking. Cutting across all the different tenurial systems is the notion that no one should be denied access to safe drinking water.

The notion of safety appears to be mixed. It is influenced by sanitary notions of disease as well as by fears that the water could be poisoned. A rule concerning use was that a well should be kept closed to be protected against animal waste or children throwing objects into it.[26] The question of poisoning appears more complicated since this seems to refer to potential acts by those who have been denied access to water. Poisoning is not possible if everyone is drinking from a well, but would be possible if there was exclusion.[27] The poisoning could be literal or through witchcraft.[28] The belief that human disasters such as poisoning, disease or death is caused by spiritual revenge must be understood in the light of ways in which health, body and law are interlinked among the Shona-speaking groups in Zimbabwe. Most people believe that accidents, deaths or disease occur because they themselves or someone in their family have done something that has caused the wrath of spiritual ancestors.

Underlying these spiritual sanctions is the socio-legal order of the society.[29] We were told on a number of occasions by villagers that water sources had dried up or deteriorated because of misconduct. People we talked to were clearly afraid of denying anyone water because they believed it could lead to poisoning. No one we interviewed could ever cite a case of poisoning, yet all the villagers seemed to avoid the well of a specific widow, and this appeared linked more to fears of witchcraft. In sum, the sense of community, trust and the moral approval of the person who possessed the water thus appears to be involved in the concept of safe drinking water. In examining people's choices as where to obtain water, kinship was often more decisive than physical closeness to the water source. It seemed, however, that a sense of entitlement, safety, trust and water quality led people to simply not choose on the basis of physical closeness and cleanliness.

Drinking water appeared to be free. All respondents reported that it was not necessary to pay money or give gifts to obtain water. Well-owners who said they never received anything for use of their wells confirmed this, and this is a pattern for the increasing number of people having wells dug on their land. Two research assistants' observations at the wells also support the congruence in this case between what people say and what people do. Anticipating that this will continue to be the case in the near future, although we recognise that when norms change people tend to justify their actions within established paradigms, we intend to continue our study of continuity and change in water management in the area.

There appears to be a difference between sharing water for drinking and cooking on the one hand, and gardening and watering livestock on the other. Many of the families in the three villages had a dry season garden. These were located at the homestead, near a dam or on a *vlei* outside the homesteads. Shallow wells for gardens were treated as family property rather than common pool property. In other words, access to the water was only for garden use or by a very close relative. We did not come across any instances where water sharing for hand irrigation took place.

In an effort to save wood for fencing materials and to place gardens closer to a permanent water source, a garden project was proposed and funded in Bangira. All villagers who wished to could obtain garden land adjacent to the dam. If the land allocated to the garden committee to distribute among the villagers was insufficient, the headman saw it as his duty to allocate more land. These practices certainly point towards an underlying norm of sharing land and water that is seen as essential for the villagers' livelihood in a wide sense. People we talked to in Bangira were reluctant to pay for water if it was moved from the dam to their gardens by a pump. The products that were grown in these gardens were both for family consumption and for sale. A wealthy couple who had worked hard to establish funding for the dam so as to raise the living standard of their own and other families argued that, since the surplus was used for livelihood essentials, such as clothes, school fees or medicine, the water use should not be seen as commercial. In the three villages, there were only two or three homesteads which employed labour to establish and water, dry season gardens. Livestock were watered in shallow wells or at nearby rivers.

In general, despite the growing investment in water and new forms of cropping, the principles of allocation of garden land and water reflected household needs and capacities. This site of more commercialised agriculture and growing investment in water has not led to the enclosure of resources.[30] It appears that in this area, customary norms and institutions have been able to respond to multiple needs, changes and as such reflect a local consensus.[31] In relation to water, it is interesting to note that it was women who over-whelmingly managed water. The observation that water is used by everyone but managed by women indicates the need to pay more attention to this highly gendered division of labour.

In the three villages we found that women were responsible for caring for children, the sick, gathering wood, cooking, along with obtaining water for domestic and garden use. Women were interested and participated in income-generating activities. They did so, however, in co-operatives and groups rather than as single entrepreneurs, often due to household responsibilities. We would hypothesise that these basic and fundamental concerns are reflected in patterns of co-operation around the key resource of water. That women play a far more central role in water management than in land management is one factor that may help explain the commodification of land in comparison to that of water. To refine and deepen our hypothesis, similarities and differences between land and water management and allocation over time in different Zimbabwean contexts is needed.

V. BUILDING A HUMAN RIGHTS-BASED APPROACH TO WATER FROM THE GROUND UP

In a more general survey undertaken, 89 per cent of the residents of Bangira and Kaondera answered yes to the question whether or not there is a basic right to water. In conversations and interviews people did not express themselves in a western rights vocabulary. People stated that they could not deny anyone water and that misconduct was associated with poisoning or deterioration of water sources. These spiritually sanctioned norms appear to be a function equivalent to law in a western sense.[32] That people not only consistently shared what was considered safe drinking water but also believed that denying people drinking water would lead to sanctions, indicates that there is an obligation to share. There is, in other words, a set of corresponding rights and obligations in place. The obligation to share extends to a well which is privately dug and on basically private land. Based on the practice of sharing, it extends to boreholes constructed for principally commercial or dedicated use. The duty to share cuts across kinship and village borders. We do not know if this is true throughout Zimbabwe, but it is the case in the areas of the three catchments where the CASS water research team had been working.

A series of studies of local water management from other parts of Zimbabwe point in the same direction. In Nkayi District in the province of Matabeleland informal rules seem to be to the effect that poor women get away with breaking new rules limiting water resources to certain individual users [*Cleaver, 1998: 357*]. The obligation to share overrode new efforts to limit access to a defined group of users. The communal area population where Sithole did her study of dambo cultivation was of the view that 'water should be available to all, rich or poor, but the person who impounds the water is the one who makes the river dry' [*Sithole, 1999*]. Sithole sees this as an expression of water as a fundamental human right. Dumisani Magadlela, who studied water conflicts between farmers within the Nyamaropa Irrigation Scheme and local villagers, showed that state initiated irrigation schemes which limit the access of outside users in times of scarcity, such as drought, are not generally accepted [*Magadlela, 1999: 127*]. This is of particular note since he was concerned with irrigation water not domestic water.

Although the origin of the right to primary water as embedded in the Zimbabwean Water Act since the 1920s and the regulations that are in place in the communal lands are of different origins, they are an expression of the same principle. Both the indigenous regulation and the concept of primary water recognise everyone's right to use water as necessary for life. The concept of primary water originally came to Southern Rhodesia via South Africa. This old idea has now been codified in the new Constitution of South Africa as 'Everyone has the right to have access to sufficient food and water'.[33]

The main concern of the water reform in Zimbabwe and the international policy framework of which it is a part, is to have water considered as an economic good and, implicitly, to have it given a price. This is far different than a right to water that remains embodied in the notion of primary water. The assumption of many water scientists and managers is that a rights-based approach would lead to undervaluing water, wasting water or mismanaging water. The local management of water that we observed has more in common with a rights-based discourse. Water is too essential not to be shared. Sharing, both with regard to safe drinking water and dry season gardens, seemed to unite the villagers in an attempt to improve their living conditions. Equal access to water in Zimbabwe does not appear to have needed water reform for what is termed primary water.[34] Yet, the fears that may underlie the sharing – sanctions of poisoning and witchcraft – is a powerful tool that may be mobilised towards ends that do not necessarily coincide with human rights ideals. Nor are we convinced that water cannot be really managed because it comes from God, as underlies many people's beliefs. In short, local understandings may lead to outcomes that result in sharing and generosity but the underlying logic is very different.

Until now, village practices of water management and the statutory recognition of primary water spoke of a bottom-up perspective on the right to water as inextricably linked to the right to livelihood. There is the potential for exploration across time and space, state and local levels of how one may build linkages between rights and water, to counter the idea that only international and nation-state water reforms are effective for equitable water management. In the implementation of new water policies rests the threat that local and more equitable systems may be destroyed. We are not arguing that this is always the case but, rather, that there need to be further studies of how widespread such practices are and how local systems include (or do not include) a right to water (primary or otherwise). This should be part of research to assess the potential for linking local systems to international human rights discourses on a right to water. This limited study gives encouragement to, yet demonstrates the complexity of, building a human rights-based approach to water from the ground up and that national law should not override local systems which manage water equitably and fairly.

NOTES

1. See Peter Gleick, 'The Human Right to Water' [*1999*]; Anne Ferguson and Bill Derman, 'Water Rights vs. Right to Water: Reflections on Zimbabwe's Water Reform from a Human Rights Perspective' [*1999*]; Anne Hellum, 'Towards a Human Rights Based Development Approach: The Case of Women in the Water Reform Process in Zimbabwe' [*2001*].
2. The Convention on the Rights of the Child Article 24.
3. See A. Eide *et al.*, *Economic, Social and Cultural Rights* [*1995*].
4. See A. Eide, 'The Right to an Adequate Standard of Living Including the Right to Food', in Eide *et al.* [*1995*].
5. South Africa, Mozambique, Zambia and Malawi are also reforming their water laws and policies as a response to new international policies and principles. See Malawi Government, Ministry of Water Development, May 1999, Draft Water Act, Annex B. Lilongwe, Malawi. National Water Act (Act No.36 of 1998), South Africa, *Draft Water Conservation and Demand Management National Strategy Framework*, South Africa [*1999*].
6. See *Report of the United Nations Conference on Environment and Development* (UNCED) (Rio de Janeiro, 3–14 June 1992. UN Doc A/CONF 151/26). The International Conference on Water and the Environment (ICWE) in Dublin, Ireland, 26–31 January 1992, was attended by 500 participants, including government-designated experts. The Dublin Statement on Water and Sustainable Development was commended to the world leaders assembled at the UNCED Conference in Rio de Janeiro in June 1992.
7. On sustainable water management see Water Resources Management: A World Bank Policy Paper [*1993*] and Desmond McNeil's article, 'Water as an Economic Good' [*1998*].
8. For an exploration of how the Dublin Principles have been adopted see: 'The Dublin Principles for Water as Reflected in a Comparative Assessment of Institutional and Legal Arrangements for the Integrated Water Resources Management' by Miguel Solanes and Fernando Gonzalez-Villarreal, Global Water Partnership, Report for the Technical Advisory Committee, Santiago, Chile [*1999*].
9. See Shiva [*2002*]; Cleaver [*1998*]; Boelens and Davila [*1998*]; van Koppen [*2000*]; Peters [*1994*].
10. Foreword by Per Pinstrup-Andersen in Bryan Randolph Bruns and Ruth Meinzen-Dick (eds.), *Negotiating Water Rights* [*2000*].
11. Water Act 1998, section 32(1).
12. Water Act 1998, section 32(2).
13. Sithole and Williams have attempted to quantify the amount of water required to supply primary water needs in the Mazowe Catchment and its sub-catchments. They suggest 50 m3/h/year be used and increased for cattle and wildlife areas. This works out to between four to six per cent of water flows required to satisfy primary needs in the various sub-catchments of Mazowe.
14. Interviews with Zeb Murengweni and Dr Hugh Williams, Harare, Aug. 2001.
15. See Scott and Coustalin [*1995: 868*].
16. Muringweni and Williams, Aug. 2001.
17. Water Act No.31/98, the Zimbabwe National Water Authority (ZINWA) Act No.11/98.
18. Water Act 1998, section 36.
19. Catchment Council Minutes for the Mazowe, Manyame and Sanyati, 2000.
20. Water Act 1998 section 21.
21. See Robinson [*1998: 37*].
22. Research Notes, Feb. 2000. At a Mazowe Catchment Council meeting there was a discussion on whether to ask the Centre for Applied Social Sciences to suggest a definition for commercial water. This discussion ended when the Council's chair suggested the technological definition.
23. See Mohammed Katerere [*2001*].
24. CASS BASIS survey data, CASS 2000–2001.
25. For a discussion of the sustainability of some of the economic activities in the area see Stewart [*1998*].
26. One woman said that her well at home was unsafe for drinking because schoolchildren played soccer and the balls fell into the well. Sometimes frogs, snakes and rubbish fall into the well. They removed the dead frog and other things, but felt that the water was contaminated because

there was no chlorine at the Health Clinic to purify the water.
27. This is not specific to Mhondoro, but rather widespread in communal lands.
28. James Ferguson reports that in the rural villages supplying labour to the Zambian copperbelt, no distinction is made between poisoning through witchcraft and poison itself [*1999: 118*].
29. Childlessness is, for example, believed to be caused by the groom's failure to fulfil the obligation of paying a beast to the bride's mother [*Hellum, 1999: 188–205*].
30. This line of argument is extensively developed by the authors in Woodhouse, Bernstein and Hulme [*2000*].
31. Jean-Philippe Platteau [*2000*] suggests that local institutions may perform better than state ones, and that individualisation is not necessarily best for land tenure evolution in Africa.
32. In line with comparative legal theory we have been looking for a functional equivalent to law in a western sense [*Zwiegert and Koetz, 1987: 32*]. We took people's actual water management and the social and cultural arrangements that guided sharing as a starting point.
33. Constitution of South Africa of 1994, Section 27 (1)(b).
34. This analysis clearly does not include water provision systems for urban areas where there are much higher expenses in the supply of water.

REFERENCES

Beinart, W., 1984, 'Soil Erosion, Conservationism and Ideas about Development: A Southern African Exploration, 1900–1960', *Journal of Southern African Studies*, Vol.11, No.1, pp.52–83.
Boelens, R. and G. Davila, 1998, *Searching for Equity: Conceptions of Justice and Equity in Peasant Irrigation*, Assen: Van Gorcum.
Bourdillon, M., 1987, *The Shona Peoples*, Harare: Mambo Press.
Bullock, A., 1995, 'Hydrological Studies for Policy Formulation in Zimbabwe's Communal Lands', in R. Owen, K. Verbeek, J. Jackson and T. Steenhuis, *Dambo Farming in Zimbabwe: Water Management, Cropping and Soil Potentials for Smallholder Farming in the Wetlands*, Harare: University of Zimbabwe Press, pp.69–82.
Bruns, B. and R.S. Meinzen-Dick, 2000, *Negotiating Water Rights*, New Delhi: Vistaar Publications.
Cleaver, F., 1998, 'Incentives and Informal Institutions: Gender and the Management of Water',
·   *Agriculture and Human Values*, Vol.15, Dordrecht: Kluwer Academic Publishers, pp.347–60.
Derman, B., 1998, 'Preliminary Reflections on a Comparative Study of the Mazowe and Mupfure Pilot Catchments in the Context of Zimbabwe's New Water Act', Harare: Centre for Applied Social Sciences (CASS), University of Zimbabwe.
Eide, A., 1995, 'Economic, Social and Cultural Rights as Human Rights', in Eide *et al.* (eds.) [*1995*].
Eide, A., 1995, 'The Right to and Adequate Standard of Living Including the Right to Food', in Eide *et al.* (eds.) [*1995*].
Eide, A. *et al.* (eds.), 1995, *Economic, Social and Cultural Rights*, The Hague: Martin Nijhoff Publishers.
Ferguson, J., 1999, *Expectations of Modernity: Myths and Meanings of Urban Life on the Zambian Copperbelt*, Berkely, CA: University of California Press.
Ferguson, A. and B. Derman, 1999, 'Water Rights vs. Right to Water: Reflections on Zimbabwe's Water Reforms from a Human Rights Perspective', paper presented at the Annual Meeting of the American Anthropological Association, Chicago, IL., Nov.
Gleick, P., 1999, 'The Human Right to Water', *Water Policy*, Vol.1, No.5, pp.487–503.
Hellum, A.,1999, *Women's Human Rights and Legal Pluralism in Africa: Mixed Norms and Identities in Infertility Management in Zimbabwe*, Oslo: TANO/Harare: Mond Books.
Hellum, A., 2001, 'Towards a Human Rights Development Approach: The Case of Women in the Water Reform Process in Zimbabwe', *Law, Social Justice and Global Development Journal (LGD)*. 2001 (1), http://elj.warwick.ac.uk/global/01-1/hellum.html.
Hoffman, H.J., 1964, *Water Law in Southern Rhodesia*, Salisbury (Harare): The Government Printer.
Lan, D., 1985 *Guns and Rain Guerrillas and Spirit Mediums in Zimbabwe*, Berkeley, CA: University of California Press.
McNeill, D., 1998, 'Water as an Economic Good', *Natural Resources Forum*, Vol.22, No.4, pp.253–61.

Magadlela, D., 1999, 'Irrigating Lives: Development Intervention and Dynamics of Social Relationships in an Irrigation Project', Ph.D. Thesis Wageningen University.

Maxwell, D., 1999, *Christians and Chiefs in Zimbabwe: A Social History of the Hwesa People c. 1870s–1990s*, Edinburgh: Edinburgh University Press for the International African Library, London/Malawi Government, Ministry of Water Development, May 1999, Draft Water Act, Annex B. Lilongwe, Malawi.

Mohammed, J.K., 1995, 'Access to Water: Right or Privilege?', *Zimbabwe Law Review*, Vol.12, No.1, pp.226–50.

Mohammed, J.K., 2001, 'Participatory Natural Resources Management in the Communal Lands of Zimbabwe: What Role for Customary Law?', *African Studies Quarterly*, Vol.5, No.3.

Moore, S.F., 1998, 'Changing African Land Tenure: Reflections on the Incapacities of the State', *The European Journal of Development Research*, Vol.10, No.2, pp.33–50.

Nyambara, P., 1999, 'A History of Land Acquisition in Gokwe, Northwestern Zimbabwe, 1945–1997', Ph.D. thesis, University of Illinois.

Peters, P.E., 1994, *Dividing the Commons: Politics, Policy, and Culture in Botswana*, Charlottesville, VA: University of Virginia Press.

Platteau, J.P., 2000, *Institutions, Social Norms, and Economic Development*, Amsterdam: Harwood Academic Publishers.

Rhodesia, The Government of, 1976, *The Water Act*.

Robinson, P., 1998, *Targeted Water Price Subsidies*, Harare: Zimconsult.

Robinson, P., 1999, 'Raw Water Pricing – Options and Implications for Zimbabwe', paper presented at the African Water Resources Policy Conference, Nairobi.

Scott, A. and G. Coustalin, 1995, 'The Evolution of Water Rights', *Natural Resources University of New Mexico School of Law*, Vol.35, pp.821–979.

Shiva, V., 2002, *Water Wars: Privatization, Pollution, and Profit*, Cambridge, MA: South End Press.

Sithole, B., 1999, 'Use and Access to Dambos in Communal Lands in Zimbabwe "Institutional Considerations"', Ph.D. thesis, University of Zimbabwe.

Skogly, S.I., 2000, 'From Human Capital to Human Rights: The Human Rights Obligations of the World Bank and the International Monetary Fund', Ph.D., Faculty of Law, University of Oslo.

Solanes, Miguel and Fernando Gonzales-Villarreal, 1999, 'The Dublin Principles for Water as Reflected in a Comparative Assessment of Institutional and Legal Arrangements for Integrated Water Resources Management', on The African Water Page: http://www.africanwater.org/SolanesDublin.html.

South Africa, Government of, 1994, *Constitution of South Africa*.

South Africa, Government of, 1999, *Water Conservation and Demand Management National Strategy Framework* (Draft), Pretoria.

Stewart, J. (ed.), 1998, *Grounding Good Governance and Democracy in Communities: An Exploration of Some Zimbabwean Experiences*, Austrian North South Institute, Vienna.

Taylor, P. and C. Chatora, 1995, 'Integrated Water Management at Catchment Level: Inventory of Catchment Management Experience in Zimbabwe', prepared by the Institute of Water and Sanitation Development, University of Zimbabwe for the Royal Netherlands Embassy, Harare.

Taylor, P., Chatora, C. and J.P. Hoevenaars, 1996, *Project Formulation: Mupfure Catchment Integrated Water Management*, Project Document on behalf of the Royal Netherlands Embassy, Harare.

UNDP, 1998, *Integrating Human Rights with Sustainable Development*, UNDP Policy Document.

van Koppen, B., 2000, 'Gendered Water and Land Rights in Rice Valley Improvement, Burkina Faso,' in B. Bruns, and R.S. Meinzen-Dick, *Negotiating Water Rights*, New Delhi: Vistaar Publications.

Woodhouse, P., Bernstein, H. and D. Hulme, *African Enclosures? The Social Dynamics of Wetlands in Drylands*, Oxford: James Currey.

World Bank, 1993, *Water Resources Management: A World Bank Policy Paper*, Washington, DC: World Bank.

Zimbabwe, Government of, 2001, *Towards Integrated Water Resources*, Management by the Water Resources Management Strategy Group (Draft), Ministry of Rural Resources and Water Development, Harare.

Zimbabwe, Government of, 1998, *The Government of Zimbabwe Water Act, No.31/1998*.

Zimbabwe, Government of, 1998, *The Government of Zimbabwe National Water Authority Act No.11/1998*.
Zimbabwe, The Government of, 2000, *Statutory Instrument 33. Water (Catchment Councils) Regulations, 2000*.
Zimbabwe, The Government of, 2000, *Statutory Instrument 47 of 2000. Water (Subcatchment Councils) Regulations, 2000*.
Zweigert, K. and H. Kotz, 1987, *An Introduction to Comparative Law*, Second Edition, Oxford: Clarendon Press.

Other documents

United Nations Conventions and Declarations:
International Covenant of Economic, Social and Cultural Rights (CESCR) 1966.
Convention on the Rights of the Child (CRC) 1989.
Declaration on the Right to Development. Adopted by General Assembly Resolution 41/128 f 4 December 1986.
The Rio Declaration on Environment and Development (1992).
Agenda 21 (1992), Chapter 18 Protection of the Quality and Supply of Freshwater Resources: Water Resources.
The Dublin Statement on Water and Sustainable Development (1992).

The Interplay Between Formal and Informal Systems of Managing Resource Conflicts: Some Evidence from South-Western Tanzania

FAUSTIN P. MAGANGA

I. INTRODUCTION

This study discusses the overlaps and interactions between formal and informal systems of managing conflicts related to land and water resources in Tanzania. The discussion adds to other studies challenging previous approaches that assume a clear separation between formal and informal institutions in natural resource management [*Mehta et al., 2001*]. The study is based on fieldwork carried out in Usangu Plains, Tanzania (see Map), an area previously very sparsely populated, but recently experiencing very rapid changes in demography and agricultural development. About 40 ethnic groups are represented in the area. Apart from the in-migration of both small-scale agriculturalists and pastoralists, competition for resources is exacerbated by the expropriation of land for large-scale agricultural enterprises, particularly rice production, wildlife conservation and power-generation projects. Agricultural encroachment on to pastoral lands has at times meant that critical dry season pastures have been lost, and herder-farmer disputes and conflicts are numerous [*Charnley, 1994, 1996; Odgaard and Maganga, 1994*]. Competition for resources is particularly pronounced during the dry season when water and grazing land are very scarce.

For the majority of the population, access to land and water is regulated according to customary and village by-laws. However, more and more private

Faustin P. Maganga, Institute of Resource Assessment, University of Dar es Salaam, Tanzania; e-mail efh@udsm.ac.tz. This study draws on two research projects. The first one was conducted during 1998–99 with Dr Ibrahim Juma (Faculty of Law, University of Dar es Salaam). Funds for this research were obtained from Danida's Enhancement of Research Capacity (ENRECA) programme. The second research was undertaken during 2000, under the DFID-financed Rural Livelihoods research project, headed by Dr Frances Cleaver, Development and Project Planning Centre, University of Bradford. The author wishes to acknowledge both Dr Juma and Dr Cleaver for their useful insights. He also wishes to thank Professor Ben Cousins, University of Western Cape (South Africa) and other participants at the Seminar on 'Formalisation and Informalisation of Land and Water Rights in Africa', Skodsborg, Denmark, for constructive comments. Finally, he thanks the two anonymous referees who made constructive comments on an earlier version.

MAP OF USANGU PLAINS, TANZANIA

individuals are trying to obtain formal rights (such as title deeds to land), because of the perceived insecurity that is associated with informal arrangements or customary rights [*Maganga and Juma, 2000*].

Writers such as Meinzen-Dick and Pradhan [*2001*] have noted that policy-makers are often influenced by approaches to property rights that regard them as unitary and fixed, rather than diverse and changing. This is the case in Tanzania, where the government, prompted by increasing pressure on land and water resources, has been busy trying to establish formal legal systems, fixing property regimes and formalising informal arrangements considered efficient and transparent institutional frameworks for the management of these resources. With regard to land, reforms have been undertaken to undo and liberalise previous socialist arrangements. Policy-makers hope that the changes brought about by the 1995 Land Policy, the 1999 Land Act and Village Land Act will be responsive to the needs of modern Tanzania in the context of a liberalised economy and the emerging land market. However, these land reform processes have led to insecurity for some [*Odgaard, 1998*], while others have used the opportunity to grab large tracts of land. With regard to water resources, the government has recently established Basin Water Offices in order to manage water utilisation by different users, that is, to allocate water rights; legalise, grant, modify and control water abstractions; protect the existing water rights and take to court defaulters of the Water Utilisation (Control and Regulation) Act. These measures have increased tensions and conflicts between different resource users, as well as between the government and the villagers [*Maganga et al., 2001*].

II. RESOURCE MANAGEMENT, CONFLICT MANAGEMENT AND LEGAL PLURALISM: A THEORETICAL FRAMEWORK

This study is inspired by a number of recent analyses of resource management, especially of the role of institutions in natural resource management (NRM), conflict management and legal pluralism [e.g., *Boesen et al. 1999; Charnley, 1996; Cleaver, 2001; Cousins, 1996, 1998; Mehta et al. 1999; Meinzen-Dick and Pradhan, 2001*]. In this section I discuss some of the theoretical issues raised by these studies and their relevance to my findings from the study area.

Some studies have highlighted the crucial role played by 'formal' and 'informal' institutions in NRM, and their importance in conflict management [*Boesen et al., 1999; Cousins, 1996; Mehta et al., 2001*]. Noting that institutions include knowledge systems, rules and norms, organisations and conflict resolution mechanisms, Boesen *et al.* [*1999*] note that demands for a resource may grow in relation to either intensification under the same use, or diversification into new uses. This demand may be made by the same user group or new user groups. We have already noted the intense competition for land and water resources on Usangu Plains, where data for this study were collected. Cousins [*1996*] writes about conflict management in the context of the utilisation of natural resources for multiple purposes, that is, by more than one user. He argues that disputes or conflicts are common in these situations, and hence the need for appropriate institutional frameworks for resolving and/or managing these disputes and conflicts. To a certain extent, the evidence from Usangu corroborates Cousins' assertions, but there is also co-operation, negotiation and accommodation, as noted by Cleaver [*2001*], and Maganga [*2000*].

According to Cousins [*1998*], formal institutions 'are those backed by law, implying enforcement of rules by the state, while informal institutions are upheld by mutual agreement, or by relations of power and authority, and rules are thus enforced endogenously'. However, it is somewhat problematic to adopt a very strict distinction between 'formal' and 'informal' institutions of managing resource conflicts, since decisions in the 'formal' primary courts are also influenced by 'informal' institutions such as tribal elders who sit in the courts as court assessors.

Theoretical studies on resource conflicts and conflict management [e.g., *Burton and Dukes, 1990; Cousins, 1996*] differentiate between causes, levels and phases of conflict; and make a distinction between management problems, disputes and conflicts. These distinctions have implications for conflict resolution. As noted by Cousins [*1996*], management problems involve arguments or differences over the choice of alternatives among persons having the same goals and interests; these are best dealt with through processes of problem-solving, improved communication and improved personal interaction. Disputes involve competing but negotiable interests: here, settlement processes such as judicial procedures, negotiations and bargaining are appropriate. Conflicts involve the development and autonomy of the individual or identity group, and are thus bound up with non-negotiable human needs and questions of identity. Hence the resolution of conflicts require in-depth understanding of relationships, and often the assistance of a third party.

Instead of focusing on conflict resolution, other writers [e.g., *Hendrickson, 1997; Cleaver, 2001*] refer to relations of conflict and co-operation, challenging the perspective that tends to see conflict as 'undesirable, a breakdown in normal relations and something to be avoided or resolved as quickly as possible'. They point out that there is a relationship between conflict and co-operation, involving various reconciliatory systems. In this analysis further evidence is provided to support the assertion that conflict and co-operation are not exclusive to each other.

Another perspective that is relevant for Usangu is legal pluralism. Meinzen-Dick and Pradhan [*2001*] note that many conceptions of property rights have focused only on static statutory law, ignoring the coexistence and interaction between multiple legal orders such as state, customary and religious laws. Tanzania has a pluralistic legal system and, hence, land and water resources are regulated by different pieces of legislation and institutions, including statutory law, customary laws of the more than 120 ethnic groups, Islamic law, and so on. Whenever there is scarcity and competition, however, the authorities pretend that the only prevailing law is state law.

The above observations have methodological implications. Research on formal and informal systems of conflict management cannot be undertaken merely through the analysis of cases from the Primary and District Magistrates' Courts. Several writers point out the limitations of relying on this official legal material alone. Van Donge [*1993b*] argues that social behaviour is a continuous construction of realities which cannot be caught in formal rules, and a court case is only a fraction of the social situation which creates a conflict. Further Bentzon [*1994*] notes how a researcher qualified in law is inclined to focus on a review of statutes, subordinate legislation, case law, court files and records, in the hope that these will yield a profile of law in books, and of how specific issues are dealt with in the court. Bentzon [*1994*] also emphasises that traditional legal material and sources may offer little insight into the lived realities of the people's lives, or reveal, except superficially, the inadequacies of the legal system as operated in practice [*Bentzon, 1994: 101–2*]

Hence, although this study is based mainly on data obtained from village files, ward tribunal records, as well as some case files in the primary and district courts, the official information is complemented by that obtained from other data collection techniques, including group discussions and key informant interviews.

III. LEVELS AND TYPES OF CONFLICTS

In this section evidence is provided to show that resource conflicts in the study area cannot simply be reduced to struggles between different ethnic groups or disputes between cultivators and pastoralists. Field data show that conflicts take place at various levels, between different actors, and that some conflicts over property are deeply embedded in marital and familial relations. The section also provides evidence to show that different types of institutions are involved in conflict resolution and that, in certain cases, more that one channel may be involved in the same conflict.

Conflicts Within and Between Families

There are frequent conflicts over access to resources within, and between, families, leading to the breakdown of marriages and a proliferation of cases related to the custody of children. These cases may be handled by tribal elders, village authorities, ward tribunals and primary courts.

An example of a conflict within families is the case heard at Rujewa Primary Court between a brother and a sister, fighting over a three-acre plot left by their deceased father (Civil Case No. 1 2000: Boniface Mfyomole vs. Mhigo Mfyomole). Both the litigants were past their fifties. The case started at the ward tribunal, where the sister won. The brother then appealed, and the proceedings commenced at Rujewa Primary Court on 6 January 2000, with the judgment delivered on 10 March 2000. The brother wanted to evict his sister from a three-acre plot she was cultivating, claiming that the land was allocated to him by a village headman (*jumbe*) during the 1940s. He claimed that he had cleared the land and cultivated it continuously between 1949 and 1972, before allowing his sister's son to borrow it, when he went to work in Rujewa town. On her side, the sister claimed that the contested plot was part of a six-acre farm which belonged to their late father who, at the time of his death, left three acres to each one of them as inheritance. The sister called an elder brother as witness to testify in favour of her claim. Before passing judgment, the magistrate and the court assessors visited the disputed plot, and heard testimony from different other witnesses. The pimary court upheld the decision of the ward tribunal that the plot belonged legally to the sister, and the brother was ordered to pay all the costs related to the case.

The above case also involved the issue of women's land rights, which has been hotly debated recently in Tanzania in the context of the National Land Policy, and the recently passed Land Bills. Some feminist scholars [e.g. *Rwebangira, 1996*] have argued that customary rules, which guide decisions in ward tribunals and primary courts do not sufficiently guarantee women's access to land and that they should be scrapped. Other studies [e.g., *Odgaard, 1998*] have used historical sources to argue that customary rules of tribes, such as the Hehe and Sangu, provide some essential rights to land and property for women. The case of Boniface Mfyomole vs. Mhigo Mfyomole shows that it is possible for women to successfully claim their land rights through formal legal channels even though, as many respondents have pointed out, men and women do not have equal access to land. It is also significant to note that the brother in the above case did not question his sister's right to inherit land, but chose to legitimise his claims by alleging that he was claiming back borrowed land.

A typical case of conflict between families occurs when married couples decide to terminate their marriage and cut connections that unite their families (for example, bride-price). One woman from Ukwaheri village, who has since remarried reported: ' ... In 1986 I was divorced. The matter was heard at the Primary Court in Chimala, where it was ordered that my parents should return six of the cattle he had paid as bride price.'

Polygamy is a common practice in the study area. Many cases of quarrels between co-wives which, on the surface, look as if caused by mere jealousy, are actually struggles for resources, including land [*Maganga, 1999b*]. The following two examples from the Ruiwa Ward Tribunal illustrate this situation:

(1)   A wife sought divorce from her husband because 'she was no longer in love with him'. However, the case details show that since 1996 her husband had started a new love affair, and that he was transferring resources, including harvested crops from their joint farm (rice and maize), to the house of his new lover. Efforts by tribal elders and the village leaders to reconcile the husband and wife failed. The wife approached the ward tribunal to seek permission to forward the issue to the primary court, the institution which is empowered to grant divorce. However, the ward tribunal ruled that the wife had failed to convince it that differences with her husband were irreconcilable, so efforts at reconciling her with her husband should continue.

(2) A wife sought to terminate her marriage with a husband she had lived with for 20 years; they had seven children. She accused him of abandoning her without any support, while he had gone to live with another woman. Her brother gave her a plot of land on which she cultivated rice, got a good harvest and bought a cow. When she sold the cow in order to buy food for her children, the husband took her to the police station, accusing her of theft. Elders tried to reconcile them, but in vain. The ward tribunal, convinced she had sufficient grounds to be granted a divorce, agreed to give her a letter to proceed to the primary court to start divorce proceedings.

These examples show how some conflicts over property are embedded in marital and familial relations. Investigations at the Ruiwa Ward Tribunal show that out of 114 issues handled between 1997 and 2000, 30 were divorce cases (filed mostly by women, in the majority of which permission was granted to continue with divorce proceedings at the primary court). There were also 27 family-related cases, mostly involving women suing their husbands for child neglect and unfair distribution of family assets. Such family conflicts may move from 'informal' to 'formal channels' of conflict management (and *vice versa*). These findings underline the complexity of finding institutional solutions to resource conflicts in the area, and the fallacy of creating formal–informal divides in a situation where there are 'overlaps and interactions between various institutional domains' [*Mehta et al., 2001: 3*].

Inter-Village Conflicts

Inter-village conflicts may result from the practice of villagers cultivating in areas where they do not reside. This occurs for a variety of reasons. One is that some of the villages (especially those created during the villagisation programme) were located according to administrative convenience and accessibility, rather than ecological considerations. Hence villagers may cultivate plots in different locations in order to spread the risk of crop failure, or to cultivate crops which thrive in specific areas, exploiting different ecological and micro-climatic opportunities. Villagers may also wish to maintain two residences because they are reluctant to give up their ancestral land, or even move to another village.

The fact that such farmers do not reside in places where they cultivate may result in their failure to adhere to any by-laws of that particular village, particularly regarding the use of natural resources. Absenteeism has also encouraged neighbours to encroach on their plots, especially if they are cultivating on high potential areas.

Rivalries Between Ethnic Groups

Inter-ethnic rivalry and competition is another possible source of resource conflicts in Usangu since most villages are ethnically heterogeneous. The fact that some ethnic groups are associated more with livestock (Sukuma and Maasai) and others with cultivation has added to the impression that competition between cultivation and livestock-keeping amounts to ethnic rivalry.

The position of writers on the linkage between ethnic identity and resource conflicts differs. Charnley [*1996*] sees a strong link between ethnic identity and resource conflicts. She insists that there is actually a cultural conflict in Usangu Plains, and links this to environmental problems caused by irrigation development, land alienation, uncontrolled immigration, demographic pressure, insecure land tenure, and ineffective resource management practices. To illustrate the conflict, she highlights the ethnic hostility between the immigrant Sukuma and other ethnic groups, which manifests itself in violence. She cites a number of cases in which Maasai and Sukuma have attacked one another with knives, and also cases of verbal abuse, social isolationism, and non-co-operation. Charnley claims there is little social interaction between the Sukuma and other ethnic groups, and that efforts between the Sukuma and other herders to co-operate in solving resource-related problems on Usangu's rangelands have been futile [*Charnley, 1996: 10*].

In contrast to Charnley's position, earlier investigations in the area [*Odgaard and Maganga, 1994*] found little evidence of conflicts due to cultural differences, although there were indications that differences could exacerbate already existing conflicts. We noted that it was difficult to establish a direct link between ethnic identity and the numerous land disputes which we encountered in the study area. Two examples illustrate how the supposedly hostile ethnic groups coexist and collaborate in the study villages:

First, at the start of an interview with a Sangu farmer in Muungano village, he carried on for some time with the usual 'Sukuma bashing', alleging the loss of livestock by the Sangu was due to the arrival of the Sukuma: 'They have brought chaos, also they use a lot of black magic', he said, which is the reason Sukuma herds kept on growing in numbers, while those of the Sangu herds dwindled. However, towards the end of the interview he confided that, although he had a plot of five acres, he lacked the ability to cultivate it all. Therefore, he cultivated 2.5 acres, while renting out the other 2.5 acres to a Sukuma person, who ploughed his land in return.

Another example illustrating the collaboration between livestock-keeping ethnic groups and others comes from Mapogoro village. A Bena farmer reported that he normally hired four oxen from his Sukuma neighbours for each farming season in order to plough his fields, paying Tshs 10,000/= for each ox. The other system used in the area is to pay Tshs 10,000/= for a team of oxen to plough one acre.

In addition to the above examples, one could add many instances of inter-marriage between different ethnic groups which served to break down walls between them. It can be said, therefore, that relations between different ethnic groups in Usangu are characterised by rivalries as well as collaboration. Not all differences between ethnic groups can be classified as conflicts. However, cultural differences may lead to tension and conflict in times of stress and scarcity. Some studies on the Usangu have noted the problem of finding consensus and conflict resolution, partly because of cultural differences between groups residing on the Usangu Plains. Charnley [*1994*] notes the following on cultural differences between the Sukuma and their hosts, the Sangu:

> If a Sukuma immigrant living on the Usangu Plains is poor, he will return to Sukumaland to find a wife rather than marry in Usangu. There is very little social interaction between the Sukuma and other ethnic groups living in Usangu. Cross-marriages are rare. The Sukuma remain socially isolated, and in general only interact with other Sukuma ... the Sukuma do not appear to be assimilating with other ethnic groups on the Usangu Plains, nor with 'mainstream' Tanzanian society and culture [*Charnley, 1994: 207*].

Data from the study area confirm some of Charnley's observations, but in some instances the data modify her findings. Inter-ethnic marriages are a good indicator of cultural assimilation and co-operation among villagers. In Usangu Plains there are some obvious exceptions: whereas there are many children of mixed African and Baluch parenthood, there is no instance of an African man marrying a Baluchi woman. Likewise, it is very difficult for a Sukuma woman to be married to someone of another ethnic group, probably because of the very high bride-price expectations of the Sukuma. A number of cases involving claims of bride-price by Sukuma litigants at the Utengule-Usangu Primary Court testify to the fact that the Sukuma bride-price obligations make it impossible for Sangu suitors, given the limited Sangu herds.[1]

In contrast to the above claims, the Sangu normally marry for about six heads of cattle, as illustrated by Civil case 14/97. In the case of the Sukuma litigants, all the above cases were later withdrawn from the primary court. Several reasons were mentioned. First of all, the Court was supposed to be guided by Sangu customary laws, but the Sukuma litigants could be wary of the possibilities of getting 'justice' in such a forum. The other possibility could be the villager's desire to 'mitigate' conflicts among themselves. Relations between different ethnic groups in the study area are characterised by mixing and accommodation up to a point, but the extent and nature of this interaction is still shaped by prevailing cultural structures.

Competition Between Different Livelihood Systems

Resource conflicts may be caused by competition between people practising different livelihood systems [*Maganga, 1999b*]. In the study area, it was possible to find villagers practising different livelihood systems competing for land resources. The most obvious example is, of course, the competition between cultivators and livestock keepers. In some areas, agricultural encroachment on to pastoral lands has at times meant that critical dry season pastures have been lost, and there are numerous occurrences of herder–farmer disputes and conflicts, as documented in Charnley [*1994, 1996*] and Odgaard and Maganga [*1994*]. Competition for resources is especially pronounced during the dry season when water and grazing are very scarce. Charnley [*1996*] notes that, although the different ethnic groups have tried to implement customary resource use and management practices, the activities of one group undermine those of another, and no one group is willing to adhere to the cultural practices of another. There are many incidents of crop destruction by livestock, as well as competition between farmers and livestock-keepers for water.

Competition between different livelihood systems is compounded by the fact that there is an overlap between ethnic and livelihood identities. In Usangu, the Maasai and Sukuma ethnic groups are normally associated with pastoralism, while other groups such as the Sangu and the Bena are more related to cultivation. However, this is a rather simplistic classification that shields the complex identities of many of the villagers, as noted by Cleaver:

> In Usangu … people's interests do not fit easily into the agriculturalist/ pastoralist divide. A large number of the 'pastoralists' are semi-sedentarised and engaged in cultivation, whilst young 'pastoralist' men and families engage in migrant labour and local gold mining in order to establish themselves economically. Similarly we see that as agriculturalists generate surplus, they may invest in cattle – evidence to support the concept of ethnic and livelihood flexibility over life courses. Neither economic activities nor ethnic identities may adequately reflect the complexity of people's interests or allegiances [*Cleaver, 2001: 30*].

Conflicts Between Government and People

A number of conflicts involve the government and villagers. They result from:

• the villagisation exercise of 1974–76;

• harassment by village leaders;

• harassment of livestock keepers by tax collectors;

• harassment by the Wildlife Department.

Between 1974 and 1976 the government relocated the rural population in Tanzania into 8,000 villages. Popularly known as Operation Vijiji, this exercise was carried out without any enabling legislation, often resulting in expropriating existing customary rights without establishing new ones in law. Villagisation was carried out under the false premise that, since all land belonged to the state, the state could allocate it and relocate the villagers as it wished without any legal consequences or obligation to the villagers. This exercise created the potential for many resource conflicts. The legal deficiencies of the villagisation exercise are summarised in URT [*1994*] and Shivji [*1994*]. A liberal era was ushered in Tanzania from the mid-1980s, with some of the former customary landowners who had been displaced by villagisation beginning suits in primary courts to claim back their land.

During fieldwork, villagers reported another example of conflict with the government which was harassment by livestock tax collectors. Under tax regulations, taxes were as follows: (a) cattle and donkeys Tshs. 500/=; (b) sheep and goats Tshs. 200/=. Taxes were collected in March/April, prior to the start of the Tanzanian tax year in July. The tax collectors would return in June, and possibly accuse livestock owners of hiding newly born animals, imposing a fine of Tshs. 2,500 on every 'hidden' animal, plus the normal tax of Tshs. 500/- per animal. Villagers also reported harassment by officials of the Wildlife Department as a result of the creation of the Usangu Game Reserve.

Conflicts between government and villagers are also related to issues of livelihoods and ethnicity. In most village governments where agricultural communities would dominate, this added to the official prejudice against pastoralists, thus fuelling policies and practices perceived as discriminatory. For example, on 12 October 1998 the *Guardian* newspaper reported that the Mbeya Regional Commissioner had ordered the 'ejection of Maasai Valley Invaders' in Mbarali, and ordered the arrest of one Maasai leader for inciting others to defy his order to vacate the Ihefu wetland, a crucial dry season grazing area for livestock-keepers. In another instance, the Mbarali District Commissioner clearly indicated the official prejudice against the pastoralists as he defended the creation of the Usangu Game Reserve:

> We have now demarcated 4,000 hectares under government control. Nobody is allowed to make a living out of that place. Mind you, we did that in national interest. The nation cannot miss electricity because of only a few pastoralists who would like to please their cattle (*The Daily News*, 30 Dec. 1998).

IV. SYSTEMS OF MANAGING CONFLICTS

There are several avenues through which resource conflicts can be resolved or dealt with, ranging from informal elders' councils to official tribunals and courts. In official channels the disputes can be styled as civil proceedings or criminal proceedings either in ward tribunals or magistrates' courts. Disputes may also be resolved administratively, by such public officers as the District Irrigation Officer, the District Land Officer or other local government officials.

Informal conflict management channels

Discussions with key informants revealed that many villagers would rather settle their conflicts through informal channels, taking their complaints for mediation to tribal elders, or sub-village chairpersons. The Maasai normally reconciled crop losses from animal grazing without compensation because 'it could happen to you tomorrow' (meaning they were all engaged in cultivation as well as animal rearing and animals could stray into a neighbour's field any time) [*Maganga and Juma, 2000*]. This is an example of villagers' preference for the maintenance of good relations with neighbours rather than encouraging inevitable conflict between different livelihood systems. Likewise, Baluch immigrant farmers never took their disputes outside their communities, preferring to settle them within their communities according to Islamic Law.

Ward Tribunals

The first 'formal' channel which plays an important role in conflict resolution involves the ward tribunals, established for each ward in Tanzania mainland. This channel attempts to combine 'informal' principles and methods of managing conflicts with the 'formal' ones.

The minister responsible for local governments is empowered to establish two ward tribunals for a ward, if it is seen that there are special circumstances that make it necessary or desirable. Each ward tribunal is made up of between four and eight members nominated by the Ward Development Committee from among residents of the ward in question. The District Council with jurisdiction over the ward will nominate a Chairman from amongst the members of the ward tribunal. Secretaries to the ward tribunals are proposed by Ward Development Committees and appointed by District Councils. The secretary serves the local government authority with jurisdiction over the ward in question.

The main responsibility of ward tribunals is the maintenance of law and order within the ward and striking a compromise and reconciliation between disputing parties. Tribunals are encouraged to try first to strike a compromise before resorting to mandatory powers. In the exercise of its criminal jurisdiction, a ward tribunal may exact a fine not exceeding Tshs. 10,000/=. In civil cases the tribunal may award damages of up to Tshs. 10 000/=. Village government may be a complainant to a criminal or civil proceeding.

Tables 1 and 2 record issues which were handled at Rujewa and Ruiwa Ward Tribunals.

TABLE 1
ISSUES HANDLED IN RUJEWA WARD TRIBUNAL (1995–1997)

Issues	1995	1996	1997
Farms	15	8	4
Divorce	23	15	13
Others	10	3	2
Total	50	27	20

TABLE 2
ISSUES HANDLED IN RUIWA WARD TRIBUNAL (1997–2000)

Issue	Number of Cases	Remarks
Land/Farms	20	Mostly related boundary problems, tenure arguments caused by villagisation
Divorce	30	Mostly by women; majority granted
Family	27	Mostly women suing fathers for child neglect; distribution of property
Others	37	Unpaid debts, bad language

As can be seen, most of the cases were divorce (filed mostly by women) or other family-related conflicts. As discussed earlier, divorce cases may be caused by competition over resources. It is interesting to note that women prefer the 'formal' legal channels (ward tribunals and primary courts) when seeking a divorce. This is due apparently to their hope that they may draw on provisions of the 'progressive' 1971 Marriage Act which is more beneficial to them than the 'conservative' tribal elders' councils.

Magistrate's Courts

In addition to ward tribunals, the magistrate's courts play an important role in dispute resolution. As with the ward tribunals, the primary magistrate's courts enforce both official statutory laws as well as customary and Islamic laws. Primary courts are established in every district to exercise jurisdiction within the district wherein a primary court is established. Any primary court has jurisdiction in proceedings of a civil or criminal nature. In proceedings of a civil nature the primary court has jurisdiction over:

- awarding any amount claimed;
- awarding compensation;
- ordering the recovery of a piece of land;
- ordering the restitution of any property;
- ordering the specific performance of any contract; and

• promoting reconciliation, encouraging and facilitating the settlement, in an amicable way, of the proceedings on such terms as are just.

In addition to the above tasks, a primary court may, on application of the party entitled to benefit from such an order in any civil proceedings, request a district court to take steps for the arrest and detention of any person who fails to comply with its orders.

A primary court therefore has civil jurisdiction in all proceedings where by-laws are applicable, be they customary or Islamic. During fieldwork it was established that the majority of people in the villages were still regulated by their respective customary laws and practices. The Magistrates Courts Act, 1984 provides that in the exercise of their customary law jurisdiction, primary courts shall apply the customary law prevailing within the area of respective jurisdiction of primary courts concerned. For the Rujewa Primary Court in Mbarali district, for example, the prevailing customary law is that of the Sangu people, which regulates use of water and land. Since currently the Sangu people are in an absolute minority in Usangu [*Charnley, 1997b*], it can be said that the system of referring to prevailing customary law is actually reproducing inequitable relations of power. However, the application of Sangu customary law is counterbalanced by the composition and role played by court assessors who sit with the magistrate in the primary courts.

The Magistrates Courts Act, 1984 provides that in every proceeding in the primary court, including a finding, the court is required to sit with not less than two assessors. Decisions of primary courts are made by the majority of court assessors and the presiding primary court magistrate. The application of the principle of court assessors helps to underscore the dynamism of customary law in conflict management. During fieldwork it was found that only the Rujewa Primary Court Assessors were predominantly Sangu (out of six assessors, five were Sangu and only one belonged to the Ngoni ethnic group). The ethnic composition of other primary courts was mixed. For example, the composition of Ilongo primary court assessors was six Sangu, one Safwa, one Nyiha and one Ngindo. The four Chimala assessors were balanced equally between Wanji, Sangu, Yao and Bena ethnic groups. The ethnic identity of assessors underlines the balance between individual agency and institutions in the application of the law. Hence, with greater flexibility and more complexity, there is greater scope for individuals to shape the outcome, making it possible for the interplay between 'formal' and 'informal' channels, as well as the varied aspects of customary law as noted by Odgaard [*1998*]:

• customary law as interpreted in courts of law (the principle of precedents);

• indigenous customary law (for example, of the Sangu people);

- customary law as interpreted by traditional authorities;
- 'customary living law' as applied by people in everyday life.

Primary courts are also vested with criminal jurisdiction to try such offences as fouling of water contrary to section 184 of the Penal Code (Chapter 16 of the Laws of Tanzania); setting fire to crops and growing plants contrary to

TABLE 3
ISSUES HANDLED IN USANGU PRIMARY COURTS

TABLE 3.1: IGURUSI PRIMARY COURT

Issue	Number of Cases	Remarks
Land	22	Mostly over rice plots, harvests
Family	19	Mostly over bride-price and *ugoni*[2]

TABLE 3.2: ILONGO PRIMARY COURT (1995–2000)

Issue	Number of Cases	Remarks
Land	14	Mostly related to plot boundaries and distribution of irrigation water
Divorce	9	Mostly by women; majority granted
Livestock theft	16	Sukuma vs Sukuma (4 cases); Sukuma vs others (2 cases); Others vs Sukuma (1 case). 8 cases settled out of court; 7 convictions (5-8 years jail), 1 case ongoing.
Others	5	Related to protection of forest, all dismissed

TABLE 3.3: UTENGULE–USANGU PRIMARY COURT

Issue	Number of Cases	Remarks
Land	1	
Divorce	2	
Livestock theft	8	Mostly settled out of court
Family	5	Related to non-payment of bride-price. Withdrawn and settled out of court

TABLE 3.4: CHIMALA PRIMARY COURT

Issue	Number of Cases	Remarks
Land	18	Mostly rice plots: boundary problems
Divorce	12	Mostly filed by women, all granted
Livestock theft	7	4 settled out of court, 2 ongoing, 1 conviction (8 years in gaol)

section 321 of the Penal Code; and absence from extra/mural employment, contrary to section 116A of the Penal Code.

Table 3 above gives an illustration of the issues which were recorded in Igurusi, Ilongo, Utengule-Usangu and Chimala Primary Courts. The table shows the proliferation of cases related to competition for irrigation water and boundary conflicts in irrigated areas. As it was the case in the Rujewa and Ruiwa Ward Tribunals, most of the divorce cases were filed by women. Family-related cases involved non-payment of bride-price and *ugoni*. The senior primary court magistrate in Rujewa noted the following points regarding resource conflicts in Mbarali primary courts:

In recent years there has been a trend for villagers to forward civil land conflicts to the court as 'criminal trespass'. Plaintiffs apparently wish to exploit Section 299 of the Penal Code, which makes it an offence for someone to enter another's property unlawfully. This is also apparently to avoid arguments and counter-arguments that are involved in civil suits, based on judgments according to customary principles. Moreover, many conflicts are caused by village land committees: once there is a change in leadership, the new leadership may not respect allocations made by the previous one. This signifies that the system of accessing land is still personalised to a greater extent, rather than institutionalised, as noted in the case of the composition of court assessors. Finally, some of the land conflicts in Mbarali District were caused by land renting and selling practices, particularly of paddy plots. An individual may rent out or sell a plot which is supposed to belong to the clan; however, once the clan members discover this, they may refuse to recognise the transaction. This observation also indicates that there is a long way to go before the institutionalisation of private property in land becomes a fact.

Early in 1999, the Tanzanian Parliament passed two pieces of legislation, the Land Act, 1999 and the Village Land Act, 1999, which created land courts and village land councils as alternative levels of official channels for dispute resolution. These new channels are yet to begin operating. However, it is clear that these policy initiatives are still focused on formalising land rights and systems of managing resource conflicts, in spite of all the evidence pointing to the interplay between 'formal' and 'informal' systems.

V. PRINCIPLES OF CONFLICT MANAGEMENT

Data from the study area reveal interesting insights about the principles of conflict management, including systems of punishment, as well as co-operation and conflict mitigation among the resource users.

Adversarial versus Reconciliatory Principles

In discussing systems of punishment, Cousins [*1996*] makes a distinction between adversarial systems, aimed at punishing the wrongdoer, and reconciliatory systems, aimed at reconciling the disputants. Distinguishing between the two, Cousins notes:

... the objective of traditional courts or tribunals in Africa was to reconcile the disputants and maintain peace, rather than to punish the wrongdoer. The 'winner-takes-all' judgements favoured by adversarial systems of law were generally avoided in favour of 'give-a-little, take-a-little' principle. ... Western systems are inherently goal-oriented and fear-based, and tend to negotiate conflicts from a position of power and in order to control people and situations. In contrast, non-Western approaches tend to be process-oriented, focused on the needs and desires of the people, rather than on the results. Values of respect, honesty, dignity and reciprocity are stressed [*Cousins, 1996: 49–50*].

Data from the study area have shown that systems of punishment in 'informal' channels generally operate along the lines suggested by Cousins. Even when fines or penalties are imposed, the proceeds are used to fund a celebration, which may also include the offender. This is what Cleaver [*2001*] terms 'celebrating reconciliation'. The ward tribunals apply both adversarial as well as reconciliatory principles. The ward tribunals were created essentially to reconcile, not to punish. However, this principle is undermined by the fact that members of the tribunal benefit from fines imposed on offenders. At one of the tribunals I was informed that members of the tribunal prefer to handle land conflicts because the litigants were required to pay Tshs. 15,000/= as 'allowance' for inspecting the contested area. Also, we have noted how the tribunals have been used mostly by women to facilitate their divorce proceedings. Courts are supposed to punish offenders; however, evidence shows instead that they tend to facilitate reconciliation, especially when allowing litigants to withdraw their cases so as to settle them out of court.

Conflict Mitigation

Villagers often practise conflict mitigation, including a preference for using informal channels, such as mediation by tribal elders and hamlet chairpersons or the application of religious principles in settlement of disputes. Examination of court records also revealed that the majority of cases involving livestock theft and claims for bride-price were withdrawn from primary courts, to be settled out of court. Another example is the compensation claimed after *ugoni*, in order to normalise relationships, after a spouse catches his/her partner making love with another person.

Writing of a related topic, Hendrickson [*1997*] mentions the notion of 'conflict avoidance', which has been explored in much of the literature coming from anthropological and resource management perspectives. He notes that many institutions associated with warfare among herder communities serve to restrict violence. These institutions and rules provide a way to mitigate conflicts and to ensure the payment of reparations when damage or homicide occurs. In our case the notion of 'conflict avoidance' is problematic, since conflicts are part and parcel of normal relations, and it is not always possible to avoid them – what remains then is to mitigate their impact.

VI. CONCLUSIONS

Although for the majority of the population access to land and water is regulated according to customary and village by-laws, more and more private individuals are trying to obtain formal rights, because of the perceived insecurity that is associated with informal arrangements or customary rights. Increasing pressure on land and water has prompted the government to try and establish what it considers to be efficient and transparent institutional frameworks for the management of these resources. While with regard to land, reforms have been undertaken to undo previous socialist arrangements; with regard to water resources, the government has established Basin Water Offices in order to manage water utilisation by different users, that is, to allocate water rights, legalise, grant, modify and control water abstractions. These measures to establish formal legal systems and to formalise informal arrangements have ignored the overlaps and interactions between formal and informal systems of managing natural resources. They have also increased tensions and conflicts between different resource users, as well as between government and the villagers.

Conflicts related to land and water resources occur at different levels: within and between families; between villages; between ethnic/livelihoods groups and between government and the people. Some conflicts over resources are deeply embedded in marital and familial relations; however, there are several avenues through which these conflicts can be handled, ranging from informal elders' councils to official tribunals and courts; disputes may also be resolved administratively by such public officers as the District Irrigation Officer; the District Land Officer or other local government officials.

Many villagers prefer to settle their conflicts through informal channels, by taking their complaints for mediation to tribal elders or sub-village chairpersons. However, women seeking divorce have preferred the 'formal' legal channels, hoping to benefit from the provisions of the 'progressive' 1971 Marriage Act. Regarding principles guiding conflict management in official channels, it is noted that ward tribunals and other official channels enforce both the official mainstream laws as well as the rules of customary law and Islamic law. The application of the principle of court assessors underscores the dynamism of customary law in conflict management. The ethnic diversity of the assessors also helps to establish a balance between the role of individual agency and institutions in the application of law, making it possible for the interplay between statutory law and the various strands of customary law. In practice, the blend is clear: contrary to the principles establishing ward tribunals, they apply both adversarial as well as reconciliatory principles; conversely, the courts also serve to reconcile villagers in some cases, contrary to their established objective.

NOTES

1. Civil Case 5/94 (Moku Nyorobi vs. Kulwa Ngassa): 55 cattle; Civil Case 8/94 (Subi Jinjiro vs. Lungunusa Rifa): 50 cattle; Civil Case 3/95 (Kulwa Machia vs. Ugali Ludano): 55 cattle.
2. Catching one's spouse making love with another person. Normally compensation is claimed in order to normalise the situation.

REFERENCES

Bentzon, A.W., 1994, 'Negotiated Law – the Use and Study of Law Data in International Development Research', in C. Lund and H.S. Marcussen (eds.), *Access, Control and Management of Natural Resources in Sub-Saharan Africa – Methodological Considerations*, Roskilde, International Development Studies, University, IDS Occasional Paper No.13, pp.92–108.

Boesen, J., Maganga, F. and R. Odgaard, 1999, 'Norms, Organizations and Actual Practices in Relation to Land and Water Management in Ruaha River Basin, Tanzania', in T. Granfelt (ed.), *Managing the Globalized Environment*, London: Intermediate Technology Publications.

Burton, J. and F. Dukes, 1990, *Conflict: Practices in Management, Settlement and Resolution*, New York: St. Martin's Press.

Campbell, H., 1987, 'Popular Resistance in Tanzania: Lessons from the Sungu Sungu', seminar paper presented at the Department of History, University of Dar es Salaam, 8 Sept.

Charnley, S., 1994, 'Cattle, Commons, and Culture: The Political Ecology of Environmental Change on a Tanzanian Rangeland', Ph.D. dissertation, Stanford University.

Charnley, S., 1996, 'Environmental Problems and Cultural Conflict: A Tanzanian Case Study', draft, Energy and Resources Group, University of California, Berkeley.

Charnley, S., 1997a, 'Environmentally-Displaced Peoples and the Cascade Effect: Lessons from Tanzania', *Human Ecology*, Vol.25, No.4 pp.593–618.

Charnley, S., 1997b, 'Pastoralism and Property Rights: The Evolution of Communal Property on the Usangu Plains, Tanzania', *African Economic History*, Vol.25, pp.97–119.

Charnley, S., 1998, 'Analyzing Environmental Degradation on a Tanzanian Rangeland: Natural and Social Science Perspectives', seminar paper presented at the Centre for Development Research, Copenhagen.

Cleaver, F., 2001, 'Institutional Bricolage, Conflict and Cooperation in Usangu, Tanzania', *IDS Bulletin*, Vol.32, No.4, pp.26–35.

Cousins, B., 1996, 'Conflict Management for Multiple Resource Users in Pastoralist and Agro-Pastoralist Contexts', *IDS Bulletin*, Vol.27, No.3, pp.41–54.

Cousins, B., 1998, 'How Rights Become Real? Formal and Informal Institutions in South Africa's Tenure Reform Programme', *Proceedings of the International Conference on Land Tenure in the Developing World*, University of Cape Town, 27–29 Jan. 1998, pp.88–100.

Hendrickson, D., 1997, *Supporting Local Capacities for Managing Conflicts Natural Resources in the Sahel: A Review of Issues with an Annotated Bibliography*, London: IIED.

Leach, M., Mearns, R. and I. Scoones, 1999 'Environmental Entitlements: Dynamics and Institutions in Community-Based Natural Resource Management', *World Development*, Vol.27, No.2, pp.225–47.

Lund, C. and H.S. Marcussen (eds.), 1994, *Access, Control and Management of Natural Resources in Sub-Saharan Africa – Methodological Considerations*, Roskilde University, IDS Occasional Paper No.13.

Maganga, F.P., 1995, 'Local Institutions and Sustainable Resource Management: The Case of Babati District, Tanzania', Ph.D. dissertation, Roskilde University Centre.

Maganga, F.P., 1999a, 'Researching Land Conflicts and Channels of Conflict Resolution: Some Insights from Babati District, Tanzania', in J. Boesen, I.S. Kikula and F.P. Maganga (eds.), *Research on Sustainable Agriculture in Semi-Arid Tanzania*, Dar es Salaam: Dar es Salaam University Press, pp.139–61.

Maganga, F.P., 1999b, 'Resource Conflicts and Conflict Management: Fieldwork Findings from Iringa Rural and Mbarali Districts', paper presented to the SASA Conference, Copenhagen, 17–18 Nov. 1999.

Maganga, F.P., 1999c, *Madibira Smallholder Agricultural Development Project: Baseline Survey of the Project Villages*, Consultancy Report to MSADP, Danagro Adviser A/S.

Maganga, F.P., 2000, *Resource Conflicts and Conflict Resolution on the Usangu Plains*, Consultancy Report for the SMUWC Project, Rujewa Tanzania.

Maganga, F.P., Butterworth, J. and P. Moriarty 2001, 'Domestic Water Supply, Competition for Water Resources and IWRM in Tanzania: A Review and Discussion Paper', *Proceedings of the Second WARFSA/Waternet Symposium*, Cape Town, pp.169–78.

Maganga, F.P. and I. Juma, 2000, *From Customary to Statutory Systems: Changes in Land and Water Management in Irrigated Areas of Tanzania – A Study of Local Resource Management in Usangu Plains*, Research Report submitted to ENRECA.

Mbonile, M.J, Mwamfupe, D.G. and R. Kangalawe, 1997, *Migration and its Impact on Land Management in the Usangu Plains, Mbeya Region – Tanzania*, University of Dar es Salaam, Report submitted to ENRECA.

Mehta, L., Leach, M., Newell, P., Scoones, I., Sivaramakrishnan, K. and S. Way, 1999, 'Exploring Understandings of Institutions and Uncertainty: New Directions in Natural Resource Management', *IDS Discussion Paper*, No. 372.

Mehta, L., Leach, M. and I Scoones, 2001, 'Editorial: Environmental Governance in an Uncertain World', *IDS Bulletin* Vol.32, No.4, pp.1–9.

Meinzen-Dick and R. Pradhan, 2001, 'Implications of Legal Pluralism for Natural Resource Management', *IDS Bulletin*, Vol.32, No.4, pp.10–17.

Moore, S.F., 1978, *Law as a Process*, London: Routledge & Kegan Paul.

Odgaard, R., 1998, 'Fathers and Daughters in the Struggle for Women's Land Rights: the Case of Hehe and Sangu Peoples in South Western Tanzania', *SASA Research Notes*, Copenhagen: Centre for Development Research.

Odgaard, R. and F. Maganga, 1994, *Local Informal Land and Water Management Systems in the Ruaha River Basin*, Draft Report, Centre for Development Research, Copenhagen.

O'Riordan, T., 1971, *Perspectives on Resource Management*, London: Pion.

Pendzich, C. 1994, 'Conflict Management and Forest Disputes – A Path Out of the Woods?' *Forests, Trees and People Newsletter*, Uppsala.

Rwebangira, M., 1996, *The Legal Status of Women and Poverty in Tanzania*, Research Report No.100, Nordic Africa Institute, Uppsala.

Shivji, I., 1994, *A Legal Quagmire: Tanzania's Regulation of Tenure Act (Establishment of Villages) Act, 1992* (Pastoral Land Tenure Series No. 5), London: IIED.

United Republic of Tanzania (URT), 1994, *Report of the Presidential Commission of Inquiry into Land Matters*, Vol.1: Land Policy and Land Tenure Structure, Dar es Salaam and Uppsala: Scandinavian Institute of African Studies.

van Donge, J., 1992, 'Agricultural Decline in Tanzania: The Case of Uluguru Mountains', *African Affairs*, Vol.91, pp.73–94.

van Donge, J., 1993a, 'Legal Insecurity and Land Conflicts in Mgeta, Uluguru Mountains, Tanzania', *Africa*, Vol.63, No.2, pp.197–217.

van Donge, J., 1993b, 'The Arbitrary State in the Uluguru Mountains: Legal Arenas and Land Disputes in Tanzania', *Journal of Modern African Studies*, Vol.31, No.3, pp.431–48.

Scrambling for Land in Tanzania: Process of Formalisation and Legitimisation of Land Rights

I. INTRODUCTION

The idea of Tanzania as a land-abundant nation needs to be altered to include the intensifying contemporary competition for arable and grazing lands. Tanzania is now experiencing an increasing number of land conflicts between different interest groups and between various types of land use. There are more and more cases of land struggles between groups of pastoralists and the state; disputes between villages over village boundaries; individual farmers against each other and/or the village government; land disputes between family and clan members, between rural and urban dwellers, between old and young people, and between men and women. There are examples of farmers joining forces to try to get their fellow pastoral villagers out from the areas where they live. The fairly recent creation of notably pastoral organisations attempting at a general level to defend the rights of pastoralists to land is an indication that some pastoralists are trying to strike back.[1] In other words, the scramble for land in Tanzania is in full swing. This situation poses challenges of how land rights are to be negotiated.

The focus in the present study is on the various types of land rights held by different groups of people in south-west Tanzania, and on how they struggle to acquire, maintain and secure land rights. In line with Berry [*1993, 1997*], Falk Moore [*1999*] and others, I look at land rights from the perspective of social relationships and as outcomes of processes of negotiation. Thus land rights are not just understood in terms of the rules and laws specifying them, but from the perspective of movement and interaction [*Berry, 1997*].[2]

Based on empirical evidence from south-west Tanzania, more specifically Iringa district, the study shows that, at present, all social groups living in the area participate in land negotiation processes, and their access to prosperity is determined by active participation in these processes. Certainly not all social

Rie Odgaard, Social Anthropologist and Project Senior Researcher, Centre for Development Research, Copenhagen.

groups are equally well positioned in relation to the type of outcome they are able to obtain, but the point is that they are all still involved. However, it is also shown that, due to the ever-increasing competition for land and pastures in the area, a new tendency of what I call 'double safeguarding' of land rights is emerging: while the formalisation of customary rights is sought, the social legitimation of 'formal' rights is also pursued. The negotiating processes hereby become more complicated, involving new barriers, especially for the most vulnerable groups, among which many women and pastoralists are found.

II. THE SETTING

The data used to illustrate the above have been collected during a number of fieldwork periods over the past eight to ten years[3] in semi-arid parts of what administratively is today referred to as Iringa district.[4] The semi-arid parts of Iringa district have previously been fairly sparsely populated but, due to natural increase and heavy immigration from other parts of Tanzania, the population has increased dramatically. People who consider themselves indigenous[5] to the area belong to the Hehe ethnic group but, as a result of immigration, the population is now ethnically very mixed.

There are wide variations in the agro-ecological conditions and the composition of the population in various parts of the Iringa district, but the villages in which data have been collected have the following general characteristics in common:

People base their livelihood on a combination of cultivation and livestock-keeping, some with more emphasis on cultivation and other livestock-keeping. Maize is the most important food crop, usually interplanted with various leguminous plants. Other crops are sunflower, sorghum, millet and, in places where irrigation is possible, different types of vegetables. Over the past 20–30 years, tomatoes have become an increasingly important cash crop, especially in the villages most accessible from the main road.

As mentioned, the population comprises a number of ethnic groups, with the Hehe as the indigenous group. The second largest group is the Bena from the neighbouring Njombe district, who started migrating to the area fairly early in the history, particularly since the late 1940s. Both the Hehe and the Bena had previously based their main livelihood on livestock-keeping with agriculture only as a complementary activity, carried out mainly by the women. Whereas women still play a very important role in agricultural production, the emphasis on livestock-keeping and cultivation respectively has changed dramatically both during and after the colonial era, and agriculture is by far the most important activity today.

Apart from the Bena, people from a number of other ethnic groups in Tanzania have found their way to Iringa district in search of land for cultivation and pastures, thus the population has increased heavily due both to natural increase and immigration. Seen from the perspective of the land rights issue the most important of such groups are Maasai herders mainly from the Dodoma and Arusha regions, the first of whom arrived in the area in the 1950s. Recent history of the area in question reveals that there is still a fairly heavy flow of immigrants into the area from other parts of Tanzania.[6]

The distinction made here between different ethnic groups needs some explanation. Many scholars have rightly shown[7] that the division of the African population into distinct tribes or ethnic groups in African countries is a colonial construct rather than something inherent in so-called 'traditional' African society. Historical accounts of Tanzania show, for example, that what has been referred to as Hehe and Bena tribes or ethnic groups since the beginning of the colonial era are in reality conglomerates of peoples, who had previously been carriers of different cultural identities [e.g., *Iliffe, 1979; Redmayne, 1968*]. It is also a well-known fact that population movements, the amalgamation of different peoples and so on have taken place in Africa since time immemorial [*Mamdani, 1996*]. Tanzania is no exception here.

Thus, when I refer to Hehe, Bena or Maasai, for example, I am not referring to tribes in the colonial sense of the word, but people who identify themselves, and are identified as belonging to these specific groups. Moreover, as part of their self-identification, each of these groups refers to specific norm sets and customary rules as forming part of their culture. But, as will be apparent, the norm sets and customary rules on which Hehe, Bena and Maasai base their self-identification, and which are used to define the rights of individuals to land and other property, are continuously being invented and/or reinvented – through the interaction of developments taking place at the local, national and global levels of society.

The Articulation of Land Rights in Iringa

The type of land rights held by the majority of rural people in the Iringa district are rooted in unwritten 'customary' rules and norms. However, this does not mean that all the people who happen to live together in a specific area have the same type of rights. Land endowments differ for different groups and individuals in the society, not only in accordance with age, status and gender, but also depending on whether one is *mwenyeji* (indigenous) or *mgeni* (guest).[8] For example, in a certain area, *wenyeji* have two types of land endowments in principle: indigenous rights and rights in accordance with socialist land policies, which are still reflected in the 1999 Land Acts [*URT, 1999*]. Hence, in principle,

Hehe men and women are endowed with two types of land rights in their respective home areas. The *wageni,* however, have land endowments in their home area, but endowments in the immigration area only in accordance with existing policies, and only if accepted as a member of a village community.

The extent to which *wawenyeji* and *wageni* (as groups or individuals) are able respectively to derive potential benefits from their land endowments, that is, to have legitimate effective command (entitlements) over such benefits (what can be produced from the land – food crops, cash from sales, etc.) depends on a number of factors of which the question of access to power and bargaining power is very important. In general, people's land rights depend very much on social relations: relations within an ethnic group, family/clan relations, marrital relations, friendship, patron–client relations, relations with authorities at various levels of the society and so forth. Thus, to a very large extent, the acquisition and contestation of land rights depend on the ability of an individual or group of individuals to negotiate with parties involved in the distribution of land rights, and the resolution of conflicts related to land. Certainly, some individuals or groups are better positioned than others in this whole game about land rights, as shown in the examples below.

In accordance with 'modern' land legislation and policies, people may have access to land through purchase and through allocation by the authorities. The involvement of local authorities in allocating land is not a new phenomenon,[9] but the form it takes at present is very much influenced by policies introduced during the socialist era in Tanzania.[10] However, under the New Village Land Act, 1999, village authorities are still assigned a very crucial role in land allocation [*URT, 1999*].

Contrary to what has been thought, landed property has, in the past, and increasingly so, changed hands across family and clan divisions. A land market has existed for a long time, with both men and women able, in principle, to buy land but, according to information obtained in the area, very few women in the two districts seem to have been able to do so.

In practice, the following are different forms of tenure found in the area and articulated as such:

• *Indigenous customary rights*, that is, rights held by people who are *wenyeji* in the area, mainly the Hehe as members of the indigenous ethnic group. Rights differ in accordance with age, status and gender.[11] Indigenous customary claims to seemingly unoccupied land have grown as a result of increased competition for land. Indigenous customary rights are considered locally to be as secure as private title deeds.[12] Customary rights are usually associated with obligations to use the land.

• *Customary rights rooted in non-indigenous customary rules and norms.* Such rights are referred to mainly by groups of immigrants who have lived in Iringa district for some time. Distribution of specific use rights are taken care of by internally recognised 'traditional' authorities to individuals and families in accordance with the way they interpret their own specific ethnic customary rules. These groups may or may not have approval from the local authorities to use the areas they occupy, however, while using the land, some of them may be involved in negotiation processes in which they try to increase their tenure security.

• *Rights through allocation by village authorities.* Many people in the area have received rights to some or all their land by this means. Such rights are held by both 'indigenous' villagers and immigrants – individuals and households – men and (some) women. However, married women are generally not allocated land without the consent of their husbands [*Odgaard, 1999*]. Some single and divorced women have been allocated land by the authorities, but they generally claim that this has been a very difficult process. Acquiring access to land through allocation by the village authorities is, however, very common in the area. The fact that not only immigrants hold such rights is related to various developments in the area. First of all, villagisation policies[13] have meant that large numbers of indigenous Hehe people were resettled in other parts of their home area and allocated land by village authorities in the new *ujamaa* villages. Since the mid-1980s, however, new agricultural policies have allowed people to move back to their original home areas, and many people have been able to reclaim rights to land they had previously cultivated. Such claims are continually being made. Village authorities are also being approached by people who want to have access to more land, either because they wish to ensure enough land for their children to inherit, or because new economic opportunities, have arisen. The tomato boom in the area is an example of new economic opportunities, and people who happen to have all their land outside areas well-suited to tomato-growing have tried to obtain rights to land in such areas, either through allocation or borrowing and renting arrangements (see below). In principle, people are allocated land free of charge, but some 'facilitation' costs are usually involved.

• *Borrowed or rented land rights* are widespread in the area, and almost all social groups are involved in such arrangements. The major distinction between the conditions associated with borrowed and rented land rights is in the nature of the relationship between landowner and borrower/renter, and the form of 'payment', for borrowing is not 'free of charge' and without conditions. For renting arrangements, the following forms of payment were identified: sharecropping; rent in cash; rent in kind or in labour (which may include the use of the renter's own equipment for ploughing a piece of land for the landowner, for example). Except for rent in cash, varying degrees of other 'payment' forms were also found with regard to the 'borrowing' arrangements but, again, depending on the type of relationship between the two parties. Both borrowed and rented rights are also often associated with the delivery of various types of services to the landowner. Renting and borrowing arrangements are usually accompanied by some restrictions related to the use of land: agreements, for example, are always short term (usually just for one year or growing season); it is not permitted to plant perennial crops such as trees, etc., or to make investments of any kind which may lead to later claims of property rights for the tenant. Renting and borrowing of land is a strategy used by landless people as well as by people who already have some land, and by Hehe and immigrants alike. Thus new economic opportunities have provided important incentives for people to borrow or rent land outside their 'home' villages.

• *Land rights obtained through commercial transaction.* An increasing number of particularly urban people try to obtain access to land this way for investment purposes. Some of these rights are formally sanctioned by an officially approved title deed, but more informal written evidence, signed by representatives for the official or traditional village authorities and witnesses, is becoming commonplace as a first step to formalisation.

• *Open access*: In some areas, defined as public village lands, there is a type of right that may best be described as 'open access'. Villagers use public village lands for various purposes such as grazing, firewood and fruit collection, etc. Everyone who is a recognised member of a certain village does, in principle, have such rights, and exercises them to varying degrees in practice. However, rights to village public lands (much of such land has been allocated to the villagers), are a frequent object of struggle, and there are many cases of village boundary disputes in the area, and disputes about whether *wageni* have the same rights as *wawenyeji* in such areas, while some people claim that they have customary rights to various pieces of land in these areas. There are also conflicts related to the relationship between customary rights and obligations. While everyone feels free to use these resources, it is difficult to hold specific individuals or groups of individuals directly responsible for sustainable management.

Although the different forms of tenure identified in the area have been described separately, it should be stressed that in practice it is very difficult to distinguish sharply between them. There is much overlap, as changes occur all the time, and new mixed forms arise. Moreover, one and the same farmer is often involved in several of the above-mentioned forms at the same time, implying that he or she has different types of rights to the various pieces of land being used. The situation is similar to that in Ghana described by Berry [*1997*].

The Land Scramble in Iringa and Processes of Formalisation and Legitimisation

In this complex and dynamic picture there is now an increasing tendency for many people to double safeguard their land rights, that is, on the one hand attempting to have customary rights 'formalised' and, on the other, to have 'modern' rights legitimised, that is, sanctioned by custom. The examples below illustrate this, but some reference to what, among the Hehe, the *wawenyeji* (indigenous) of the area, is understood as customary land rights today is needed as background.

The Hehe word for land held under Hehe custom is '*lilungulu*' – a word more generally understood in Swahili as '*lungulu*'. *Lungulu* land is a person's land sanctioned by Hehe custom. According to Brown and Hutt [*1935*], '*lilungulu*' means settlement, that is, an area with only a few houses, perhaps between one and ten houses, and usually inhabited by families bound together by kinship ties. Previously, when the area was very sparsely populated, the Hehe lived in very scattered settlements, there was plenty of land available and people moved very frequently because of livestock. Thus, people did not associate themselves strongly with a specific territory. According to the interpretations of land rights at the time, people had the right to the place where their houses were situated, and to cultivate as much land as access to labour and other resources would allow. The Hehe headman was authorised to distribute user rights to land to people living in their area, and to people from outside – both Hehe and people from other ethnic groups, who asked for it – as long as there was enough land available.

Until fairly recently, there has been enough arable land and pasture available. However, the situation described above, with increasing population, heavy immigration, alienation of large areas for plantations, conservation and other purposes, combined with the increased focus on cultivation and expansion of the cultivated area, has eventually led to pressure on arable land and pastures. Besides, people are now more permanently settled and increasingly cultivating the same fields with some rotation and fallowing. From having previously been the place where one has lived at any given time, that is, a settlement with scattered houses and fields belonging to close relatives, *lungulu* has now become the epitome of rights to land sanctioned by Hehe custom – an integral part of Hehe culture – the place where forefathers used to live, and the place where ancestors are buried.

Prior to European occupation, bodies of the dead were generally not buried but left in the bush. However, during the German occupation[14] it was ordered that all corpses had to be buried. Since then, the dead have generally been buried in their *lungulu*, with a small plantation to mark the position of the grave. Only people considered the rightful heirs to the property of the deceased may be allowed to use land where ancestors are buried. In the eyes of the Hehe, the presence of graves is itself a justification for legitimate land claims.

Some of the other ethnic groups living in the area have developed similar burial customs. The presence of graves is therefore a strong justification for making land claims, and not immediately disputed. Claiming rights to specific pieces of land with reference to the presence of graves is a very much used – and misused – strategy, but unless the position of the graves is clearly marked, it is of course difficult to prove their existence. To deal with this problem, it has now become common practice to make graves very visible by investing in large tombstones and developing plantations around them. Thus, during the course of the past ten years, there has been a remarkable increase in very visible graves and even graveyards in the district, particularly in areas where there is most pressure on land. I shall refer to this process as *'lungulisation'*.

Generally, any sort of visible investments on the land may be used to make claims, implying that the person investing in such a piece of land may eventually acquire rights to it.[15] It is in this light that the rules prohibiting any such type of investment in relation to the renting and borrowing of land should be seen. Previously, long-term use of a piece of land was sufficient enough to make claims, but this is becoming more and more difficult. Nowadays, investments have to be seen to be more tangible, due to the increased competition for land.

In general, customary rights may only be retained if the land is used, and if it is obvious that it is being or has recently been used. In most villages there are rules specifying the number of years that land can be left fallow. In principle, if the number of years is exceeded, the land (in a case where there are no visible graves or tree plantations on it) may be diverted by the village authorities and made available to other people. Even though there are some people who are better positioned in relation to the decision-making bodies in the villages, and may therefore be able to bend the rules in retaining their land somehow, these rules have generally implied that people having more land than they are able to cultivate by their own means are interested in letting other people use their land, while at the same time being able to derive extra income from the arrangement. This is the reason why renting and borrowing arrangements are so widespread. To double safeguard customarily-owned land, some *lungulu* owners have tried to obtain documentation in writing from village authorities or other respected authorities to avoid other people trying to gain rights to it. It is also becoming increasingly common that some landowners, particularly those coming from outside, try to have land rights formally registered (see the example below).

However, to have land rights formally registered (granted right of occupancy) is a very cumbersome and expensive process. The first step is that local authorities and witnesses have to certify the land in question actually belongs to the person wanting the right to it, and that there are no other claims. This involves time and 'facilitation' costs. The village land committee has to approve (that is, fees to be paid or at least 'facilitation' costs), then technicians have to be involved to measure the plot, a plan drawn up, and an application with documentation taken to the land registrar's office in Iringa town. According to people's experiences, a number of 'push' visits (involving time and transport costs), and 'facilitation' costs have to be paid. Finally, registration fees have to be paid if the application is approved.[16] In other words, it is perhaps no surprise that none of the smallholders interviewed possessed a granted right of occupancy. However, it is also possible to have a granted customary right of occupancy which can be issued at the village level, and some people who have the means and connections pursue this option.[17]

It is interesting to note that *'lungulisation'* is not something involving only the Hehe. There is general agreement among immigrants – and some Hehe – that there are now two different types of *lungulu*: there is the old type – hereditary over many generations; and there is the new one 'in being'. People argue that to obtain *lungulu* rights is a process – something that can be obtained over time – through investments, etc. Thus, land which people have been allocated by the authorities may in time become *lungulu,* and immigrants, who are generally farmers, are preoccupied with making sure that there are graves and other visible investments on their land, on which to base their claims for secure tenure. Some Hehe are not too willing to accept that immigrants can have *lungulu* but, on the other hand, they themselves may have pieces of land allocated to them by the village authorities, and which they may also want to call *lungulu,* so it is difficult to deny immigrants secure rights, even if they are not *wawenyeji* but *wageni*.

The following example, involving two immigrants (Mosi and Charles)[18] who belong to different ethnic groups and live in one of the fieldwork villages, illustrates that the divide in perceptions about the relationship between *lungulu* and *wawenyeji/wageni* is complex and not just a matter of the Hehe being on one side and the immigrants on the other:

Mosi belongs to the Gogo ethnic group, but has been born in this area to which his father migrated a long time ago. The original home area of the Gogo is in the neighbouring region, where the Gogo used to derive their main livelihood from livestock-keeping. Mosi's father has managed to get access to some land in another village nearby and, according to Mosi, the land now has the status of *lungulu*. The parents still use their *lungulu,* and Mosi lives here with his two wives, and borrowed some land from paternal relatives. The relatives are also immigrants, but have been allocated land from the village authorities. Mosi emphasises that the land he is using at present will never become his land – he has only borrowed it, but he will eventually inherit his father's *lungulu*.

While I am talking to Mosi one of the neighbours (Charles) comes by, and when he hears that we are talking about *lungulu,* he says to Mosi: 'But why should you as a Gogo be so concerned about *lungulu* – it is not part of the Gogo culture to establish strong long-lasting relations to a specific piece of land. For the Gogo, access to pastures used to be the important issue.' Mosi, however, emphasised that he grew up among the Hehe and is now part of the Hehe system, and *lungulu* is therefore also very important for him.

The preceding day I had interviewed Charles, who had told me that he belonged to the Sagara ethnic group. The Sagara used to be close neighbours to the Hehe, but were traditionally mainly hunters with some shifting cultivation, moving very frequently from one place to the other. *Lungulu,* therefore, was not previously a strong concept for them, according to Charles. However, during the British colonial era, the Sagara were amalgamated with the Hehe, and they now consider themselves part of the Hehe. Charles moved to the village some time ago, and when he came, he was allocated land by the village authorities. He has been using that land ever since, and now considers the land as his *lungulu.* Charles stressed during the interview that *lungulu* rights are now part of the Sagara/Hehe culture.

An interesting thing to note here is that Charles seemed to look at his own and Mosi's situation in different terms, and that he found it more legitimate for him than Mosi to be concerned about *lungulu* rights, and to consider such rights as an integral part of *his* culture rather than Mosi's. The example shows that there are different perceptions about what it takes to become part of another culture. It is clear from the example that Charles looked at himself as more *wenyeji* than Mosi, even if Mosi was born in the area, while Charles actually moved to the area later in his life. There is also another interesting aspect, namely that the traditional Gogo pastoral way of life was actually more akin to the traditional Hehe life-style than the traditional Sagara. Hence the important thing for Charles seemed to be that Sagara and the Hehe came to share the same traditional leadership through amalgamation and thereby became like one people.

The example also illustrates that while there are processes of *lungulisation,* there are also processes of *wenyeji-sation.* It appears that it is quite possible for a person to be referred to as a *mwenyeji* if he or she has lived in the area for a long time, has acquired *lungulu,* perhaps married into a Hehe family, and is a good leader and so on.[19]

Lungulu Land Rights are Not for Everyone

I have stressed above that all the social groups in the area are actively involved in negotiation processes in relation to land rights, and also pointed out that negotiation processes do not take place on equal terms for everyone. The degree of success in terms of quantity and quality of land rights is very much related to the nature of the relationship between negotiating parties, access to power and bargaining power, and other socio-economic factors, such as access to other resources (cash, labour, technology, etc.) The study clearly reveals that there is very unequal distribution of land in the studied villages and that the increasing pressure on land is intensifying the land struggle in the area, as well as giving rise to increased inequalities [*Odgaard (work in progress)*].

However, apart from being related to the issues above, inequalities in access to land rights are also related to the question of land use patterns and gender. As will appear from the following brief discussion, pastoralists and women are generally more unfavourably positioned in the negotiation processes than most other groups, and harder hit by the increased pressure on land.

Pastoralists have generally been continuously marginalised throughout modern history in Tanzania.[20] The reason why so many pastoralists from northern Tanzania live in Iringa and other parts of southern Tanzania[21] is that large areas where they used to live have been alienated and turned into fields, plantations, national parks, etc. as a result of colonial as well as post-colonial policies.[22] As appears below, processes of marginalising pastoralists are also taking place in Iringa district.[23]

The problem of marginalisation as reflected in the situation of immigrant pastoralists in Iringa may be summarised generally as follows: as long as nobody else wants to use land for agricultural purposes, the pastoralists and other villagers with livestock may use pastures on village public land, but as soon as there is a need to extend the agricultural area due to increased demand, or if somebody wants to invest in large-scale agricultural activities, the pastoralists have to move. Almost all pastoralists in the area are also engaged in cultivation as a supplementary activity to pastoralism but, due to the transhumance nature of pastoralism, they have either mainly small temporary fields close to their homesteads, or rent, and in some cases own, land in areas set aside for cultivation. As appears from the example below, there is a conscious strategy on the part of many pastoralists not to have fields in grazing areas. Very few pastoralists leave visible investments on the land they use and, therefore, generally do not gain more permanent rights to it (*lungulu*). There are many examples in the area of pastoral families having had to move several times, either because part of the pastures has been distributed to farmers, or because access to remaining pastures and water resources has been blocked by newly established farming areas.[24]

These problems are illustrated by the following example:[25]

An enterprising Maasai, who was among the first Maasai to settle in the area, had managed to be considered the legitimate owner of approximately 400 acres of land bordering the area set aside for grazing in the village. According to the information obtained, he used approximately 70 acres for cultivation, with the remainder for grazing. Finding himself in serious social and economic problems, he sold the 400 acres of land to an urban-based Hehe businessman who wanted to invest in large-scale agriculture. The village government approved the transaction in 1995 and allowed the businessman to start procedures for the registration of ownership. With the newly acquired land as a basis, the Hehe businessman subsequently managed to acquire land allocations or buy[26] land from the village government in the grazing area adjacent to his newly acquired land, and he then had approximately 1,500 acres at his disposal.

A group of Maasai herders, who had been living in the area in question since the 1950s, have since 1993 tried to have the same area set aside for herders to be used only for grazing. The Maasai were concerned about the continuous reduction of the grazing area and felt it more and more impossible to keep their cattle out of the many fields established in the grazing area. Moreover, there were increasing conflicts in the village between the Maasai and newly established farmers due to cattle invading fields. However, the village government has continuously rejected the request from the Maasai.

When discussing with the village government and some of the villagers interviewed whether this was fair, the answer was that the Maasai had not acquired any rights to the area and there was not enough land in the village to allow for any part to be set aside for herders. However, based on additional information obtained in the area, and the fact that the village files revealed that numerous land allocations to farmers both from the village and from outside were undertaken during the same period of time, it is hard to avoid the conclusion that there has been a conscious strategy on the part of the village government and some supporters to try to squeeze the Maasai out of the area.[27]

Women comprise another social category of people for whom access to land in their own rights is constrained. As mentioned above, it has turned out to be very difficult for women in practice to be allocated land in their own right, and also to buy land, even though women are granted the same rights as men in the Constitution and also in the 1999 Land Acts.[28] The major obstacles in relation to women's possibilities to exercise such rights in practice are, first, that such rights are being considered in the light of a woman's marital status, and made conditional on the consent of her husband. Secondly, the cumbersome procedures and the costs involved are prohibitive, particularly for female-headed families and the poor.

Many women in the area, at least as far as Hehe women are concerned, are in a much better position in relation to customary land rights [*Odgaard, 1999*]. Space does not allow me to enter into a detailed discussion here about the reasons why this is so, but generally the following principles are important: negotiation processes related to customary land rights takes place mainly between parties within the family and/or local so-called traditional authorities. Such forums are much more easily accessible to most women (and poor people in general) than district authorities, expensive bureacratic procedures, court rooms, lawyers and so on. Secondly, as appears from Odgaard [*1999*], customary rules strongly link the ability to exercise a right with the fulfilment of obligations. The relation between right and obligation often plays a major part in family decisions related to inheritance rights. The flexible nature of unwritten customary rules allows for interpretations that take into account changes over time in the roles and responsibilities between various parties in the family, men and women, parents and children and so on. Provisions in formal written legislation do not allow for such flexibility.[29]

III. CONCLUDING REMARKS

In the discussion about the dynamic processes involved in the scramble for land rights in Tanzania, I have emphasised that all social groups are presently involved, but stressed that they are not equally well positioned in relation to influencing the outcomes of the land negotiation processes. Based on empirical evidence from the Iringa district in Tanzania, the main point to be made here is that the increased focus on formalisation and *de facto* privatisation taking place at present, which is strongly influenced from outside, is more exclusive than inclusive for the majority of rural people, whose land rights are defined in accordance with customary and local rules and norms. As shown, privatisation and formal title deeds imply the involvement of experts such as land titling authorities, village authorities, courts and lawyers and so on. Such experts, of whom there are relatively very few in a country such as Tanzania, are beyond the reach of the majority of rural people.

Not surprisingly, it appeared that some people with ample access to financial resources, power and bargaining power may obtain large tracts of land even though land is becoming increasingly scarce for other groups. But, as pointed out, factors other than wealth in resources are, however, of vital importance for people's opportunities to ensure land rights. People who are indigenous (*wenyeji*) in a specific area have, for example, a much better starting point than immigrants (*wageni*). However, farmers among the *wageni,* whose type of land use is similar to that of the *wawenyeji,* and who have similar perceptions about what it takes to gain secure rights to land, stand a much better chance than, for example, pastoralists, who have a different land use pattern.

Gender inequalities, particularly in relation to access to the formal or more 'modern' land distribution systems (allocation from the village authorities and commercial land transactions), have implied, as stressed, that many women are excluded from accessing the mentioned types of rights. Women are generally in a much better position when land negotiation processes take place in family and local settings, and in accordance with interpretations of customary rules and norms. In such rules, the relation between right and obligation is stressed, and the unwritten nature of customary rules makes them open to flexible interpretations that can take general changes in the society into account. Emphasising this is not the same as arguing for a 'return' to customary law, as some may think. Customary rules and norms have always been there and still comprise part of Tanzania's legal pluralism but, as shown by Moore *1978* among others, they should always be understood from the perspective of changing contexts and process. Customary land rights in Tanzania should therefore be respected and recognised as on an equal footing with other types of rights for all social groups, including women and pastoralists.

NOTES

1. The Indigenous World [*1997–98*]; The Indigenous World [*2000–2001*]; Johnsen [*2000*].
2. A number of studies: Moore [*1986, 1999*]; Berry [*1993, 1997*]; Lund [*1998*] to mention just a few, have proved that this approach is very fruitful in understanding the articulation of land rights in Africa.
3. The major part of the information presented here has been obtained during my involvement in Subproject 3 under the research programme: Sustainable Agriculture in Semi-Arid Africa (SASA) from 1995-2000, financed by the Danish Council for Development Research. This fieldwork was carried out in Ismani and Mazombe Divisions, Iringa Rural District, in close collaboration with Jannik Boesen and Faustin P. Maganga. Other fieldwork periods in Iringa Rural District have been as part of my involvement in two studies carried out for The Danish International Development Agency (DANIDA), together with Hildegard Kiwasila, and for the World Bank with Faustin P. Maganga. See Kiwasila and Odgaard [*1992*], and Odgaard and Maganga [*1994*].
4. Administrative boundaries have changed frequently in Tanzania.
5. Indigenous population not to be confused with the term Indigenous People. Indigenous peoples are referred to as *watu wa asilii* in Kiswahili.
6. Further details about the population increase and immigration are found in McCall [*1982*], URT [*1978, 1988*], Odgaard [*1987, 1994*], Odgaard and Maganga [*1994*], Kiwasila and Odgaard [*1992*].
7. Lema [*1993*], Mamdani [*1996*], Ranger and Hobsbawn [*1983*], Ranger [*1993*], Chanock [*1998*] – just to mention a few.
8. It also depends on the nature of land utilisation pattern (for example, pastoralism/cultivation). This is further elaborated in Odgaard (work in progress).
9. Hehe headmen in the precolonial and colonial periods in Tanzania had the authority to distribute land both to members of the Hehe and to people coming from other groups.
10. See below and URT [*1983*]; Fimbo [*1992*]; James and Fimbo [*1973*]; URT [*1994*].
11. There are detailed analyses of the way indigenous Hehe customary rights historically have been allocated in practice in the area in accordance with age, gender and status, and how such practices have been changing over time in, for example, Brown and Hutt [*1935*]; Mumford [*1934*]; TNA Secretariat Files Nos.: 7794 and 7794/3 [*1925*]; Accession No. 157, file No.6/42 [*1938*] and Odgaard [*1999*].
12. For an in-depth discussion of the security in tenure of so-called traditional rights versus other types of rights, for example, individual private rights, see also, for example, Migot-Adholla *et al.* [*1991*]; Havnevik [*1995*]; Sjaastad and Bromley [*1997*].
13. The ujamaa policy was introduced with the Arusha Declaration in 1967 and aimed at the establishment of socialist villages. During the first years Ujamaa was a volunteer movement, but in 1973 an order was issued that within three years the whole rural population had to be settled

in such so-called development villages. For a detailed analysis of the ujamaa and villagisation policies and experiences, see, for example, Nyerere [1969]; Raikes [1975], Boesen et al. [1977]; McHenry [1979]; von Freyhold [1985].

14. The German Occupation lasted from 1894 to 1918. During this period Tanzania, by then called Tanganyika, was a German Protectorate.

15. Planting of trees and perennial crops is a commonly used way of acquiring more permanent property rights to land. See, for example, Chachage and Nyoni [2001] and Odgaard [1986].

16. The procedure described here is in accordance with information obtained from village informants and members of village land committees. As appears, with the exception of the 'facilitation' costs and 'push' visits, it conforms to the provisions in the 1999 Land Act Part VI, Sub-part 1, section 25.

17. Procedures to be followed appear from the Village Land Act [URT, 1999], Part IV, Village Land B, 22-47.

18. Boesen, Maganga and Odgaard [1997].

19. The situation is very similar to the situation existing in other areas in South-West Tanzania. See, for example, Odgaard [1987].

20. Many studies have shown that. The following are a few examples: Århem [1985, 1986]; Lane and Pretty [1990]; Mustafa [1993]; Tenga and Kakoti [1993]; Lane [1993]; Odgaard and Maganga [1994]; Talle [1999].

21. See Odgaard [1994]; Odgaard and Maganga [1994], for example.

22. The problems related to pastoral land rights and the consequences for the pastoral communities in Tanzania are very well documented in the literature referred to above as well as in Tenga [1992], Shivji [1994], among others.

23. Processes of land allocation in areas used for pasture are described in Boesen, Maganga and Odgaard [1996 and 1997] based on interviews and village files.

24. In response to this some pastoralists have realised the importance of lungulu in relation to security of tenure. But due to the type of land management compatible with pastoralism in semi-arid areas, lungulu, for most of the pastoralists living there, seldom means an area beyond the size of a settlement composed by houses and other structures belonging to close relatives. The word, therefore, has a similar meaning for these pastoralists as the lilungulu concept used for the Hehe previously.

25. The example is described in detail in Boesen, Maganga and Odgaard: Fieldnotes [1996 and 1997].

26. It is not quite clear to what extent the land transactions involved payment to the village government [Boesen, Maganga and Odgaard, 1996: Fieldnotes].

27. Much literature documents that there are similar examples in many other parts of Tanzania. See, for example, Mustafa [1993]; Århem [1985, 1986]; Odgaard and Maganga [1994]; Lane and Pretty [1990], just to mention a few.

28. This in spite of the fact that the Village Land Act [URT, 1999] contains several provisions to prevent discrimination of women in relation to customary land rights, allocation of land by village authorities, and registered rights.

29. For further discussion of the relationship between customary law and formal legislation please refer to Odgaard [1999] and Bentzon and Odgaard [2000].

REFERENCES

Århem, K., 1985, Pastoral Man in the Garden of Eden: The Maasai of the Ngorongoro Conservation Area, Tanzania, Uppsala.
Århem, K., 1986, 'Pastoralism under Pressure: The Ngorongoro Maasai', in J. Boesen, K.J. Havnevik, J. Koponen and R. Odgaard (eds.), Tanzania – Crisis and Struggle for Survival, Uppsala: Scandinavian Institute of African Studies, pp.207–24.
Bentzon, A.W. and R. Odgaard, 2000, 'Rural Women's Access to Property in Patrilineal

Communities in East Africa – In a Web of Norms', paper presented at WLSA Colloquium, Kariba, Zimbabwe, July.

Berry, S., 1989, 'Social Institutions, and Access to Resources', *Africa*, Vol.59, No.1, pp.41–55.

Berry, S., 1993, *No Condition is Permanent: The Social Dynamics of Agrarian Change in Sub-Saharan Africa*, Madison, WI: University of Wisconsin Press.

Berry, Sara, 1997, 'Tomatoes, Land and Hearsay: Property and History in Asante in the Time of Structural Adjustment', *World Development*, Vol.25, No.8, pp.1225–41.

Boesen, J., Storgård Madsen, B. and T. Moody, 1977, *Ujamaa – Socialism from Above*, Uppsala: Nordic Africa Institute.

Boesen, J., Maganga, Faustin P. and Rie Odgaard, 1997, 'Rules, Norms, Organizations and Actual Practices – Land and Water Management in the Ruaha River Basin', in Tiia Riitta Granfelt (ed.), *Managing the Globalized Environment*, London: Intermediate Technology Publications, pp.114–32.

Boesen, J., Maganga, Faustin P. and Rie Odgaard, 1996 and 1997, Fieldnotes.

Boesen, J., Maganga, Faustin P. and Rie Odgaard (work in progress), *Managing Natural Resources: The Role of Rules, Norms, Policies and People's Practices in South Western Tanzania* (working title for book manuscript).

Brown, G. and A. McD.B. Hutt, 1935, *Anthropology in Action. An Experiment in the Iringa District of the Iringa Province, Tanganyika Territory*, International Institute of African Languages and Cultures, Oxford: Oxford University Press.

Chachage, S. and J. Nyoni, 2001, *Economic Restructuring and the Cashew Industry in Tanzania* (Tanzania Agricultural Situation Analysis Report), Dar es Salaam: Dar es Salaam University Press.

Chanock, M., 1998, *Law, Custom and Social Order: The Colonial Experience in Malawi and Zambia*, London: Heinemann.

DANIDA, 2001, Review of MEMA Phase I (unpublished report).

Fimbo, G.M., 1992, *Essays in Land Law Tanzania*, Dar es Salaam.

Havnevik, K., 1995, 'Pressing Land Tenure Issues in Tanzania in the Light of Experiences from Other Sub-Saharan African Countries', *Forum for Development Studies*, No.2.

Iliffe, J., 1979, 'A Modern History of Tanganyika', 'African Studies Series 25', Cambridge: Cambridge University Press.

IWGIA, 1998, *The Indigenous World 1997–98*, Copenhagen.

IWGIA, 2001, *The Indigenous World 2000–2001*, Copenhagen.

James, R.W. and G.M. Fimbo, 1973, *Customary Land Law of Tanzania: A Source Book,* Nairobi and Dar es Salaam: East African Literature Bureau.

Johnsen, N., 2000, 'Placemaking, Pastoralism, and Poverty in the Ngorongoro Conservation Area, Tanzania', in V. Broch-Due and R.A. Schroeder (eds.), *Producing Nature and Poverty in Africa*, Uppsala: Nordic Africa Institute.

Kiwasila, H. and Rie Odgaard, 1992, 'Socio-cultural Aspects of Natural Forest Management in the Udzungwa', Report prepared for DANIDA, Copenhagen: CDR.

Koda, Bertha, 1998, 'Changing Land Tenure Systems in the Contemporary Matrilineal Social System: The gendered dimension', in P. Seppälä and B. Koda (eds.), *The Making of a Periphery*, Seminar Proceedings No.32, Uppsala: Nordic Africa Institute, pp.195–221.

Lane, C., 1993, 'The State Strikes Back', in Veber, Dahl, Wilson and Wæhle (eds.) [*1993*].

Lane, C. and J.N. Pretty, 1990, 'Displaced Pastoralists and Transferred Wheat Technology in Tanzania', IIED, Gatekeeper Series, No.SA20.

Lema, A., 1993, *Africa Divided. The Creation of 'Ethnic Groups'* (Lund Dissertations in Sociology 6), Lund: Lund University Press.

Lund, C., 1998, *Law, Power and Politics in Niger*, Hamburg: LIT Verlag.

Mackenzie, F., 1989, 'Land and Territory: The Interface Between Two Systems of Land Tenure, Murang'a District, Kenya', *Africa*, Vol.59, No.1.

McCall, M.K., 1982, *The Population Pressure on Natural Resources in Mbeya Region and Potential Solutions,* Mbeya RIDEP, Tanzania.

McHenry, 1979, *Tanzania's Ujamaa Villages: The Implementation of a Rural Development Strategy*, Institute of International Studies, University of California.

Mamdani, M., 1996, *Citizen and Subject. Contemporary Africa and the Legacy of Late Colonialism*, Princeton, NJ: Princeton University Press.

Manji, A., 2000, 'Her Name is Kamundage: Rethinking Women and Property among the Haya of Tanzania', *Africa*, Vol.70, No.3, pp.482–500.

Mbilinyi, M., 1991, *Big Slavery*, Dar es Salaam: Dar es Salaam University Press.

Migot-Adholla, S.E., Hazell, P., Blarel, B. and F. Place, 1991, 'Indigenous Land Rights Systems in Sub-Saharan Africa: A Constraint on Productivity?', *World Bank Economic Review*, Vol.5, No.1.

Moore, S.F., 1978, *Law as Process*, London: Routledge & Kegan Paul.

Moore, S.F., 1986, *Social Facts and Fabrications. 'Customary' Law on Kilimanjaro, 1880–1980*, Cambridge: Cambridge University Press.

Moore, S.F., 1999, 'Changing African Land Tenure: Reflections on the Incapacities of the State', in Christian Lund (ed.), *Development and Rights*, London: Frank Cass, pp.33–49.

Mukangara, F. and B. Koda, 1997, *Beyond Inequalities: Women in Tanzania*, SARDC, Tanzania.

Mumford, W.B., 1934, 'The Hehe, Bena and Sangu Peoples of East Africa', *American Anthropologist*, Vol.36, No.2, pp.203–22.

Mustafa, Kemal, 1993, 'Eviction of Pastoralists from Mkomazi Game Reserve in Tanzania: A Statement', unpublished paper, IIED, March.

Mwaikyusa, J.T., 1993, 'Community Rights and State Control in Tanzania', in Veber, Dahl, Wilson and Wæhle (eds.) [*1993*].

Nyerere, J., 1969, *Socialism in Tanzania*, Uppsala: Nordic Africa Institue.

Odgaard, Rie, 1986, 'Tea – Does It Do the Peasant Women in Rungme Any Good', in J. Boesen, K. Havnevik, J. Koponen and R. Odgaard, *Tanzania: Crisis and Struggle for Survival*, Uppsala: Scandinavian Institute for African Studies, pp.207–24.

Odgaard, Rie, 1987, 'De tog til Usangu! – Bondemigration i det sydvestlige Højland', *Den Ny Verden*, Vol.20, No.3, pp.69–90.

Odgaard, Rie, 1994, 'Jordbesiddelsesformer og baeredygtig ressourceudnyttelse' [Land tenure and sustainable resource use], *Den Ny Verden*, Vol.27, No.2, pp.50–67.

Odgaard, Rie, 1997, 'The Gender Dimension of Nyakyusa Rural–Rural Migration in Mbeya Region', in Ngware, Odgaard, Shayo and Wilson (eds.), *Gender and Agrarian Change in Tanzania – with a Kenyan Case Study*, Dar es Salaam: Dar es Salaam University Press (DUP), pp.46–70.

Odgaard, Rie and F.P. Maganga, 1994, *Local Informal Land and Water Management Systems in Ruaha River Basin*, Working Paper, Copenhagen: CDR.

Odgaard, R., 1999, 'Fathers, Daughters and Sons in the Scramble for Women's Land Rights: The Case of the Hehe and Sangu Peoples of South West Tanzania', paper presented at SASA International Conference, Copenhagen, Nov. 1999.

Odgaard, Rie, 'Land Above all!! Continuity and Change in the Articulation of Land Rights in South Western Tanzania', in Boesen, Maganga and Odgaard [*work in progress: Ch.4*].

Raikes, Philip, 1975, 'Ujamaa and Rural Socialism', *Review of African Political Economy*, No.3, pp.33–52.

Ranger, T. and E. Hobsbawn (eds.), 1983, *The Invention of Tradition*, Cambridge: Cambridge University Press.

Ranger, T., 1993, 'The Invention of Tradition Revisited: The Case of Colonial Africa', in T. Ranger and O. Vaughan (eds.), *Legitimacy and the State in Twentieth Century Africa*, London: Macmillan Press, pp.62–111.

Redmayne, A., 1968, 'The Hehe', in A. Roberts (ed.), *Tanzania before 1900*, Nairobi: East African Publishing House, pp.37–58.

Shivji, I.G., 1994, 'A Legal Quagmire: Tanzania's Regulation of Land Tenure' (Establishment of Villages Act, 1992), *Pastoral Land Tenure Series No.5*, IIED.

Sjaastad, E. and D.W. Bromley, 1997, 'Indigenous Land Rights in Sub-Saharan Africa: Appropriation, Security and Investment Demand', *World Development*, Vol.25, No.4, pp.549–62.

Talle, A., 1999, 'Pastoralists at the Border. Maasai Poverty and the Development Discourse in Tanzania', in D.M. Anderson and V. Broch-Due (eds.), *The Poor Are Not Us: Poverty and Pastoralism in Eastern Africa*, Oxford: James Currey.

Tenga, R., 1992, 'Pastoral Land Rights in Tanzania', a review, IIED Drylands Programme, Pastoral Land Tenure Series.

Tenga, R. and G. Kakoti, 1993, 'The Barabeig Land Case', in Veber, Dahl, Wilson and Wæhle [*1993*].

TNA (Tanzania National Archives), Secretariat files Nos. 7794 and 7794/3, 1925. Accession No. 157, file No. 6/42, 1938.

URT (United Republic of Tanzania), 1978, *Population Census.*

URT, 1983, *Agricultural Policy of Tanzania*, Government Printer.

URT, 1988, *Population Census.*

URT, 1994, *Report of the Presidential Commission of Inquiry into Land Matters, Vol.I: Land Policy and Land Tenure Structure* (published in co-operation with The Nordic Africa Institute, Uppsala).

URT, 1998, *The Constitution of the United Republic of Tanzania of 1977.*

URT, 1999, *The Land Act 1999.*

URT, 1999, *The Village Land Act 1999.*

Veter, H., Dahl, J., Wilson, F. and E. Wæhle (eds.), 1993, ' ... *Never Drink from the Same Cup'*, IWGIA Document No.74, Copenhagen.

von Freyhold, M., 1985, *Ujamaa Villages in Tanzania: An Analysis of a Social Experiment*, London: Heineman.

When Farmers Use 'Pieces of Paper' to Record Their Land Transactions in Francophone Rural Africa: Insights into the Dynamics of Institutional Innovation

PHILIPPE LAVIGNE DELVILLE

in memory of Lacinan Paré

I. EVOLVING LAND RIGHTS, WITHIN A PLURALITY OF NORMS

Debate on land tenure policies in rural Africa over the last few decades has hinged on two main issues: land registration and cadastral systems; and the emergence of a land market, as the supposed prelude to the spread of individual private ownership. The conceptual framework used by international institutions, the evolutionary theory of property rights[1] acknowledges the dynamic, efficient nature of so-called customary rights where population density is low and there is little economic competition. However, it argues that individual private ownership, guaranteed by the state, needs to become widespread: in substance, it claims that when the stakes are raised, land rights become uncertain, leading to conflict. This results in an 'induced demand for institutional innovation' addressed to governments which, to meet farmers' expectations, must then issue ownership title, triggering a process of economic development.

Many aspects of this theory can be challenged. In particular, the expected effects of providing land title are far from guaranteed [*Shipton, 1988; Bruce and Mighot-Adholla, 1994; Platteau, 1996; Deininger and Feder, 1998*]. Moreover, the view that the collapse of customary systems of regulation is the main cause of insecurity and conflicts, thus justifying state intervention, is itself highly debatable [*Le Roy, 1997; Lavigne Delville and Karsenty, 1998*]. Keen analysis of tenure dynamics over the long term highlights a wide variety of processes that are not exclusively driven by demography and the market. It cannot be denied that, in certain cases, processes are under way whereby

Philippe Lavigne Delville, GRET, 211-213 rue La Fayette, 75010 Paris; e-mail: lavignedelville@gret.org. This contribution was written as part of the INCO-CLAIMS programme funded by the European Union.

property rights over land are becoming more individual and land is increasingly seen as a commodity. However, such processes are neither systematic or mechanical. Moreover, they do not necessarily conflict with the existence of customary land tenure regulations, essentially based on local rules and/or authorities. A large number of current tenure practices are hybrid, cross-bred and flourish 'in the shadow of modern law'. Rather than linear evolution towards individual private ownership, we find partial developments within composite local land-use systems, based on variable evolving mixtures of individual prerogatives and collective regulations, which differ for the various land and natural resources.

Furthermore, looking closely at conflicts and insecurity of tenure, they appear to be due less to the internal contradictions of custom than to the effects of proliferating norms and contradictions and competition between those (customary authorities, political leaders, local governments, state agents, and so on) with power over land [*Chauveau, 1997; Lavigne Delville, 1998a; Lund, 2001*]. The contrasts between local rules, themselves multifaceted and evolving, and complex official rules that are largely or completely unknown to rural communities, as well as frequently contradictory (different regulations for different sectors, clashes between the legal framework and unofficial policy, etc.), provide opportunities for opportunistic claims. Furthermore, one may rely on one or other line or argument or whichever authority can be persuaded to give support. Because of the eminently political nature of tenure regulations [*Berry, 1993; Le Meur, 1997, 2002*], the openness of the authorities to corruption, ignorance of the realities of local land-use systems on the part of public sector employees and the lack of continuity in judgements given, the relative confusion on the tenure scene has increased. This has been to the advantage of powerful players, those who know what the law says or have access to the government apparatus [*Mathieu, 1996b*].

Nevertheless, the emphasis rightly placed on land-related conflicts and insecurity should not detract attention from the many cases where effective regulation is gaining ground: either because the above-mentioned contradictions are minimised in practice by the undisputed pre-eminence of customary rules, or because new, hybrid rules involving local stakeholders and public officials have come into being.

Another weak point of the evolutionary theory of ownership rights is that it implicitly assumes that stakeholders are unable to innovate and invent, or to come up with solutions for the problems they face. According to the theory, stakeholders are well aware of the problems (uncertainty over rights and insecurity) but remain powerless. Their 'demand for institutional innovation' is addressed to government and relates exclusively to the radical innovation of bringing land title into general use. However, stakeholders are neither passive nor totally powerless. For instance, new institutional arrangements are emerging to govern temporary transfers of cultivation rights [*Lavigne Delville et al., 2001*]; management rules for communal resources are being redefined; and neo-customary forms of settling conflicts between cropping and animal husbandry are being invented. Even where different authorities (customary authorities, administrative chiefs, politicians, state agents, etc.) compete for power over land issues, there is some consistency (albeit contingent and strongly connected with the balance of power) in the way stakeholders engage authorites to try to win their claims, thus, introducing some stability into what one might call 'pathways towards increased security of tenure'.

We shall focus here on a particular form of institutional innovation, namely, use of the written form for cash-based land transactions, delegating cultivation rights (essentially rental) and 'sales'. In some places, 'sales'[2] are the subject of customary procedures, as in northern Cameroon for instance (where handing over a hoe marks the transfer of ownership) [*Hallaire, 1991*] or some areas of Ghana [*Kasanga, 2002*]. Elsewhere, the development of market transactions in land does raise the question of norms and procedures able to regulate them, in a context where such sales are often discreet, if not entirely hidden, and usually not explicitly acknowledged as normal practice.

The question of the existence and meaning of land sales in Africa has provoked much debate, all too frequently muddled by a combination of ideological premises and methodological problems in describing and interpreting the processes seen on the ground. A number of recent studies, based on a careful description in social and anthropological terms of cash-based land transactions (where they exist), their dynamics and the perceptions that underpin them, have made it possible to move forward and gain a better understanding of the inherent ambivalence of such transactions. Moreover, this research has shown that the use of 'pieces of paper', in some form or another, is common and sometimes almost systematic in respect of 'sales' and other 'transfers', whether or not public officials are called upon to validate the contracts.

There is still much to be learned about these matters. Nevertheless, the presence of a number of consistent features in very different contexts justifies a preliminary overview. Drawing on a series of case studies, mainly in West Africa (Ivory Coast, Burkina Faso and Benin) but also in Rwanda and the Comoros, this contribution offers a framework for description and analysis of such popular use of the written form for land transactions.[3]

II. WRITING IT DOWN: TRANSACTIONS, CERTIFICATES AND PIECES OF PAPER

Land Transactions and Insecurity

In rural areas of Africa, the gap between legislation and local rules and, above all, the unregulated coexistence of different types of arbitration authorities (customary, religious, administrative, judicial and so on) has been one of the major sources of insecure tenure, since the colonial era. This situation has been exacerbated by the independent states which have maintained and stepped up their claims to a state monopoly on land and resources. It produces uncertainty about legitimate rules and space for opportunistic ploys and manipulation. Land tenure is one of the areas where investment in social and clientelist networks has been and remains a condition of access to resources [*Berry, 1993*]. However, the players in the game are not all equal and the main beneficiaries are those who are best placed within the state apparatus, can use complex, little-known legislation to their own advantage or can make money from arbitrating conflicts. Providing greater security of tenure is a political process in every sense of the word [*Mathieu, 1996a*].

Although the proliferation of rules and the competition between authorities in arbitration arrangements may be the major causes of insecure tenure, contradictory principles can coexist even within customary regulatory systems [*Breusers, 1999*]. Such contradictions and the nature of customary systems, based on negotiation, provide the various stakeholders with room for manoeuvre to confirm or attempt to renegotiate their access to land and resources. Among the processes observed are harsher conditions for access to land, restrictions on access rights and challenges to former arrangements. However, these changes are determined above all by problems in regulation and arbitration related to the differing perceptions of the state and local communities.

While rural communities are, on the whole, not in a very secure position, they do not all live in a state of permanent insecurity – far from it. Studies of conflicts show that forms, patterns and degrees of insecurity of tenure vary considerably among regions, within regions and from one type of stakeholder to another.[4] Generally speaking, apart from the risks inherent in the registration procedure and cases of exclusion within family units,[5] the major factors in insecure tenure seem to be related to the transmission of rights:

– calling into question an open-ended loan; or dispute about the content of rights granted to a 'stranger' when he was authorised to settle;
– 'sale' of some of the lineage landholding by a rights-holder without the agreement of the others, leading to the transaction being challenged;
– multiple sales of the same plot;
– disputes over inheritance.

Consequently, insecurity in relation to farmland hinges to a significant degree on the issue of transactions. Long-standing arrangements may be called into question or disputed by the descendants of those who concluded them; new forms of transactions may emerge for which rules have yet to be fixed; and stakeholders may not belong to the same social circles and not share the same tenure rules or a single acknowledged arbitration authority. This is where the contradictions of the tenure issue are most evident, in contexts where economic conditions and types of stakeholders are evolving rapidly.

In most cases, forms of non-definitive transfer of cultivation rights, often termed derived rights to stress the contractual relationship, are not particularly insecure [*Lavigne Delville et al., 2001*]. New arrangements come into being to cope with new challenges, loans tend to become shorter and fees to become the rule, turning – gradually or otherwise – into rental. Moreover, the terms of crop share contracts become stricter. While conditions of access have become harsher in certain cases and risks of opportunistic manoeuvres related to dysfunctional arbitration systems exist, there is really no mass insecurity connected with the actual procedures for delegating rights. In a given area, there will be a more or less extensive range of institutional arrangements, the clauses of which are clear to the parties and which pose few problems in enforcement.[6] Conversely, in areas where there is tension over land, there may be unilateral renegotiation of contract terms, or even strategies to recover previously ceded land and earn income from land, through systematic withdrawal of land loaned to migrants in order to rent it to other parties [*Baud, 1999; Paré, 2001; Zongo and Mathieu, 2000*]. We also find conflict where preparations for tenure legislation or an operation to register rights have triggered anticipatory strategies by both parties, each of them seeking acknowledgement as the 'owner' (see Lund [*1993*] on Niger) or 'main manager' (see Chauveau *et al.* [*1998*]; Chauveau [*2002*], on rural land-use plans in Ivory Coast).

The question of sales is more complex. It touches upon deeply held social values and upon the often inalienable nature of the lineage landholding, as well as, in some case, the religious overtones of indigenous communities' relationship with the land. However, in southern Benin, on the banks of the river Niger in Niger and in south-eastern Ghana, sales have existed since at least the beginning of the twentieth century. In some cases, pledging has been a way of getting around the prohibition on sales [*Coquery-Vidrovitch, 1982*]. Cash-based land transactions are developing in a number of regions[7] for a variety of reasons. Changes in social norms, urgent need for cash on the part of some rural people, and the growing presence of urban stakeholders wishing to establish a landholding, or migrants who have become wealthy seeking to consolidate their land rights, all contribute to this. Where the principle of sale is accepted under local rules, these are explicit. A distinction is then clearly made, within the family landholding, between inherited land (about which the extended family has a say, at least in the event of transfer outside the group) and bought land, which is a personal asset of the purchaser. Where they are not acknowledged as legitimate practices (and even if they are quite common in practice), such sales are discreet, if not secret, and are often euphemistically called 'cessions' in French (that is, transfers) or gifts. The financial transfer will be concealed or presented as simple compensation. This use of euphemism also reflects the fact that sales are illegal in some countries. Finally, it allows for some ambiguity, either deliberate or unavoidable, about what has actually been transferred (the asset itself or simply cultivation rights). This encourages misunderstandings between protagonists, manipulation (for example by urban residents who register land whereas the customary holder thought he had merely granted cultivation rights) or even later reinterpretation by the parties or their descendants.

The matter is all the more complex in that protagonists do not necessarily make the content of their transaction clear and may have different perceptions of what they are entering into. Moreover, such sales often indicate either financial difficulties that the party wishes to hide, or financial opportunities he wishes to keep for himself. Consequently, they are often made without the family's knowledge. If concluded by an individual (often, but not always, the head of family),[8] sales may be disputed by other rights-holders, who will call for them to be cancelled ... or for additional payments to be made. Zongo [2000] reports the case of a rights-holder living in town who challenged a sale made in secret by the head of family, who had kept the money for himself. During his next visit, he found that his brothers, who had also originally contested the sale, had changed their minds. In the meantime, they had in their turn received money from the buyer ...

The risks of insecurity and conflict in these sales seem to hinge on two main questions:

• Can a rights-holder (even a head of family) cede a portion of something which is not a personal asset but part of a family or lineage holding and, if so, under what circumstances?
• Is what is at stake in the transaction the alienation of the underlying asset (a land sale in the real sense) or a transfer of cultivation rights *inter vivos* (without alienation of the asset, with or without the possibility for the purchaser to pass on these rights; with or without a possibility of redemption)?[9]

It is above all where the answer to these questions cannot be provided by shared rules that monetary transactions cause conflict.

Amassing Various 'Pieces of Paper'

In terms of local social organisation, the fact that stakeholders know each other well, combined with the memory of the elders and successive judgements given by the authorities dealing with land use, should suffice, in principle, to ensure peaceful use of resources by regulating access to land in a legitimate manner. In many rural areas, this is still the case. However, the emergence of new institutional arrangements which are not regulated in this way, along with an increasing number of challenges to former arrangements, has meant that customary procedures may no longer be seen as adequate and sufficient by all. More and more, current customary authorities are former migrants or former public servants who have lived for some time outside the village and no longer have this built-in memory of tenure history. Moreover, experience of relationships with the state and development projects, and cases of conflict going beyond local level show the importance of putting things down on paper. Where tenure practices are evolving rapidly, writing things down is now increasingly seen as an essential tool in managing relationships, even by rural people themselves. Faced with the risks of legal insecurity, small farmers try to amass documents, without always knowing what they are for, hoping that they will have the right one when required. We see 'a strategy of keeping track in writing and piling up papers to safeguard acquired rights' [*Koné, Basserie and Chauveau, 1999*]. Where there is no possibility of making copies or no register exists, such documents are often unique and very precious.

Some documents are issued by the administration and have official value, while others derive from projects or the extension services: maps, various certificates, etc. Others are written directly by farmers. They can come in many forms:

- contracts between individuals, on ordinary paper or sheets from a notebook;

- contracts between individuals, validated by the customary or administrative authorities dealing with land use (including the *certificats de palabre* [literally 'certificates of palaver/discussion'], a colonial procedure reactivated when the law on agrarian reform in Burkina Faso was last amended and which, by validating a land 'transfer', allows the taker to start the registration procedure [cf. *Tallet, 1999*]);

- reports on arbitration or court cases (whether they are issued by the customary authorities, as in Niger where the latter are legally obliged always to draw up a report, the administration or the courts);

- certificates of land allocation, issued by the canton chief in Niger, the rural council in Senegal, or the administration when migrants settle (AVV [Volta Development Scheme] in Burkina Faso, for example);

- 'livrets de terre', such as the land record books issued by colonial administrators in the early 1950s in the Gao and Timbuktu region in Mali, listing the fields belonging to the various families;

- *certificats de notoriété* [attesting to something that is common knowledge], drawn up by cadis in the Comoros or burgomasters in Rwanda (pre-1994) and serving as certificates of ownership;

- official documents having no legal value (such as receipts for applications to register rights, issued by local land commissions in Niger); and

- miscellaneous documents, issued by the administration but theoretically having no fundamental value: various certificates issued by extension workers (plantation certificates in Ivory Coast; papers referring to settlement within development schemes); etc.

In addition to these documents that may be held by rural parties in connection with their own rights, there are documents held by the local authorities:

- lineage land registers, as in north-western Rwanda [*André, 1999*] and Savé in Benin [*Edja, 1997*];

- maps of plot division, indicating the holders of plots within development schemes (AVV villages in Burkina, hydro-agricultural schemes, etc.) and considered as proof of rights; etc.

Some Insights into the History of Written Contracts

The history of this use of the written form in different contexts has still to be documented, but some pointers can be given. In Zahia, in the forest region of Ivory Coast [*Koné, Basserie and Chauveau, 1999*], the oldest document found (referring to settlement of a tenure dispute) dates from 1950. Plantation certificates as demanded by customs officials became more common in the 1970s. A local government official (*sous-préfet*) then began to encourage people to put things on paper and this is a rapidly growing trend. Nowadays, two types of document, known as 'little papers' and 'agreements', are used in local tenure arrangements, mainly between migrants and indigenous parties, both referring to commercial transactions, that is 'sales'. The indigenous seller is often urgently in need of cash. 'Sales' are concluded on payment of part of the agreed price, with full payment often being staggered over several years. 'Little receipts' confirm the amounts of money paid, the sale actually being concluded when the entire sum has been received. This is when an 'agreement' will be established before witnesses. Until all the purchased land has been put to productive use (seen as the only genuine proof of ownership) and full payment is made, the process of sale may remain incomplete for a long period which, although it does result in a degree of insecurity, can nevertheless have advantages for both protagonists. The seller can continue to claim assistance from the buyer, for whom not paying everything until he has been able to develop all the land is a way of protecting himself against the risk of the uncultivated portion being sold to someone else, or of a promise of sale being made simply because of an urgent need for money and disputed immediately afterwards. In this way, the various parties develop strategies aimed both at gaining more security and exploiting the room for manoeuvre left by imprecise clauses.

In Burkina Faso, *certificats de palabre* (literally 'certificates of palaver', that is, minutes of a discussion) were instituted by the colonial authorities to 'transcribe agreements following tenure disputes or quarrels over access to natural resources ... . When discussions (hence the term 'palaver') result in agreement, the certificate puts this on a formal basis' [*Tallet, 1999*]. The signature of the parties, customary leaders and government representatives gives the certificate official validity, making it binding on third parties. The procedure does therefore exist, it was not abolished in subsequent legislation and has even been put forward again in the latest version of the law on agrarian reform (1996). 'Minutes of discussion' (PVP) must in fact accompany all applications for cultivation permits or land allocation orders (the two procedures used in allocating state-owned land to private individuals). In the western cotton production region (the Banwas), rural residents use the PVP as a way of legalising sales which are theoretically illegal. The document is drawn up by a public official outside working hours and then legalised at the police station; the minutes do not mention the amount paid and refer to 'transfer' to avoid the appearance of a sale, but there is in fact often another version of the contract, kept by the parties, that mentions the precise amount of the transaction [*Zongo, 1999*]. Elsewhere in the same region, farmers who use the above-mentioned certificate in transactions with civil servants may not be aware that this document can be used to start a registration procedure, leading to disputes when survey operations are carried out [*Paré, 1999*]. Although very discreet, 'transfers' between rural parties are gaining ground, especially in the southern region (the pioneer farming area) at the request of returning migrants who have imported these procedures from Ivory Coast. Some transfers are informal while others, especially where civil servants or migrants returning from Ivory Coast are concerned, will be the subject of a document drawn up before witnesses or possibly a *certificat de palabre* [*Paré, 2001*].[10]

In north-western Rwanda, an area where the lineage landholding structure is still strong, pressure on land, prior to the 1994 genocide, resulted in splitting up holdings and increasing individual land ownership, although lineage regulations continued to apply to transactions [*André, 1999*]. Since the early 1990s, the crisis in the peasant economy has led to greater diversity, marked by an expansion in the land market (essentially to the benefit of urban residents) and the growing exclusion of marginalised stakeholders (widows, divorced women, emigrants, etc.) [*André and Platteau, 1996*]. Purchased land is held strictly individually and evades all family control. The written form is gradually becoming used as evidence not only of cash transactions, but also non-cash transactions between different lineages and even within the same family (regarding inheritance, for example). It is widespread in respect of sales and becoming more common with regard to rental. Sales are made before witnesses, particularly members of the lineage who will check that there is no alternative. The contract is held by the purchaser and shows the type of transaction, parties involved, date and amount. The oldest contract found dates from 1933. Sales sometimes cause disputes due to the lack of evidence supporting the transaction (or some part of its content). They may be challenged by the seller's family. To protect themselves, buyers sometimes falsify the contract of sale: they show an amount much higher than the amount paid, thereby guarding against cancellation by making it more costly for the seller or his family. Over time, information on the plot in question becomes more specific (sketch map, boundaries and so on).

There is also a system for registering land with the *commune* (municipality), which is also not legal although it involves the municipal authorities and is therefore 'official'. People who think their rights are in danger will register their plot with the *commune*. On the basis of the documents they submit and confirmation from one or other witness, the authorities will issue an *attestation de notoriété* (certificate recording statements made by several people attesting to commonly known facts) in respect of ownership of the plot (no field survey is performed and payment has to be made). Only people who are well informed and/or have connections with the administrative authorities register their plots in this way and often only plots that are in dispute [*André, 1999; Mathieu, 1999*].

These few examples show that the use of the written form is not always a recent innovation. But such practices seem to have become more common lately (in the last few decades or less) as the population and number of transactions grow, making it more difficult to rely on memory alone (as in the Comoros and Rwanda), some aspects of customary rules are breached and 'sales' develop. Events such as the redistribution of land from colonial estates and ensuing land exchanges, in the Comoros, or the expulsions and purchases of land involved in establishing a mission in Rwanda, also played a part, as did the plantation certificates demanded by customs officials in Ivory Coast in the 1970s and encouragement from the previously mentioned *sous-préfet* in that country. There, as in Burkina Faso, the presence of numerous migrants was undoubtedly a factor. Market transactions and the establishment of documents primarily involve indigenous and migrant farmers or urban dwellers.

III. NEGOTIATING AND VALIDATING TRANSACTIONS: WHY PUT
     THEM IN WRITING?

It is significant that the written form is mainly found in connection with 'transfers', 'sales' and pledging, that is to say definitive transactions (or likely to become such) involving money. Furthermore, the transfer of money and the sum involved are often mentioned more explicitly than the actual content of the transaction or the location of the plot. It seems to be mainly where sales are rare and illegitimate that they are found without written contracts. Such documents are less common where cultivation rights are delegated. Use of written contracts for pledging or rental is seen in less systematic or more recent fashion in Rwanda, where the practice seemed to be spreading in the early 1990s, as well as in Ivory Coast (where a 'little paper' is drawn up in respect of any cash payment, including for rent), southern Benin and, more rarely, western Burkina Faso. It is extremely unusual for contracts based on crop sharing to be on paper, which seems to confirm the link between the transfer of money and use of the written form.[11] At the study sites, they were only found in the citrus belt of Ghana [*Amanor and Diderutuah, 2001*], where plantation crop-share contracts are the main way of gaining access to land outside the family group and a private oil palm company makes contracts with farmers. In this case, contracts based on those suggested by the company may even be typewritten.

Whether in respect of procedures for drawing up contracts, the involvement or otherwise of witnesses or authorities, the actual content of documents, the language in which they are drawn up, or how explicit their clauses are or how many copies are produced, the pieces of paper recorded and analysed are extremely diverse, varying from one region to another as well within in the same region. Can any common features be identified?

Incomplete Contracts

Written contracts are often short and a number of important clauses may not be made explicit or in any event not be formalised. While the identity of parties and names of witnesses are always mentioned, the precise content of the transaction often remains vague ('transfer'), details of the plot in question may be limited or absent and the amount paid is not always mentioned (sometimes because such payment is illegal). Those 'clauses in land tenure agreements that are not related to land itself', the expression used by Chauveau to describe the social obligations related to the tenure relationship, are never made explicit.

Even where changes in the content of these pieces of paper can be seen over time, contracts are still largely incomplete according to contract theory. They do not make all clauses explicit, either because that is not felt necessary in local networks where everyone knows one another, or because such vagueness reflects deliberate misunderstandings or the wish of at least one of the parties to take advantage of ambiguity. The written form can also be manipulated, as in Rwanda where the purchaser will put down an amount exceeding that negotiated and paid, to protect himself against cancellation, or in Burkina where the minutes lodged at the police station may not be the same as those kept by the parties. Varying degrees of literacy within local society do in fact provide new opportunities for trickery.

Witnesses, Publicity and Validation

An important factor in the security of a transaction is its public nature. Third parties must be aware that rights have been transferred. Practices in this regard are quite varied, depending on the legitimacy of land sales in the local area, whether or not the family agrees to the sale and why it is being made.

Even discreet transactions involve witnesses, in almost all cases, and very often authorities who are asked to validate or certify them. Witnesses (one or two for each party) are therefore a more vital aspect of the transaction than the content of the document itself. They are often relatives or friends, perhaps people who hold neighbouring plots. Attempts by relatives to find an alternative to sale in order to preserve the integrity of the family landholding actually form one of the stages in the procedure used in the Mandara mountains.

Apart from witnesses, in the majority of cases – and for almost all sales? – the parties look for official validation of the transaction. It is then a matter of approaching an authority (customary, religious[12] or administrative – village chief, mayor, burgomaster, sometimes *sous-préfet* or even the police as in Burkina Faso) to make the transaction official. Here again, there is a difference between a transaction concluded before an authority who will authenticate it by signing the contract with the witnesses and one concluded between parties who will then ask an authority to validate the existence of the transaction, by either stamping or signing the contract, or issuing an administrative certificate ratifying it (*certificat de palabre* in Burkina Faso, *certificat de notoriété* issued by the burgomaster in Rwanda).

The protagonists usually approach an authority connected with the state, thereby seeking to safeguard locally-negotiated arrangements *vis-à-vis* the state (or at least the local administrative authority, as the procedure is often not legal).

> In fact, the intervention of someone from the local administration (*commune* in Rwanda or rural council in Senegal) serves to validate or confirm – make more secure – a transaction which has just been conducted at the level of private relationships between local stakeholders in a local society, within the context of social relationships they have chosen [*Mathieu, 1999: 24*]. [In north-west Rwanda,] the *communes* have a survey carried out (by a councillor or agricultural extension worker) before a sale to check that it is acceptable to the family and neighbours. The proposed sale and purchase is then examined by the *commune's* development committee before being approved through issue of a *certificat de notoriété* by the commune. This is just a

declaration recorded at the municipal offices in the presence of witnesses, stamped by the *commune* and signed by the burgomaster, certifying that such and such a person is now the owner of the field located at such and such a place' (Mathieu [*1999: 26*] adapted from André [*1994*]).

Elsewhere, the procedure may involve the government extension services, for example to survey a plantation purchased by migrants in centre-west Ivory Coast [*Koné, 2001*].

Combining customary principles, contractual principles and validation by the local authority, such procedures are not generally provided for in law, but are often openly practised by the local administrative authorities, with or without government encouragement, sometimes making use of statutes diverted from their original purpose [*Mathieu, 1999*]. In north-western Rwanda, Ivory Coast, southern Benin and Senegal (and probably elsewhere), we find these regular procedures established by local authorities, on the fringes of the law, to meet stakeholders' social requirements. We see 'informal formalisation' of contracts [*André, 1994*], provided by the authorities and universally recognised, although outside or alongside legal procedures,[13] and involving a more or less standard payment (to witnesses, the customary authorities and public officials).

Registration and Land Registers

Apart from the contracts themselves, we have noted the existence of registers. These may be informal or follow a more systematic approach. For example, in north-west Rwanda, lineage chiefs used to record all transactions or arbitration decisions in a notebook, with a brief description. These notebooks were embryonic land registers, keeping track of changes in tenure on the hill. They allow transfers or arbitration to be traced and can therefore be used in the event of dispute. In central Benin, in a migrant settlement area, Edja [*1997*] has shown how, under the influence of lineage members living in urban areas, lineage chiefs have transformed arrangements to settle migrants into rental agreements, keeping a proper land register recording the migrants settled, land allocated and fees paid.

Surprisingly, such registers are sometimes absent where one would most expect to find them: in the hands of the government authorities involved in land-use management. For example, what farmers call 'registration' with the *commune* in Rwanda actually refers to the issue of a certificate of ownership, a copy of which is apparently not systematically kept. This means that there is no gradual establishment of a system of tenure information which would make it possible to check whether a particular plot had already been 'registered'. In Senegal, where the rural councils are officially empowered to allocate land from the national estate, certificates of allocation are supposed to be given to beneficiaries and a record kept of all land allocation decisions. In the area of Kounghel at least, tenure researcher G. Blundo [pers. comm.] was never able to gain access to this supposedly public register of which councillors constantly speak but that no-one has ever seen.[14] It would not be surprising if this register did not actually exist, this being quite consistent with the clientelist, factionalist way land is managed by elected members of the rural councils [*Blundo, 1996*].

CONCLUSION

Although still very partial, knowledge of popular use of the written form in land transactions sheds new light on contemporary tenure practices and the dynamics of institutional innovation. In rapidly changing socio-economic contexts, where there are many different rules and competition between arbitration authorities, stakeholders do not stand idly by. They make up new institutional arrangements and new contractual procedures. Even though they may be informal and not yet fully consolidated, rules and procedures are followed by the parties involved who try, with varying degrees of success, to bring in elements of stability.

In their various forms, the 'little papers', agreements and *certificats de palabre* used in land transactions are amongst these institutional innovations. Beyond the level of bilateral arrangements between parties, the latter also involve authority systems, through mechanisms employed to have contracts validated in one way or another by the local administration and the various means of informal formalisation we have mentioned.

As stressed by Chauveau [*Chauveau and Lavigne Delville, forthcoming*], where (i) social networks are the main way of access to land and natural resources, (ii) a stable, respected legal framework does not really exist, and (iii) land tenure and use have complex features, stakeholders are pursuing innovations along two lines, trying as best they can to establish new rules or institutional arrangements and consolidate particular negotiation or arbitration procedures to back them up. Outside or in parallel with the market or rules guaranteed by the public authorities, these systems are designed to provide a minimum of predictability in day-to-day interaction and a degree of security for acquired tenure rights in the longer term. They involve both local officials belonging to official public organisations (acting according to unofficial rules but in the name of the acknowledged legitimacy of government departments) and private parties invested with local legitimacy, thereby finally achieving more secure tenure by combining both types of legitimacy.

Writing things down is only one aspect of these institutional arrangements. Alone, the written form is not sufficient to guarantee transparency in transactions or avoid all ambiguity. There are two related reasons for this: the incomplete nature of written contracts and the strongly socio-political dimension of land-use regulation. First of all, not all stakeholders are asking for transactions to be clarified, or at least not all aspects of them. Urban residents want to make their land purchases secure but not necessarily to have it known that they own land. Indigenous sellers anxious for money and buyers seeking title may both prefer to keep the actual content of the transaction as a grey area. Consequently, the incomplete nature of the contract cannot be seen only as a phase, arising from lack of experience in drafting. It also reflects strategic issues. The above-mentioned plantation sales described by Koné, Basserie and Chauveau [*1999*] provide a particularly clear illustration of this. When the content of a transaction does not come under explicit, shared social rules, putting it on paper does not get rid of the ambiguity.[15] This reflects the way parties both suffer from and utilise this lack of precision, attempting to limit the risks of opportunistic behaviour by the other party, while retaining as many options as they can for themselves. Secondly, while noting the introduction of a more explicit contractual dimension, we can see that use of the written form, what is and is not written down, is deeply rooted in the socio-political context of tenure relations, where arbitration is also dependent on the balance of power and where agreements or arbitration can be renegotiated.

The many different authorities that can be called upon, the uncertain status of local rules and practices in the eyes of the law and the semi-informal character of local ways of validating transactions are amongst the reasons why a piece of paper or written contract cannot usually be considered adequate, quite apart from its formal limitations. The existence of a written contract is not always a necessary and, above all, rarely a sufficient guarantee of tenure security. Even where validated by the administration, a document may be challenged or not accepted by arbitration authorities, as in several cases described by Lund [*1999*] in Niger.

Consequently, stakeholders put transactions on papers not so much to make their content of the transaction comprehensively and unambiguously clear as to certify that they have indeed taken place and before which witnesses. Rather than the *substance* of rights, it is primarily their very *existence* that is at stake and amassing pieces of paper is an attempt to substantiate this. The various papers 'signal the existence of a right and associate it [with] one or several persons which seems often to be the necessary proof considering the nature of disputes' [*Lund, 1999: 120*].

In this context, it is not certain that the interplay of actors alone can bring further clarification of sales, avoiding the main sources of insecurity faced by the different stakeholders. It might be thought that a number of conditions need to be fulfilled if contracts are to play a more important part in providing greater security of tenure:

- clarification of locally accepted rules governing 'sales' (is it possible, under what conditions and according to which procedures guaranteeing agreement amongst rights-holders, to transfer some of the family landholding? Which rights have actually been transferred? Are there restrictions on transfers outside the local community?);

- legal recognition by the various official bodies of private contracts relating to land;

- legalisation of 'informal formalisation' procedures involving the local administration and empowerment of the latter to enforce the above rules.

More than a systematic titling process, is it not this type of state-led institutional innovation, increasing the stability of local arrangements, that rural dwellers (or some of them at least) are really asking their governments to pursue?

NOTES

1. I am drawing here on the presentation and analysis made by Platteau [*1996*].
2. Because of the ambiguities of this term, I am using 'sale' as a generic term, in inverted commas without predicting the type of rights that are actually transferred. I shall come back to this later.
3. Some of the following points are taken from research into use of the written form co-ordinated by the author with Paul Mathieu [*Lavigne Delville and Mathieu, 1999*], which brings together a number of case studies on Niger [*Lund, 1999*], Burkina Faso [*Tallet, 1999; Pare, 1999; Zongo, 1999*], Ivory Coast [*Koné, Basserie and Chauveau, 1999*], Rwanda [*André, 1999*], the Comoros [*Saïd, 1999*] and Haiti [*Dorner, 1999*]. This enquiry arose from our earlier work [*Lavigne Delville, 1998a; Mathieu, 1996a, 1996b; Mathieu et al., 1999*] focusing on the issues involved in providing greater security of tenure. More recent research into land transactions in Burkina Faso [*Baud, 1999; Triollet, 1999; Mathieu, Lavigne Delville, Ouedraogo, Paré and Zongo, 2000*] and procedures for delegating cultivation rights in West Africa [*Amanor and Diderutuah, 2001; Edja, 2001; Koné, 2001; Pare, 2001; Lavigne Delville, Toulmin, Colin, Chauveau, 2001*] have shed further light on the subject. See also de Zeuw [*1997*].
4. Even in areas of tension, such as western Burkina Faso, the social configuration at micro-level is decisive: in villages where the village chief and the chief of the migrant community still want to maintain social peace, there will be no problem; in migrant hamlets, the risk of land being withdrawn by the indigenous parties is lower than in mixed villages; and migrants who have achieved economic success do not feel insecure (see the work of Paré and Zongo).
5. Total exclusion of dependants in certain areas of Rwanda before 1994 [*André and Platteau, 1996*], as well as inability of family rights-holders who have migrated to reclaim rights on their return as in southern Benin [*Mongbo, 2002; Edja, 2001*]; and appearance of forms of negotiating access to land within family units [*Chauveau, 1997*].
6. Even though the existence of a 'market' in derived rights raises the 'opportunity cost' of granting a portion of family land to dependants and tends to make conditions of access harsher for the latter.
7. But not all: during a systematic survey going into the history of plot tenure, Guigou, Pontié and Lericollais [*1998*] did not find any sales in their study area, the part of Senegal inhabited by the Serer ethnic group, an area with high population density and long-standing involvement in cash cropping.

8. Baud [*1999*] reports cases of land sales, on the fringes of the family landholding, by young people wishing to migrate to the city.
9. This issue arises particularly in the case of plantations.
10. The two types of sale actually have different names in the Dioula language: *sany féré: purchase/sale* and *sébé sany* (or *sébé féré*): documented purchase (or sale) [*Paré, 2001*].
11. In Bodiba (centre-west Ivory Coast), a new arrangement known as *pukudre pakré* covers investments in rehabilitating former plantations [*Zongo, 2000*]. It has three phases corresponding to the three stages of gradually bringing the plantation back into production, with different contractual conditions. Only the phase involving the payment of money by the operator is put on paper.
12. The religious authorities are only called upon in the Comoros where they do have an acknowledged place in the administrative set-up.
13. The PVP ('minutes of discussion') is an exception, because it was reintroduced when the law on agrarian reform in Burkina Faso was last amended. However, ways still have to be found to get around the ban on sales.
14. Mathieu [*1987*] had made similar remarks a few years earlier about the Senegal river valley.
15. Except where subsequent use of another, legal procedure removes any vagueness in interpretation, such as going on to apply for registration.

REFERENCES

Amanor, K.S. and Diderutuah, M.K., 2001, *Share Contracts in the Oil Palm and Citrus Belt of Ghana*, London: IIED/GRET.
André, C., 1994, 'Evolution des droits fonciers au Rwanda: une main invisible?', Rapport préparatoire de la commission 2 du 11ème Congrès des economistes belges de langues française, CIFOP.
André, C., 1999, 'Pratiques foncières et "formalisation informelle" des transactions (Nord-ouest du Rwanda)', in Lavigne Delville and Mathieu [*1999: 126–53*].
André, C. and Platteau, J.-Ph., 1996, *Land Tenure under Unendurable Stress, or the Failure of the Evolutionnary Mecanisms: The Tragic Case of Rwanda*, Cahier de la Faculté des sciences économiques et sociales de Namur, Université de Namur.
Baud J., 1999, *Etude des transactions foncières dans les départements de Bama et de Padéma au Burkina Faso (Province du Houet)*, Ministère de l'Agriculture du Burkina Faso/Service de Coopération et d'Action Culturelle/GRET.
Berry S., 1993, *No Condition is Permanent, the Social Dynamics of Agrarian Change in Subsaharan Africa*, Madison, WI: University of Wisconsin Press.
Blundo, G., 1996, 'Gérer les conflits fonciers au Sénégal: le rôle de l'administration locale dans le sud-est du bassin arachidier', in Ph. Tersiguel and C. Becker (eds.), *Développement durable au Sahel*, Paris/Dakar: Karthala/Sociétés, espaces, temps, pp.103–22.
Breusers, M., 1999, *On the Move; Mobility, Land Use and Livelihood Practices on the Central Plateau in Burkina Faso*, Münster: LIT/APAD.
Bruce, J.W. and S.E. Migot-Adholla (eds.), 1994, *Searching for Land Tenure Security in Africa*, Dubuque, IA: Kendall/Hunt Publishing Company.
Chauveau, J.-P., 1997, 'Jeu foncier, institutions d'accès à la ressource et usage de la ressource', in B. Contamin and H. Memel-Foté (eds), *Le modèle ivoirien en crise*, Paris/Abidjan, GIDIS/Karthala, pp.325–60.
Chauveau, J.P., 1998, 'La logique des systèmes coutumiers', in Lavigne Delville (ed.) [*1998: 66–75*], Paris: Karthala/Coopération française.
Chauveau, J.P., Bosc, P.M. and M. Pescay, 1998, 'Le plan foncier rural en Côte d'Ivoire', in Lavigne Delville (ed.) [*1998: 553–83*].
Chauveau, J.P., 2002, *Rural Land Plans, How to Establish Relevant Systems to Identify and Record Rights?*, Workshop on 'Making Land Rights More Secure', Ouagadougou: GRAF/GRET/IIED.

Chauveau, J.P. and Lavigne Delville Ph., forthcoming, 'Pour des politiques foncières intermédiaires', in M. Lévy (ed.), *Inégalités et politiques publiques en Afrique*, tome 2, Paris: Karthala.

Colin, J.Ph., 1995, 'De Turgot à la nouvelle économie institutionnelle: brève revue des théories économiques du métayage', *Économie Rurale*, Vol.228, pp.28–34.

Coquery-Vidrovitch, C., 1982, 'Le régime foncier rural en Afrique noire', in E. Le Bris, E. Le Roy and F. Leimdorfer (eds.), *Enjeux fonciers en Afrique Noire*, Paris: Karthala, pp.65–84.

de Zeeuw, F., 1997, 'Borrowing of Land, Security of Tenure and Sustainable Land use in Burkina Faso', *Development and Change*, Vol.28, No.3, pp.583–95.

Deininger, K. and G. Feder, 1998, *Land Institutions and Land Markets*, Working paper, World Bank Land Policy Network, Washington, DC.

Dorner, V., 1999, 'Titres fonciers, indivision et transactions informelles en milieu rural haïtien', in Lavigne Delville and Mathieu [*1999: 154–81*].

Edja, H., 1997, *Phénomènes de frontière et problèmes de l'accès à la terre. Le cas de la sous-préfecture de Savè au Bénin* (Working Papers on African Societies No.12), Berlin: Das arabische Buch.

Edja, H, 2001, *Land Rights under Pressure ; Access to Resources in Southern Benin*, IIED/GRET.

Guigou, B., Pontié, G. and A. Lericollais, 1998, 'La gestion foncière en pays Sereer Siin (Sénégal)', in Lavigne Delville (ed.) [*1998: 183–96*].

Hallaire, A., 1991, *Paysans montagnards du Nord-Cameroun, les monts Mandara* (coll. a travers champs), Paris: Orstom.

Kasanga, K., 2002, 'Land Tenure, Resource Access and Decentralisation in Ghana', in C. Toulmin, Ph. Lavigne Delville, S. Traore (eds.), *The Dynamics of Resource Tenure in West Africa*, London: IIED/James Currey/Heinemann, pp.25–36.

Koné, M., 2001, *Gaining Rights of Access to Land in West-Central Côte d'Ivoire*, London: IIED/GRET/GIDIS-CI.

Koné, M., Basserie, V. and J.P. Chauveau, 1999, '"Petits reçus" et "conventions": les procédures locales de formalisation des droits fonciers et les attentes de "papiers", étude de cas dans le centre-ouest ivoirien', in Lavigne Delville and Mathieu (eds.) [*1999: 52–76*].

Lavigne Delville, Ph., 1998a, *Foncier rural, ressources renouvelables et développement en Afrique*, Coll. Rapports d'études, Ministère des Affaires Etrangères – Coopération et francophonie, Paris. (includes English version *Rural Land Tenure, Renewable Resources and Development in Africa*).

Lavigne Delville, Ph., 1998b, 'La sécurisation de l'accès aux ressources : par le titre ou l'inscription dans la communauté?' in Lavigne Delville [*1998: 76–86*].

Lavigne Delville, Ph., 2000, 'Harmonising Formal Law and Customary Land Rights in French-Speaking West Africa', in C. Toulmin and J. Quan (eds.), *Evolving Land Rights, Policy and Tenure in Africa*, London: DFID/IIED/NRI, pp.97–121.

Lavigne Delville, Ph. and A. Karsenty, 1998, 'Des dynamiques plurielles', in Lavigne Delville (ed.) [*1998: 215–42*].

Lavigne Delville, Ph., Toulmin C., Colin J.Ph. and J.P. Chauveau, 2001, *Negotiating Acess to Land in West Africa: a Synthesis of Findings from Research on Derived Rights to Land*, final report, London: IIED/GRET/IRD.

Lavigne Delville, Ph. (ed.), 1998, *Quelles politiques foncières en Afrique noire rurale ? réconcilier pratiques, légitimité et légalité*, Paris: Karthala/Coopération française.

Lavigne Delville, Ph. and P. Mathieu (eds.), 1999, *Formalisation des contrats et des transactions: Repérage des pratiques populaires d'usage de l'écrit dans les transactions foncières en Afrique rurale*, working document, London: GRET/IED/UCL.

Le Meur, P.Y., 1997, 'La politique du foncier', synthèse de l'atelier 'Tenure foncière et droits de propriété', in Th. Bierschenk, P.Y. Le Meur and A. von Oppen (eds.), *Institutions and Technologies for Rural Development in West Africa*, Werkersheim: Margraf Verlag.

Le Meur, P.Y., 2002, 'Trajectories of the Politicisation of Land Issues. Case Studies from Benin', in K. Juul and C. Lund (eds), *Negotiating Property in Africa*, Portsmouth, NH: Heinemann.

Le Roy, E., 1996, 'La théorie des maîtrises foncières', in Le Roy *et al.* (eds.), *La sécurisation foncière en Afrique*, Paris: Karthala, pp.59–76.

Le Roy, E., 1997, 'La sécurité foncière dans un contexte africain de marchandisation imparfaite de la terre', in Ch. Blanc-Pamard and A. Cambrézy (eds.), *Terre, terroir, territoire, les tensions foncières*, Coll. Dynamique des systèmes agraires, Paris: Orstom, pp.455–72.

Lund, C., 1993, *En attendant le Code rural: réflexions sur une réforme de la tenure foncière au Niger* (Programme Réseaux des zones arides, dossier n° 44), London: IIED.

Lund, C., 1998, *Law, Power and Politics in Niger – Land Struggles and the Rural Code*, Hamburg/ New Brunswick, NJ: LIT Verlag/Transaction Publishers.

Lund, C., 1999, 'A Note on Property, Paper and Proof', in Lavigne Delville and Mathieu (eds.), [*1999*], pp.119–25.

Lund, C., 2001, ' Les réformes foncières dans un contexte de pluralisme juridique et institutionnel', in G. Winter (ed.), *Inégalités et politiques publiques en Afrique ; pluralité des normes et jeux d'acteurs*, Paris: Karthala/Ird, pp.195–208.

Matthieu, P., 1987, 'Agriculture irriguée, réforme foncière et stratégies paysannes dans la vallée du fleuve Sénégal, 1960–1985', thesis, Fondation Universitaire Luxembourgeoise, Arlon, 2 vols., 414pp.

Mathieu, P., 1996a, 'La sécurisation foncière, entre compromis et conflits: un processus politique', in P. Mathieu, P.J. Laurent and J.C. Willame (eds.), *Démocratie, enjeux fonciers et pratiques locales en Afrique, conflits, gouvernance et turbulences en Afrique de l'Ouest et centrale* (Cahiers africains n° 23–24), Paris: CEDAF/L'Harmattan, pp.26–44.

Mathieu, P., 1996b, 'Pratiques informelles, gestion de la confusion et invention du foncier en Afrique', in G. de Villers (ed.), *Phénomènes informels et dynamiques culturelles en Afrique* (Cahiers Africains), Paris: Cedaf-L'Harmattan, pp.64–87.

Mathieu, P., 1999, 'Les paysans, la terre, l'Etat et le marché: sécurisation et formalisation endogène des transactions foncières en Afrique', in Lavigne Delville and Mathieu [*1999*].

Mathieu, P., Mugangu Mataboro, S., Mafikiri Tsongo, A. and P.J. Laurent, 1999, 'Enjeux fonciers et violences en Afrique. Quelques réflexions pour la prévention des conflits à partir du cas du Nord-Kivu (1940–1994)', *Réformes agraires et coopératives*, Rome: FAO.

Mathieu, P., Lavigne Delville, Ph., Ouedraogo, H., Pare, L. and M. Zongo, 2000, *Sécuriser les transactions foncières au Burkina Faso* (rapport de synthèse de l'étude sur l'évolution des transactions foncières), GRET/Ministère de l'Agriculture/Ambassade de France au Burkina Faso.

Mongbo, R., 2002, 'Land Availability and the Land Tenure Regime in Rural Benin', in C. Toulmin Ph. Lavigne Delville and S. Traore (eds.), *The Dynamics of Resource Tenure in West Africa*, London: IIED/James Currey/Heinemann, pp.98–109.

Paré, L., 1999, 'Les pratiques de formalisation des transactions foncières dans l'ouest burkinabé', in Lavigne Delville and Mathieu [*1999: 89–94*].

Paré, L, 2001, *Negotiating Rights: Access to Land in the Cotton Zone*, Burkina Faso: IIED/GRET.

Platteau, J.-Ph., 1996, 'The Evolutionary Theory of Land Rights as Applied to Sub-Saharan Africa: A Critical Assesment', *Development and Change*, Vol.27, No.1, pp.29–86.

Saïd, M., 1999, 'Formalisation des transactions et contrats fonciers à Anjouan (Comores)', in Lavigne Delville and Mathieu [*1999: 99–118*].

Shipton, P., 1988, 'The Kenyan Land Tenure Reform : Misunderstandings in the Public Creation of Private Property', in Downs and Reyna (eds.), *Land and Society in Contemporary Africa*, University Press of New England, pp.91–135.

Tallet, B., 1999, 'Le certificat de palabre comme instrument dans les transactions (Burkina Faso)', in Lavigne Delville and Mathieu [*1999: 95–8*].

Triollet, K., 1999, *L'évolution des transactions foncières dans une région de fronts pionniers du Sud Ouest du Burkina Faso, département de Mangodara*, Ministère de l'Agriculture du Burkina Faso/GRET.

Zongo, M., 1999, 'Transactions foncières et usages de l'écrit dans la zone cotonnière du Burkina Faso: exemples à partir de la région des Banwa', in Lavigne Delville and Mathieu [*1999: 77–88*].

Zongo, M., 2000, *Etude des groupements imigrés burkinabés dans la région de Oumé (Côte d'Ivoire). Rapports fonciers avec les groupes autochtones et les pouvoirs publics locaux, et organisation en migration*, Ouagadougou: IRD/REPFO.

Zongo, M. and P. Mathieu, 2000, 'Transactions foncières marchandes dans l'ouest du Burkina Faso: vulnérabilité, conflits, sécurisation, insécurisation', in A.S. Fall, Ch. Gueye and I. Dia (eds.), *Les interactions rural-urbain: circulation et mobilisation des ressources (Bulletin de l'APAD, No.19)*, LIT, pp.21–32.

Monetary Land Transactions in Western Burkina Faso: Commoditisation, Papers and Ambiguities

PAUL MATHIEU, MAHAMADOU ZONGO
and LACINAN PARÉ

I. INTRODUCTION

In the cotton provinces of West Burkina Faso, exchanging land for money, which was once unthinkable, is now becoming common practice. Although customary land management principles do not condone this, some lineage chiefs cede family or lineage land holdings for good against payment in cash. Those who acquire the land can be other local peasants, migrants or indigenous, or investors living in town. Increasingly, they are also 'new actors' originating from outside the local communities, who have money earned in non-agricultural activities and who intend to farm using hired labour and mechanised equipment.

As these new practices expand, traditional land allocations agreed on 20 or 30 years previously between autochtonous peasants and migrant families are now being contested by those who granted the land (or their children): lands granted to migrants on a long-term basis (sometimes with rights of transmission to their descendants, under certain conditions) are now being withdrawn unilaterally, and then sold, more often than not, to people from outside the village. The victims of this ceding of family land outside the lineage are sometimes those members of indigenous families who are more vulnerable than others because they are absent from the village. All these new practices (land sales and rentals, land withdrawals) increasingly imply tensions and conflicts. In these new conflicts and transactions, actors use various procedures to make their agreements visible. These practices of validation are

Paul Mathieu, Researcher, Fonds National de la Recherche Scientifique (FNRS) and professor, Institut d'Etudes du Développement – UCL (Belgium), when this paper was completed; currently with the Land Tenure service, FAO, Rome. Mahamadou Zongo, Consultant, teaching part-time at the University of Ouagadougou, and associate member of the research unit 'Régulations foncières', (IRD), France. Lacinan Paré, geographer and consultant, deceased in 2002. The authors dedicate publication of this study in tribute to his memory. They thank two reviewers and Michael Kevane for useful comments, all remaining errors being theirs alone.

MAP 1
WESTERN BURKINA FASO – THE PROVINCES OF THE COTTON-GROWING AREA
(ADAPTED FROM PARÉ, IIED, 2001)

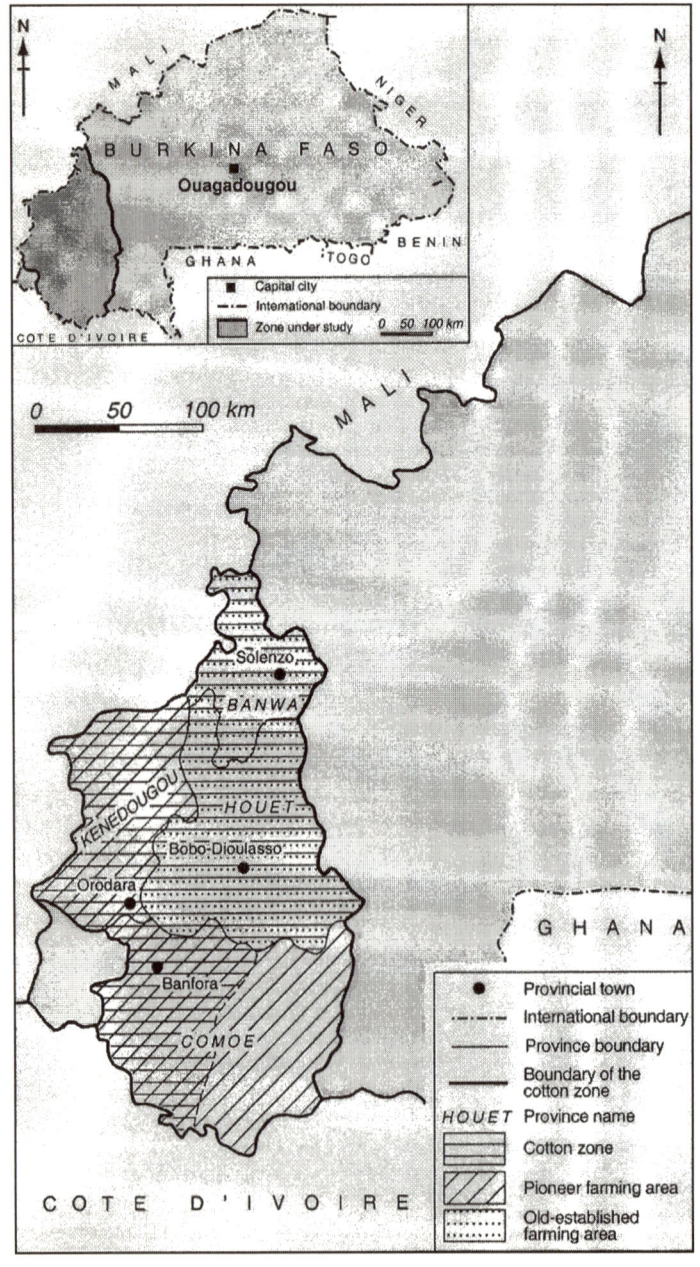

of various types. Some are quite formal and codified, while others are more informal and grounded in local forms of sociability and social relations.

This study presents certain aspects of these new monetary land transactions, while underlining the procedures of 'formalisation' which accompany them. Our arguments are based on field observations made during several enquiries in western Burkina Faso, which the three authors carried out between 1998 and 2001. The first part of the study presents the context of traditional land rights, the structural mutations that have occurred over the last 30 years and the new transactions involving payment in money. The second part presents an account of land withdrawal, which took place in 1997 and 1998. The third part provides a résumé of the various 'signs' and means that the actors in land transactions use in order to obtain social acknowledgement of these acts. In the fourth part, we analyse the functions of the various forms and 'signs' used in the new transactions, focusing on the concepts of security and legitimacy of rights, enforcement, normative pluralism and the aspect of ambiguity in transactions.

II. THE CONTEXT OF RECENT CHANGES IN LAND TENURE

The Traditional System of Land Ownership: Migration, Access to Land and the Institution of 'Sponsorship'

According to the traditions of the rural areas of West Africa, 'strangers' (migrants, people from elsewhere) could obtain relatively lasting and secure rights to land, subject, however, to certain relational conditions. Their access to land was possible through a personalised, 'dependent inclusion' within a space governed by the authorities (village chief, land chief) of an indigenous group [*Gruenais, 1986*]. This acknowledgement of the fact that the indigenous group had control of the space implied respect of the indigenous authorities and an acceptance of the dependent relationship as well as gratitude towards lodgers and sponsors ('tuteur' in Côte d'Ivoire, 'logeur' in Burkina Faso) who took in the migrant and gave him land to cultivate.

> Acknowledgement is shown by means of compensation, usually symbolic, agreed on at the time of the grant. A small portion of the annual production is generally given to the sponsor. Otherwise, the grantee might make a contribution to expenditure incurred by the sponsor during specific social events (death, funerals) or in the case of financial problems, which crop up now and then. This 'gratitude' that must be shown to the sponsor is passed down from one generation to the other. Migrants readily accept this, as long as the claims laid by sponsors remain moderate [*Chauveau, 2000: 15*].

Customary land tenure relationships are structured around the idea that the land is a living entity, appropriated by a local group and linked to ancestors and supernatural forces. In keeping with these conceptions, land provides the grounds on which social cohesion and community life are based, and can in no case be seen as individual property. Village land is shared out to the different founding lineages. The lineage chiefs are responsible for the management of family land, settling of internal conflicts surrounding field boundaries, welcoming and settling strangers and according temporary farming rights to them. This conception of land tenure relationships also required the granting of land to those really in need of it, generally migrants who ask for 'some land to cultivate in order to feed their family'. Once a long-term right on land was granted to a migrant, the indigenous owner could no longer – while remaining faithful to the spirit of customary provisions – withdraw this right as long as the beneficiary cultivated the granted land on a regular basis, remained on 'good terms' with his sponsor and respected local rules and taboos. This right was transmissible to the descendants of the initial beneficiary, as long as they, in turn, respected the same conditions.

Structural Changes During the Last 20 Years: Population, Land Use and Access to Land

Recent changes in land tenure are strongly influenced by three major structural transformations which have occurred during the last 40 years:

- a continuous inflow of migrant *mossi* farmers and their families, between 1960 and 1990, from the densely populated and ecologically unfavourable lands of the centre and north towards the fertile and inviting lands in the West;

- the rapid extension of cotton farming, from the 1960s to the present, strongly encouraged by the State and backed by external financial support;

- the 1984 Land Reform Act (*Réorganisation Agraire et Foncière*), later revised in 1991 and 1996. This Act defines the entire rural space as a 'National Domain', belonging exclusively to the State. In the two years succeeding its promulgation (1984–1986), this reform became a byword in official political discourse, aimed at undermining the 'autocratic feudalistic' powers of customary chiefs.

The first two factors led to a rapid increase in the total area of farmlands, particularly following the spread of animal traction for ploughing. The substantial incomes gained from cotton cultivation led to a rapid monetisation of rural societies and economies, with the consequences which usually follow in cases such as this: the individualisation of social behaviour, the erosion of the norms on which family discipline and cohesion are founded and so on. On the other hand, the migration of *mossi* people coming from the central and northern plateaux have attained such massive proportions that in many localities in the Banwa and Houet provinces the indigenous people are now largely outnumbered. Land farmed by migrants cover an ever-increasing surface of land, due to their numbers and to the dynamic expansion of cotton farming. Superior in numbers and often in wealth, these migrants are easily tempted to affirm themselves as independent proprietors, in fact, if not by right, by progressively ignoring the limits and conditions of farming rights defined by the indigenous people. In the 1980s, this led to rising social tensions between migrants and the indigenous *Bobo, Bwaba* and other autochthonous groups who detain customary rights to the land.

Since the awareness of land 'saturation' has dawned on peasants, migrants are more and more concerned about the precariousness of their hold on the land, while certain indigenous youth also fear that they will have to face up to a scarcity of land in the near future. Given the tense demographic and ethnic context, the Land Reform Act or RAF (*Réorganisation Agraire et Foncière*) triggered diffuse and growing protests against the customary rights migrants have to the land. Although it is generally acknowledged that the RAF may not be really applied, and that it may be unfamiliar to most rural actors, it still serves to aggravate the state of confusion and uncertainty about what the legitimate principles and who the legitimate authorities are, as far as land management is concerned. This erosion of customary authority over the land, which does not erase the significance of custom and the ideological weight of tradition, results in a situation in which pluralism is gaining ground, accompanied by growing confusion over the norms and rules of land tenure. These social evolutions over the last 30 years have also weakened the degree of collective control the land chief and the lineage elders exercise over the way land is managed in the village. As a result, there has been a shift in the real centre of management, which has moved from lineage chiefs to the new people in charge of family farm lands, and a fragmentation of the lineages' patrimonial holdings.

New Practices in Land Tenure

In this context, marked by uncertainty and a plurality of legal references, emerging situations of competition for land and the increasing awareness that land is getting scarce have generated various types of strategies. It has become increasingly common to find cases in which indigenous peasants take back land from migrants to whom it was granted 20 or 30 years earlier (often by the parents of the current decision-makers). This is often carried out in a brutal and unilateral manner (in the province of Banwa, for example). Sometimes, but this is more unusual, indigenous proprietors suggest to the migrants that they could stay on the land if they made a substantial increase in gifts or in produce (which used to be purely symbolic). Tension and conflict usually follow in the wake of this retrieval of granted land. Those migrants, who can afford to do so, generally try to secure their rights to the land through monetary means. Others who cannot afford this, but who are faced with increasingly hostile indigenous land managers, move further to the south in search of a new settlement in a less populated zone where there might be agricultural space still available for newcomers. In recent years (five to ten, depending on the locality), new transactions have been observed which have very little to do with customary practices. The following summarises these new land tenure practices: land withdrawals, land rentals with payment in money, permanent land acquisition by purchase in money.

Withdrawal of land formerly allocated to migrants: This is a case in which the indigenous proprietor or his descendants withdraw the right to cultivate land formerly granted to a migrant who has been settled for 20 to 30 years. This usually occurs when one or the other of the original partners in the transaction dies, either the indigenous peasant or the migrant. When this happens, the grant, which, as a tacit customary rule, is transmissible to the next generation, has to be renewed for one more generation. This incurs the risk of the grant becoming permanent. If the person who made the grant, or his son, wishes to retrieve the land, either to merge it with the family's patrimonial holdings or to sell or rent it, he takes it back from the migrant's family to whom the land was initially 'given'.

Land rental agreements: The land is ceded for a few years in return for an annual rent paid in cash every year at the beginning of the cropping season. In 2000, rent for cotton cultivation cost about 10,000–20,000 CFA francs[1] per hectare annually in some regions (north of Houet province, south of Banwa province). These land rental contracts, unheard of even ten years ago, are becoming increasingly common in these two regions.

Rapid increase in the sale of land: What we are referring to by sale is a permanent ceding of land in return for money, despite the fact that the indigenous people themselves are generally anxious to avoid the use of terms like 'land sales and purchases', in words spoken in public or in writing. These transfers are permanent and thus offer the buyer the possibility of marking off the boundaries of the plot, the right to plant trees, and, in some cases, the right to set about obtaining a modern title to the property. In the Banwa and Houet provinces, where these monetary transactions have been in practice, albeit discretely, for over ten years, these transactions are generally considered by both parties as permanent with no strings attached, or, in other words, as a 'sale' in the modern or western sense. In the province of Banwa, prices range from 50,000 to 100,000 CFA francs per hectare, but can exceptionally rise as high as 200,000 CFA francs per hectare. These transactions are almost always concluded in the presence of a witness, and sometimes result in the establishment of some kind of document.

III. MONETARY LAND TRANSACTIONS AND SOCIAL RELATIONSHIPS: DISPUTES OVER LAND AS DISPUTES OVER MEANINGS AND RELATIONSHIPS

New transactions give rise to internal tension in the families involved, within the indigenous community, among kin, between indigenous peasants and migrants. The story below illustrates a fundamental aspects of these new practices. These conflicts and quarrels over land transactions occur in a variety of instances. Here a key issue is the framing and the legitimacy of diverging interpretations regarding rights, obligations and relations, the main question being: what are the relationships between actors, and what are the land tenure rights and obligations generated by these relationships?

A civil servant visiting his family in the village discovers that family lands are being sold with the agreement of family elders

This story was related in 1998 to M. Zongo by a civil servant working in Kouka [*Zongo and Mathieu, 2000*]:

> During my vacation, I went back to the village to visit my parents. One day, while walking in our old fields, I noticed that the migrant to whom my parents had given some land to cultivate had planted mango trees. Yet our parents had explained to him well that it was totally forbidden to plant trees on the land we were giving him. So I went to tell our old man (the elder of the family) so he could remind the migrant of this prohibition. I told my brothers and my uncles; we decided to hold a family meeting, to call the migrant to tell him to go and remove the trees if he wanted to continue exploiting the piece of land.

> The day of the meeting, the migrant came to tell us that one of our brothers had given him the piece of land with permission to plant trees. The brother in question had lived in Ivory Coast for a long time, he had come back to settle here but he is having a hard time. He confirmed what the migrant had said.

> I asked the old man to tell the migrant to uproot the mango trees that he planted to put an end to the brother's error. My other brothers agreed

with me. But strangely, the old man did not want to comply. We asked our brother whether he had received money from the migrant, at first he denied this then later admitted that he had received money, while specifying that there was no connection with the land. Neither did he remember the amount he had received. The meeting was starting to get tense; we did not understand our elder's attitude. Finally, he suggested to end the meeting and to meet again another day when we had calmed down. I found that odd. We ended the meeting without saying anything to the migrant. That was not normal but we could not go against the old man's word. During my subsequent stays in the village, I kept bringing up the problem, but my uncle always found reasons to explain why there was no meeting to ask the migrant to uproot his trees.

Long afterwards, a childhood friend told me that the migrant was having a well dug. To me, this was provocation because digging of a well figures among the prohibitions. So I returned to the village to tell the old man and the other members of the family.

When the meeting was held, only two of us thought the migrant's behaviour was not normal. The others had all changed their position or said nothing; some brothers had not even come to the meeting. When I tried to speak up, our uncle got annoyed with me, he even told me that I no longer respected the customs, since I dared to bother him and to contradict him. He started to explain that the migrant is now part of the family because he has been there a long time and he respects our customs well. This is not true. The others agreed with him. I was isolated, so I gave up.

Later, one of my aunts told me that after the first meeting, the migrant brought the uncle an expensive embroidered boubou, he also bought him shoes, and that sometimes he came to his house for chat, always with little presents like sugar or cola nuts. To some brothers he also gave presents; it even happened that he offered dolo to some on the day of the market or in the village cabarets.

An Interpretation of the Story

Although this account presents the point of view of a single actor (and one who sees himself as the victim of an unfair action), we can, none the less, draw some tentative conclusions from this story. We observe that the lineage chief engaged in a monetary transaction. But he was anxious to legitimate his dealings in money by resorting to traditional references. This legitimising discourse appears to be designed for the benefit of the local scene. It comes across as an opportunistic process which is more concerned with making a show of symbols of custom than with actually conforming to its fundamental principles, namely that property is owned by the community and the inalienable character of the land excludes sale.

The successful actors in this story are those who actually managed to conclude and ratify a transaction that custom forbids and that is contested by one family member: the brother who has come back home and initiated the monetary transaction; the migrant who secured rights in land formerly received as a 'conditional long term grant'; the family elders who accepted gifts and money. These are the actors who have agreed to 'make a deal' (possibly implicit), exchanging the rights to plant trees in exchange for money and other gifts, while at the same time finding the means to make a public display of the signs of tradition with regard to social relations and relations to land. They manage to respect at least the outward signs of socially acceptable behaviour while, at the same time, adapting to new circumstances: land has become scarce and valuable; one actor was in need, looking for land and ready to pay for it, while others in need (or ready to accept) gifts and money, in exchange for ceding land.

This transaction obviously occurs somewhere in between two sets of norms, namely, the norms of customary principles (land is not a commodity, it belongs to the family and it cannot be 'sold') and those of the market. The actors who are best able to manage this plurality and find their way in the new circumstances are those who have the ability to play several games with meanings on different stages, while the losers are those who still believe that there is only one game being played, as defined by custom. In this context marked by a plurality of norms, the winner of disputes is the player who is better at fighting symbolic and relational battles. He knows how to use various kinds of meanings and craft innovative arrangements while still remaining in the realm of acceptable social behaviour. Some 'forms' or visible signs of the actions that perform the transaction play a key role in this process: paying visits, offering gifts, planting trees ... .

IV. FORMALISATION: THE DIVERSITY OF FORMS AND PAPERS IN THE NEW LAND TRANSACTIONS INVOLVING MONEY

Between 1998 and 2001, the authors of this study investigated more than 60 cases of land transactions involving either sales or the granting of long-term rights in exchange for money, in three specific areas of the south-west region: 35 in Kenedougou [*Paré, 2002*], 10 in the provinces of Banwa and of Comoé [*Zongo, 2000*], and more than 20 in the northern part of the province of Houet, in a village situated at 30 kilometres from the town of Bobo-Dioulasso [*Zougouri and Mathieu, 2002; Baud, 2001*].

We will first summarise the findings of these investigations with regard to the various kinds of papers and other socially meaningful signals accompanying these transactions. In the following section and in the conclusion, we will suggest some hypotheses regarding the logic and the strategies underlying the use of papers, and the reasons for the diversity of practices among various actors and between localities.

The Various Kinds of Papers and the Formalisation of Land Transactions

(a) No document, no witness and no formalisation. Exhibiting marks of custom to justify new practices in order to secure land transactions: As regards their immediate social environment (the village, the family, migrant families allowed to settle on granted land), the indigenous land managers involved in the transactions are anxious to legitimate their practices *vis-à-vis* tradition. In this case, there is no formal registration or official administrative document in writing. What we observe, to the contrary, is a displayed 'traditionalisation' of certain types of behaviour: gifts, customary sacrifices, public display of gratefulness from the receiver to the grantor of land rights, according to the 'official customary' model of migrant/sponsor (guardian) relationships. The display of traditional signs is no doubt meant to legitimate, on the local scene, a type of behaviour which breaches tradition. This kind of formalisation transits via customary forms and signs. It entails an opportunistic formalisation in the traditional idioms in order to legitimise, and maybe to conceal, something which is quite new and different, when the main object of the transaction is a transfer of land in exchange for money. In Mangodara, such a case has been documented in 2000 [*Zongo, 2000*]. In this case, the buyer (a civil servant) first told a foreign young researcher 'here we do not say "buying" and "selling", these [transactions] are gifts in exchange for something'. A year later, the same person told M. Zongo that 'with the person who sold me the land, we agreed that I should say [in public] that he gave me the right to plant trees because we are on very good terms. Even when I will go to get official papers from the administration, that is what I will say, because the law forbids the sale of lands.'

(b) Witnesses, customary signs of long-term land rights, but no paper: The planting of trees (and other visible long-term investments, such as wells, houses, etc.) is often used to express and assert claims of ownership. Most local small farmers who acquire land by purchase neither ask for nor receive a written 'registration' of the transaction. However, they see to it that the agreement is concluded in the presence of a local eyewitness (of their choice) and rapidly proceed to plant trees or make other kinds of durable and visible investments. In these monetary but non-formalised transactions between peasants, occurring on the borderlines of the law and of administrative

procedure, the 'seller', for his part, usually acts on his own, without inviting witnesses. Being customary marks of rights of ownership, the planting of trees and other visible investments (wells) are also acts of 'formalisation' which have a high degree of social visibility, and which, without being documents, convey the message: 'I am [visibly] really the owner of this land', as well the implicit corollary: 'if any one wants to challenge this, he'd better be quick about it, since I publicly claim my legitimate ownership through this act of investment'. It is in keeping with this logic that the man (a migrant residing in the village) who buys land in the first account digs a well with the consent of the indigenous lineage chief. If this act remains unquestioned in the short term by the traditional owner, this means that the latter agrees that the migrant farmer has permanent rights. Digging a well (or planting trees) is thus the visible social sign, which signifies a public claim, on the part of the buyer, and a public acceptance, by the traditional indigenous owner, of the permanent transfer of land rights.

(c) 'Little receipts': a local informal paper in writing: In some localities (near towns and where monetary property transactions are the most frequent), monetary transactions between peasants involving land have recently been accompanied (over the last five years, according to our enquiries) by little documents or 'little receipts', which are very simple, and prepared on the spot with the help of someone who can write. These handwritten papers in French (usually using a very basic and simple vocabulary), bear witness to the transaction, that is, to the agreement between two people who consider that such and such a plot of land, covering this area (the approximate surface, mentioned in hectares, is often, but not always, mentioned) and located at such place, now belongs to Mr X. This paper uses very simple terms and is often deliberately left incomplete, to the extent that the terms it employs are quite vague, make no mention of payment in money, and carefully avoid terms such as 'sell', 'buy', 'allocate' (since the state alone has the prerogative to allocate land, as mentioned by one author of such a study). The aim here is obviously to leave a trace of the agreement, which the acquirer can keep, without acting overtly counter to the law or tradition. The advantage of these easily manufactured little receipts [*Kone and Chauveau, 1998*] is their low cost and accessibility to peasants of lower social ranks, thus producing a written, permanent 'proof' of the agreement that can be used later to try to prevent the transaction being cancelled or challenged by the seller himself or by other actors.

(d) The 'grant certificate': a local, typewritten semi-formal paper: In a version that is even more sophisticated, this paper, often titled 'certificat de cession', is typewritten and framed in an administrative style, with a letterhead imitating administrative documents, such as mention of the province, of the department,

of the state's official motto (*La Patrie ou la Mort. Nous Vaincrons*) and so on, pretending thus to belong to the realm of the administrative papers.

The document mentions the date, the identity of the seller and of the buyer, the surface area of the land, its locality, and sometimes a brief definition of boundaries. Finally, there are the signatures of the two parties, that of the witness as well as the references on their identity cards. The terms used to designate the parties vary from document to another, the purchaser being referred to as the beneficiary or as the buyer, the seller as the grantor or as the owner of the land. The sums involved are not mentioned on the document, which simply mentions that the land has been ceded [*Zongo, 1999*].

The document is typed in two copies, one for each party. Later on, both parties, or at times the purchaser alone, will go the police station or to the *Prefecture* to have the signatures on the document validated. This authentication is not a validation of the property transfer. It merely certifies that the signatures are genuine. Hence, in this way, the local administration plays the role of a witness whose weight makes it difficult to challenge the transaction. This intervention thus reinforces the future effectiveness of the rights acquired in the transaction, in the event of it being disputed.

(e) The record of palaver ('procès-verbal de palabre'): a bridge between local custom and legal property rights procedures: Finally, the most complex and the most precise of all locally established document attesting to a transaction is the '*procès-verbal de palabre*'. This document was used in colonial times to officialise a resolution or to finalise a decision (usually one made under local customary authority) and was meant to arbitrate and to put an end to disputes over land ownership. This was a written document recording the terms of the decision, and carried the signatures of land authorities implicated in the agreement. The document still had some legal meaning and acknowledgement after independence, according to law No. 77/60/AN of 12/07/60. Later, the 1996 revision of the Land Reform Act revived this practice under the name of '*procès-verbal de palabre*'. The parties involved in the decision, the customary authorities and the administration, must sign this document. The involvement of the local authorities (the village chief, usually, and/or land chief) is to ensure public discussion of the transaction at the village scene (which is not usually the case with the other documents mentioned above) and shows that is has been approved of as correct or legitimate by the local authorities. The law and recent administrative practice require this document in order to deliver a legal title (*Arrêté d'attribution*), granted by the Préfet, only after approval by the *Service des Domaines* (Land Administration Office).

The *procès-verbal de palabre* is therefore a hybrid and legally organised procedure, at the interface between administrative procedures and custom. The first stage of the decision, involving the customary authorities, takes place in the village, but the document that attests to this local decision is made at the administrative scene (in town, or the district capital). The document is approved and registered there, at the *Service des Domaines*, and this opens the way for the procedures resulting in a complete legal title of ownership, according to the law. Acquirers who wish to obtain this document (and this practice is now on the rise), are generally non-rural purchasers coming from outside the village. Urban investors (labelled and praised, by the current political discourse, as the 'new actors' of modern agriculture) readily ask for this document, which they need to obtain a legal title. Recent enquiries [*Zougouri and Mathieu, 2002*] indicated that in areas close to towns, the establishment of *procès-verbaux de palabre* has substantially increased over the last three years.

The Social Variability of Papers and Forms Accompanying Transactions

Even in the sub-zones where these various kinds of formalisation are encountered, there is a clear social logic defining which actors want and can afford what kind of formalisation practices. For instance, in a village in the department of Bama where land sales have been occurring for more than 30 years, all the above practices have been recently observed, and the following social determinants have been identified:

– The practices pertaining to the category (a) above existed until recently, but they have almost disappeared, as the frequency of sales and withdrawals are increasing and situations described as 'just good relationships' between a buyer and seller, or between a settled migrant and indigenous landowners, are becoming increasingly rare.

– The practices of category (b) above (land transaction followed by the planting of trees) are most often performed by migrants settled long ago, and who obtained land from their customary 'guardians' or sponsors. This too is becoming rare, as the first generation of 'old migrants' who were given land with long-term usufruct rights some 20 years ago, when land was abundant, are becoming less numerous, as compared to recent migrants and urban investors.

– Only new migrants and a small number of the older migrants buying land are asking for 'little receipts' or for a 'grant certificate'. The majority of recent migrants who buy land ask for some kind of paper, even the most basic. The two kinds of papers mentioned above are relatively easy to produce, but the buyer still has to pluck up the courage to ask for the paper, and must consider it as a necessity; it is not spontaneously proposed (on the contrary) by the seller, and there is nothing like a standard procedure for all the operations involved in the purchase of land.

– Rich, new migrants (for instance, those returning from Ivory Coast, with some financial capital and experience gained in a much more market-oriented rural economy) and small 'new actors' ask for the *procès-verbal de palabre*, which involves going to government offices in the district administration, dealing with officials and facing additional costs in order to have the papers certified, with the necessary government stamps.

– Finally, the big investors from the city, who buy between 20 and sometimes 100–200 hectares, choose the most complete procedure, involving the most official and most recent type of *procès-verbal de palabre*. They go through the entire process, with the intervention of the Service of Land Administration, the mapping out of the limits of the field with physical boundary markers and, finally, the application for a 'certificate of attribution', which is the first legal step towards obtaining a legal title of ownership.

It is thus observed that the various actors in the new monetary land transactions use different methods and means of formalisation to give visibility to these transactions. The different categories of acquirers in monetary land transactions also have different perceived needs for securing their rights in the future and in this global space. And finally, they have very different means of producing the various kinds of formalisation noted above. This is very important, because the cost involved in formalisation are different for each of the five categories mentioned above. Costs in terms of money obviously increases dramatically from (a) to (e) above. It is important to note here that money is not the only price to pay for formalisation. Other resources such as information, time, trust and good local relations, means of transportation, political connections, and so on can play an influential role. These are not equally available to all of the various actors involved.

Variability of Papers and Formalisation Strategies According to Geographic Location

Moreover, we observe a great variety in the formalisation practices used depending on the region. In the area close to and north of Bobo-Dioulasso, where cotton cultivation and other crops of high monetary value (fruit trees, vegetables), massive migration and the presence of urban people investing in agriculture have been noted for a long time (more than 30 years), all kinds of formalisation practices are observed. However, the more formalised types of practices, incurring higher expense, are obviously on the increase over the last five years.

In the area of Mangodara, which has the lowest population density of our four locations, and where migration and market-oriented agriculture are the most recent (in a region that is also quite a remote area, situated far from roads and big cities), land sales are still very carefully concealed, not easily discussed, and the only frequent modes of formalisation are types (a) and (b). Securing land rights implies constant investments (of time, gifts, money if requested) in order to maintain good relations with the landowner. Once these relations are well established, and only when certain of the mutual trust between the owner and himself, does the 'potential purchaser' dare to plant trees with the approval of the owner. Usually there is no clearly formulated claim or request that this investment be considered as the equivalent of a permanent transfer, amounting to the sale of land.

In the area of Kouka (province of Banwa), cotton cultivation and migration were introduced a long time ago, and population densities are high (43.5 inhabitants per square km in 1993, according to Paré and Tallet [*1999*]). But relatively 'rich' newly settled migrants, stakeholders and urban investors are relatively rare as the area is less suited to market-oriented agriculture. Here, 'little receipts' are exchanged between indigenous owners and second-generation young migrants or new migrants; records of palaver (*procès-verbal de palabres*) also exist, but use of them is infrequent. This is a region in which the rental market is quite limited compared to the other cotton-growing areas further south (those nearest to Bobo-Dioulasso). It is also one in which violent conflicts related to land withdrawals are the most frequent (source: interviews of M. Zongo and L. Paré with notables and Préfets, 1999–2000).

Finally, in the province of Kenedougou, and especially in the fruit-growing area near Orodara, Paré [*2002*] observed that numerous *Procès-verbaux de Palabre* (PVP) were made during the 1976–83 period, then ceased to exist during 'the Revolution' period (under Thomas Sankara), with its prevalent anti-'feudalistic' political discourse, its 'Committees for the Defence of Revolution' (CDR) present in every village. Later, there was a new surge of the PVPs as of 1996, after the third revision of the land reform which had officially recognised the use of PVPs. Between 1983 and 1995, it seems that the use of all kind of papers became very rare, except in the case of a few 'little receipts' claimed by urban-based stakeholders, investing in fruit farms.

The purchasers in this area are mostly civil servants or other people investing in orchards. During the years 1976–90, the local (*Senoufo*) indigenous landowners had usually agreed to the plantation of fruit trees, usually stating in clear and precise terms (by word of mouth and before witnesses, not in written PVPs) that this permission to plant trees did not mean ownership of land. In the 1990s, many customary land owners realised that some investors considered themselves as having purchased land and had managed to obtain official legal titles. Consequently, many violent conflicts and the burning of orchards occurred in the late 1990s in the area close to Orodara [*Paré, 2002*]. It is interesting to note that the new PVPs, after 1996, sometimes clearly stipulate that both the owner and the investor consider and accept that the land is NOT sold and remains the property of the indigenous traditional owner. It remains to be seen if this new approach will result in a decrease in conflicts related to orchards and land sale.

III. ANALYSIS

Transactions

Why do people perform transactions through social signals and various formal means with visibility and/or durability (papers, etc.)? The various social practices aimed at formalising transactions are geared towards securing, as far as possible, the rights resulting from the transactions, that is making them more durable and less likely to be challenged in the future. In order to obtain this security, the actors who pay to obtain land rights try to get these transactions achieved through or accompanied by forms that are:

(a) legitimate, or at least socially acceptable and accepted in the local social milieu in which the transaction takes place, and

(b) durable and visible, so that the proofs they present will be convincing and justifiable in the face of future threats or challenges concerning the rights claimed as a result of the transaction.

The condition (a) takes place in the local setting, and it includes various local persons in the social space closely related to the transaction (the seller, his family, the local community ... . But the various categories of acquirers of land, as well as the buyer and the seller in a given transaction are not equally dependent on this local space more or less characterised by face to face relationships. An urban dweller depends on this to a limited extent, and for a limited period (except if his orchards are burned down ten years later); the son of a migrant who has settled in this space for 20 years, and who wants to stay on the land, is a lot more dependent on this local relational factor, shaping the legitimacy and recognition of his rights. In this respect, it is totally right to say that 'the point is that, if property does not have legitimacy, it is not property because it lacks the basic ingredient of property, acknowledgement by others' [*Platteau, 1996: 46*].

From the 'buyers' point of view, factor (b) is clearly essential in the medium and long term, property being in essence valuable only if possessed permanently, not just for the time being. A major issue at stake in the formalisation of transaction is thus the enduring legitimacy and the *future* enforcement and strength of the rights resulting from the transaction. The point made by Platteau above should thus be completed in the following way: acknowledgement and legitimacy are one thing (basic, indeed), but, especially in periods of transition and normative pluralism, enforcement is another necessary condition for a *claim* to property to become an actual and secure property *right* [*Bromley, 1992*]. Hence, it seems important to pinpoint two conditions that are equally necessary for the securing the rights resulting from land transactions:

- the acknowledgement and acceptance of the transaction in the short term and by a local constituency or community, which recognises it as legitimate;

- recognition *and* enforcement of the resulting new property rights in the medium or long term, and in a broader social space. In this second respect, the security of rights encompasses the various factors and actors of enforcement, including local administrations, courts, ministries (and the persons in them) in the global space of the national state, within the political and juridical realm of the law and its application.

Different Actors and Different Signs

Different actors use different signs to make their claims visible and their rights more secure: In the practices of formalisation presented above, we noted that different actors use different signs to make a social display of the transaction, thus also producing a lasting trace. For instance, when the buyer is a non-peasant investor who lives in town, the sale is almost always validated by a paper (record of palaver, or 'deeding certificate' – '*certificat de cession*'), which is then used to begin a legal procedure aimed at obtaining an official title to the land. Peasant acquirers do not usually go through with this procedure (which is drawn-out and expensive), but they make a point of quickly investing in visible and durable works on the parcel – planting of trees, digging a well – as soon as the transaction is concluded. This is another way (one which is closer to traditional perceptions and customary conceptions) of obtaining recognition of the transaction and of ensuring one's rights.

The diversity of practices of formalisation is a reflection of the diversity of resources and expectations actors have as far as securing rights is concerned. Each actor is eager to have his transaction validated in conditions that will be effective, from his point of view, for the legitimacy and for the future enforcement and effectiveness of his property rights. The strategies of formalisation chosen depend on the means, the needs and the priorities of each actor, within his specific context of action and anticipations: all actors do not face the same constraints, do not have the same needs for security, the same resources (local trust can be as good as a paper, for some persons and in certain contexts), the same time-horizons and so forth.

Role of Local Administrations

The important role of local administrations at the interface between the local scene and the state: In fact, the intervention of the police or of the *prefecture* provides acquirers with a written and durable trace of the transaction, duly witnessed by the administration and carried out in keeping with the forms it defines. In this sense, the legalised little receipt and the record of palaver are effective as semi-official (and semi-unformal) signals and mechanisms[2] which are practical and accessible, and provide for the visibility and acknowledgement of some claims. Through the administrative validation of records of palaver and 'little receipts', the local administration plays two essential roles. First, it plays the role of a 'super-witness' at the interface between local practices and state legitimacy. Secondly, the local administration is an official authority, and this confers some effectiveness and weight to its acts, even if the legal meaning of these acts is not strictly defined in the Land legislation. This administrative acknowledgement plays an important role, as it is perceived as ensuring a greater capacity to defend one's rights in the future, although the papers are not legal titles of ownership.

VI. CONCLUSION

An Evolutionary Process ...

The first obvious conclusion of the above analysis is that there is at least some truth in the evolutionary theory of land rights. When rural population and market-oriented agricultural production both increase, land becomes scarce and acquires an economic value. As a result, there is a social demand for more individualised, precise and formalised land ownership rights.[3] That is obviously the primary concern of the acquirers (buyers) of land in exchange for money, a practice that is now clearly on the rise. But this change is not so simple, nor is it linear and automatic, which leads us to a second conclusion.

... with Deep Contradictions

The process of commoditisation and formalisation of land rights appears to be totally embedded in social relationships: these are primarily local, but also include relationships at the interface between local and non-local actors. The changes in land transactions are therefore slow, quite dependent on local circumstances, contradictory, exclusionary (that is, there are winners and losers in the new transactions),[4] complex and ambiguous.

Legal Pluralism and the Necessity of Ambiguity

Actors in land transactions who wish to take advantage of the new opportunities linked to the acquisition of land for money cannot simply pretend that land is unrelated to meanings inherited from the past. These meanings are still very much alive, retain their significance in the local social reality and cannot be avoided in the course of transactions. Moreover, innovative actors who carry out property transactions in contradiction with tradition are obliged to produce visibility and legitimacy, in order to secure their rights presently and in the future. To do this, they must manipulate signs, relations and meanings in order to gain the approval of the social authorities (customary and/or administrative) who intervene in land management and who can guarantee the outcome of land transactions. A skilful manipulation of signs allow these actors to combine discourses, symbols and practices which carry meanings and refer both to the discourse of custom and to the logic of commercial exchange. For the actors involved in these transactions, some degree of communication skills and a creative use of ambiguity are clearly needed in order to conclude the transactions and to bridge the gaps and ideological tensions between short-term local legitimacy and the search for long-term security of land rights.

Translated from the French by Antoinette Tidjani Alou

NOTES

1. 1,000 CFA francs amount approx. to 1.5 euros.
2. This is clearly a case of effective 'institutional bricolage', as defined by Cleaver [*2001*], with an 'untold consensus' [*Hesseling and Mathieu, 1986*] between peasants and administration for the design and use of this institutional *ad hoc* invention.
3. This is obviously a very rough and simple summary of the theory. For a detailed discussion and analysis, see Platteau [*1996*].
4. See Gray and Kevane [*2001*]; Mathieu *et al.* [*2000*]; Zongo and Mathieu [*2000*].

REFERENCES

Baud, J., 2001, *Transactions et conflits fonciers dans l'ouest du Burkina Faso*, Grafigéo (Coll. mémoires et documents de l'UMR PRODIG), no.2001–13.

Bromley, D.W., 1992, 'Property Rights as Authority Systems: The Role of Rules in Resource Management', in P. Nemetz (ed.), *Emerging Issues in Forest Policy*, Vancouver: University of Columbia Press, pp.453–70.

Chauveau, J.P., 2000, Note de préparation du projet 'Frontière', Montpellier: IRD, Working note for the research unit 'Régulations foncières' (IRD), mimeo, 21 pp.

Cleaver, F., 2001, 'Institutional Bricolage, Conflict and Cooperation in Usangu, Tanzania', *IDS Bulletin*, Vol.32, No.4. pp.26–35.

Crousse, B., Le Bris, E. and E. Le Roy (eds.), 1986, *Espaces disputés en Afrique Noire. Pratiques foncières locales*, Paris: Karthala.

Gray, L. and M. Kevane, 2001, 'Evolving Tenure Rights and Agricultural Intensification in Southwestern Burkina Faso', *World Development*, Vol.29, No.4, pp.573–87.

Griffiths, J., 1997, 'Une législation efficace: approche comparative', in D. Darbon and J. du Bois de Gaudusson (eds.), *La création du droit en Afrique*, Paris: Karthala, pp.41–71.

Gruenals, M.E., 1986, 'Territoires autochtones et mise en valeur des terres', in Crousse, Le Bris and Le Roy [*1986: 309–25*].

Hesseling, G. and P. Mathieu, 1986, 'Stratégies de l'Etat et des populations par rapport à l'espace', in Crousse, Le Bris and Le Roy [1986].

Koné, M., and J.P. Chauveau, 1998, 'Décentralisation de la gestion foncière et "petits reçus". Pluralisme des règles, pratiques locales et régulation politique dans le Centre-Ouest ivoirien', *Bulletin de l'Apad*, no.16, pp.141–63.

Mathieu, P., 1996a, 'Pratiques informelles, gestion de la confusion et invention du foncier en Afrique'. in G. de Villers (ed.), 'Phénomènes informels et dynamiques culturelles en Afrique', *Cahiers Africains*, Cedaf-L'Harmattan, no,19–20, pp.64–87.

Mathieu, P., 1996b, 'La sécurisation foncière entre compromis et conflits: un processus politique ?' *in* P. Mathieu, P.J. Laurent et J.-C. Willame (eds.), 'Démocratie, enjeux fonciers, pratiques locales en Afrique', *Cahiers Africains* (CEDAF- L'Harmattan), no 23-24, pp. 26-44.

Mathieu, P., Lavigne-Delville, P., Ouedraogo, H., Paré, L. and M. Zongo, 2000, 'Sécuriser les transactions foncières au Burkina Faso', unpublished report, Ouagadougou and Paris: Ministry of Agriculture and GRET.

Mathieu, P., 2001, 'Transactions informelles et marchés fonciers émergents en Afrique'. in T. Benjaminsen and C. Lund (eds.), *Politics, Property and Production in the West African Sahel: Understanding Natural Resource Management*, Uppsala: Nordic Africa Institute, pp.22–39.

Paré, L., 2001, *Les droits délégués dan l'ouest du Burkina Faso*, Paris/London: GRET-IIED, Report for the research project 'Land Tenure and Resource Access in West Africa', mimeo, 85 pp.

Paré, L., 2002, 'L'usage des procès verbaux de palabre dans le Kénédougou: évolution, acteurs et dynamique', draft field research report (synthèse d'observations et entretiens), Ouagadougou.

Paré, L. and B. Tallet, 1999, 'D'un espace ouvert à un espace saturé – Dynamique foncière et démographique dans le département de Kouka (Burkina Faso)', *Espace, populations et sociétés*, 1, pp.83–92.

Platteau, J.P. , 1996, 'The Evolutionary Theory of Land Rights as Applied to Subsaharan Africa: A Critical Assessment', *Development and Change*, Vol.27, No.1, pp.29–86.

von Benda-Beckmann, F., 1992, 'Introduction', in von Benda-Beckmann, F. and M. van der Velde (eds.), *Law as a Resource in Agrarian Struggles*, Wageningen: Agricultural University (Wageningen Studies in Sociology, 33), pp.1–22.

Zongo, M. and P. Mathieu, 2000, 'Transactions foncières marchandes dans l'ouest du Burkina Faso: vulnérabilité, conflits, sécurisation, insécurisation', *Bulletin de l'APAD*, no.19, numéro spécial 'Les interactions rurales et urbaines: circulation et mobilisation des ressources', pp.21–32.

Zongo, M., 2000, 'Migration, mutations et stratégies d'accès à la terre dans une zone de front pionnier au Burkina Faso', paper presented at the conference on 'Population et développement' (Louvain la Neuve, Nov. 2000), mimeo.

Zongo, M., 1999, 'Transactions foncières et usages de l'écrit dans la zone cotonnière du Burkina Faso: exemples à partir de la région des Banwa', in P. Lavigne-Delville and P. Mathieu (eds.), *Formalisation des contrats et des transactions. Repérage des pratiques populaires d'usage de l'écrit dans les transactions foncières en Afrique rurale*, working paper, GRET-IED, pp.77–88.

Zougouri, S. with P. Mathieu, 2002, 'Nouvelles transactions et formalisation des transactions foncières dans l'ouest du Burkina Faso', paper presented at the APAD conference on 'The Governance of Daily Life in Africa: Public and Collective Services and Their Users', Leiden, May 2002, draft research document, mimeo.

Race for the Prize: Land Transactions and Rent Appropriation in the Malian Cotton Zone

TOR A. BENJAMINSEN and ESPEN SJAASTAD

I. INTRODUCTION

This study describes how agricultural land in peri-urban areas of the Malian cotton zone is converted, at a remarkable pace, from inalienable customary tenure to various forms of exclusive and alienable holdings. Around the rapidly expanding and densely settled urban centres, in a rough circle with a radial stretch of some 10 to 20 kilometres, agricultural fields have become vehicles in a race. The prize pursued in this race is not so much the land itself as its value; the winner is not necessarily the one who, at the end, holds legal possession but, instead, the individual who has managed to extract the maximum portion of the land's rent.

The participants are numerous and varied. We find customary land chiefs, farmers with customary rights to till the land, merchants, middlemen, commune employees, district and regional government bureaucrats and, finally, the Malian state, providing the separation of the latter's objectives from those of its servants is at all meaningful. An equally rich mix of strategies, legal and otherwise, is employed, and not just because of the multitude of objectives; in a transitional environment characterised by both legal pluralism and governmental impotence, novel ways to gain advantage thrive.

This text is exploratory, and much work remains to be done with regard to land transactions and rent appropriation in the study area. As cities in the cotton zone expand, a succession of new plots are targeted, and as one race concludes, another begins. Ultimately, however, the findings in this analysis support an old adage. As we shall see, it is mostly the wealthy, the powerful, and the informed who succeed in a race contested under such murky conditions. Although the social fall-out of these processes have yet to fully

Tor A. Benjaminsen and Espen Sjaastad, Noragric, Agricultural University of Norway. The authors would like to thank the Nordic Africa Institute for a travel grant that made this research possible. Further research funds were in part provided by the Norwegian Research Council. The authors are also grateful to Camilla Toulmin, Thea Hillhorst and Christian Lund for valuable comments on earlier drafts.

settle, it is plain to see that few winners will be found among the farmers who hold original rights to the land.

The information on which much of this study is based was collected during a visit to the Malian cotton zone in February and March 2001. Besides gathering data on the particulars of 40 odd land transactions in the central part of the zone,[1] interviews were carried out with district and regional officials, middlemen, land chiefs, court officials, surveyors, and researchers. The main part of the fieldwork took place in the towns of Koutiala (74,000 inhabitants) and Sikasso (114,000 inhabitants).[2] Remaining information was obtained through official documents and literature.

II. THE MALIAN COTTON ZONE

The Malian cotton zone is situated in the south-eastern corner of Mali, bordering Guinea, the Ivory Coast and Burkina Faso (Figure 1). Mean long-term annual rainfall ranges from 600-800 mm in the northern part of the region to 1,200–1,400 mm at the southern fringe. Besides the cultivation of food crops such as millet, sorghum and maize, production of cotton as a cash crop has increasingly gained importance during the last decades. The region is among the most densely populated areas in Mali. Cotton is Mali's biggest export product, and the relatively well-developed infrastructure of the region is a result of its being based in that part of the country where all of Mali's export cotton is produced. The cotton boom in southern Mali during the last decade has resulted in the Malian cotton zone often being referred to as an African success story.

The population in southern Mali has grown rapidly for several decades. Administrative reports from the 1940s and 1950s indicate a considerable population growth in the area. After independence, three censuses were carried out (1976, 1987 and 1998). In addition, surveys of the population were undertaken by the *cercle* (district) administrations in 1967, 1982, 1996, and 2001. In the Koutiala district, which is the core area of the cotton zone, the size of the population increased from 122,000 in 1967 Sanogo, 1989] to 396,500 in 2001 (administrative census) which implies a current population density in the district of 41 inhabitants per square kilometre.

Population pressure is also increasing through agricultural development. From 1952, cotton production has been based on a guaranteed price announced in advance by the parastatal cotton company (the CFDT until 1974, thereafter the CMDT).[3] This has led to an increase in commercialised cotton from only 150 tons in 1952 to 3,900 tons in 1958, which was only the beginning of a rapid rise in cotton production: in 1972 it reached 68,000 tons; in 1992: 310,000 tons; and in 2002: 600,000 tons. This development has made Mali the largest producer of cotton in sub-Saharan Africa.

FIGURE 1

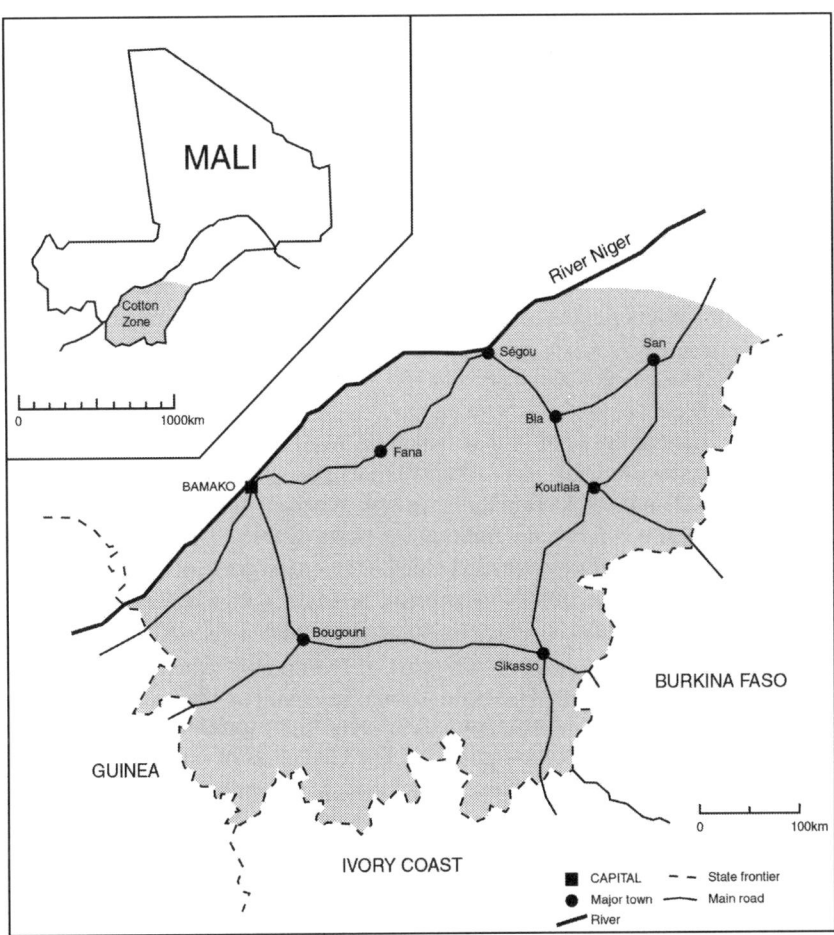

The overall growth in cotton production has also implied an extension in area from the core one around Koutiala towards the south-west. The process included both periods of intensification through rapid extension of the cultivated area and that of an application of additional inputs of labour and capital per hectare [*Benjaminsen, 2001*]. This technological change has also been of benefit to food crops grown in the area, resulting in increased food security during the last decades [*Dioné, 1989; Raymond and Fok, 1995*]. Thus the cotton zone in southern Mali is today a net exporter of grains to other parts of the country as well as to neighbouring countries.

The main ethnic groups in southern Mali are the Minyanka, the Bambara, and the Sénoufo, in addition to the pastoral Fulani. Land tenure systems in the three farming groups are fairly similar.

III. INSTITUTIONS AND ACTORS

Customary Land Tenure

In all cultures, custom is dynamic and changes over time. This is also the case in the Malian cotton zone, as this study will try to show. Some practices and institutions may, however, show greater resistance to external pressures, and a 'customary' system in the cotton zone can be described with some justification [*Benjaminsen, 2002; Colleyn, 1988; Colleyn and Jonckers, 1983; Coulibaly and Joldersma, 1991; Crowley, 1991; Jonckers, 1987; Rondeau, 1980; Sanogo, 1989*].

In the farming communities in southern Mali, membership in a lineage determines access to land. Agricultural production is organised in residential patrilineages. These production units are also generally the consumption units. Each production unit holds the right to use a part of the village land. This land is distributed to the unit by the land chief – the oldest male descendant of the founding lineage in the village. Tenure and management of land is thus tightly linked to religious beliefs, whereby the first settlers in an area establish a sacred alliance with the earth divinities and become, through this direct link, responsible for managing the land. However, land is said to belong to the divinities and to the ancestors and is, therefore, considered inalienable by chiefs and members of original lineages. The land chief or villagers who have received land from him, or those whose lineage in earlier generations have received land, should not sell or give away land to outsiders. The role of the land chief in this context is to allocate use rights to the land. Furthermore, the land chief is by far the biggest landholder in the villages. However, the village chief who holds an administrative position normally comes from the second lineage established in the village. His task has been, since the French colonial power established this position, to act as the contact person and spokesman of the village *vis-à-vis* the state. Sometimes the land and village chief are one and the same person.

Villages usually have at least one sacred forest, and it is the land chief who is responsible for making sacrifices in this forest to the earth divinities, to God, and to the ancestors on behalf of the village. Failure to comply with the norms and taboos related to land and natural resource management may lead to sanctions, decided on by the land chief. These may include not only an interdiction to participate in ceremonies, but also rituals designed to inflict health problems on offenders or pest damage on their crops. Failure to comply with rules may also bring misfortune to the whole village. 'Thus, the fundamental sanction which the land chief controls to encourage villagers to follow prescribed resource management is a spiritual link to promote well-being, health and fertility' [*Crowley, 1991: 42*]. These are 'customary' rules and sanctions which today are said to be disintegrating and less respected than before, due to factors such as the spread of Islam, the influence of modern legislation and state management of forests, and increased market integration [*Coulibaly and Joldersma, 1991*]. Today the extent to which one finds elements of these customary rules in the individual villages varies considerably depending on local political and religious struggles over leadership.

Customary Land Transactions

Even though the cotton zone is one of the most densely populated areas in Mali, it nevertheless has a relatively low density compared to other African regions with similar amounts of rainfall and with noticeable agricultural development [*Benjaminsen, 2001*]; it is currently only the core area (Koutiala district) which is experiencing a prospective shortage of land. The relative abundance of agricultural land has so far led to an open and hospitable system of lending land to outsiders. Hence, when all land has been distributed to the diverse lineages settled in a village, plots may still be obtained through borrowing from other farmers, but on one condition: investments on the land are not allowed because they may signify longer-term claims. Tree planting, the digging of wells, or construction of buildings would thus be a reason to terminate a contract.

Borrowing of land is basically free of charge, but requires important symbolic gestures. In order to obtain land, borrowers need to extend gifts of token material value to the head of the lineage holding the land. Such gifts have traditionally been cola nuts, a white cock, or cowri shells. Since land chiefs have been the largest landholders, they have also been the most frequent lenders of land. The land chief interviewed in Baramba village in the core cotton area (25 kilometres from Koutiala town) said that allocation of land traditionally required a gift of one white cock and 80 cowri shells. In addition, a basket of grain was given to the land chief after the harvest. Other informants said that it was only necessary to give a few grains of the harvest in order to maintain the contract. This should not be regarded as rent, but rather a symbolic gift manifesting a political allegiance to the village community [*Gruenais, 1986; Jonckers, 1987; Platteau, 1993*].

Land can be withdrawn when the holder needs it, or if the contract is broken by the borrower through investments. In the former case, the lender would usually feel a moral obligation to find some new land for the borrower. A loan arrangement, however, is not necessarily the one-way street that it may seem at first. Borrowed fields are often found on marginal land, and borrowers may improve this land, initially by clearing it, and subsequently through perennial tilling and use of fertilisers. Moreover, the borrower, after working a given plot for some years, may be moved by the lender to another marginal area to carry out similar improvements.

However, due to the increased pressure on land, earlier generations' land loans are giving rise to conflicts today. This occurs either when the lending family attempts to retrieve land or when the borrower tries to invest in the land. The latter is considered an attempt at appropriation and is immediately sanctioned. As confirmed by lawyers in the district court in Koutiala (*Palais de la Justice*), both these practices appear to be widespread as land conflicts are on the increase with most of these conflicts linked to earlier loans of land.

In accordance with these findings, Zongo [*1999*], studying land transactions in the cotton zone in neighbouring Burkina Faso, found that reclamation of land by lenders was increasing (see also Mathieu [*2001*]). This usually happened after 20 to 30 years and often at the occasion of the death of one of the original parties to the transaction. There was also a diminution and, in some places, a disappearance altogether of land loans.

Formal Law

In the colonial period in French Sudan, the state and individuals with title deeds were the only possible landowners. This idea came from the French *Code Civil* or *Code Napoléon* from 1804 stating in its article 713 that '*Les biens qui n'ont pas de maîtres appartiennent à l'Etat*' ('property without a master belongs to the state'). Further, in its article 539, the *Code Civil* states: '*Tous les biens vacants et sans maître ... appartiennent au domaine public*' ('all vacant property without a master belongs to the public domain') (see Rochegude [*1977*] for a review of colonial law in French Sudan). Hence, only the state and individuals with titles have property rights to land. Although over time a more realistic recognition of customary rights developed within the colonial administration, the system nevertheless only acknowledged customary holders as holders of use rights, not property rights.

Similarly, according to the Forest Code of 1935 (*Code forestier*), fallow land, pastures and forests were formally under the authority of the state. Only customary rights to land that had been *mise en valeur* (put to use, or to which value was added) were acknowledged. This meant in practice that only farming gave a community or individuals customary use rights.

As a heritage from colonial law, the Land Code of 1986 (*Code domanial et foncier*) acknowledged property rights only in the case of individually held title deeds. Customary rights were defined as use rights with a much weaker status than titled land. On registered residential plots, people hold *permis d'habiter* which are provisional titles implying a right to occupy the plot and to resell it to a third individual (incurring a tax of 24,250 CFA to the commune).

Since the emergence of Malian democracy from 1991 and the new government's decentralisation policy, several of the old laws originating in the colonial period have been revised. There were only minor revisions made to the Forest Code in 1968 and 1986, but in 1995 a new Forest Code, designed to be more in tune with decentralisation efforts, was introduced. However, the state is still the owner of all 'vacant' land such as forests, pastures, and land left fallow more than ten years. On cultivated land and land left fallow less than ten years, customary use rights are acknowledged.

The Land Code of 1986, at the time of writing, is being replaced by a current Land Ordinance[4] (*Ordonnance du 22 Mars 2000 portant code domanial et foncier*).[5] In the spirit of decentralisation, this new law allows for the titling of land also in the name of groups (*collectivités*), either in the form of residential lineage groups, villages, nomadic *fractions*, or communes.[6] However, the main question that remains is how these groups can form legal and moral entities; the definition of a group is a dynamic problem, raising issues of permissible entry and exit as generations succeed each other, and is difficult to solve once and for all. As long as the groups have not registered their land, they can only hold customary use rights.

The 2000 ordinance aids decentralisation; it stipulates, for instance, that procedures related to the authorisation of expropriation and to foreclosure of mortgaged land should be handled at lower administrative levels than before. It may also strengthen the security of customary rights holders by making it possible to convert individual, as well as collective, use rights to full property rights. However, such conversions will weaken customary rights in the long term; the fate of holders of customary rights will thus depend on their ability to avail themselves of the opportunities provided by the new ordinance and the outcome of the conflicts that will inevitably arise. Finally, the new law makes it simpler and easier to expropriate land. Previously, expropriation had to be authorised at the ministerial level but, with the new law, this can be done by district authorities.

Neither the old 1986 code nor the new 2000 ordinance consider transactions of non-titled land to be illegal. While the former has not explicitly recognised these transactions, the latter does, but in practical terms there is no difference. When a seller and a buyer agree on a transaction, the two parties and two witnesses usually sign a written attestation. To make a sale legitimate, it is sufficient to take this letter of sale to the local commune administration and have it signed and stamped.[7]

The requirements for obtaining a provisional title are that: (1) there should be no conflict about ownership; and (2) a sketch map made by the district topographer should be completed. As far as no dispute about ownership is concerned, a commission of six people is set up whose responsibility it is to investigate contesting claims to the relevant land. A letter is sent to the relevant commune, and an announcement is made on local radio and in a couple of newspapers, indicating when the commission will be present in the village to hear potential objections to the title.

Upon receiving a provisional title, the landowner has five years in which to complete improvements deemed necessary for a full title to be granted. These improvements are specific to each case, depending on location and intended use. Holders of provisional titles meanwhile pay a tax to the district of 4,700 CFA per hectare per year. Once improvements are completed, the landowner may apply to the regional authorities for a freehold title. Improvements are inspected and a more detailed map is made. Within a minimum of 75 days, providing no competing claims appear and upon the payment of 197,000 CFA for every hectare held, the owner can be in possession of a full title.

Actors

The main actors in the evolving land markets around the towns of Koutiala and Sikasso are the following groups:

Land chiefs: Generally descendants of the first family to settle in an area, land chiefs are the biggest landholders and consequently the most important sellers of land. Land chiefs in villages within a radius of ten to 20 kilometres from Koutiala and Sikasso are currently selling land cheaply and frequently. Their status and prestige among the subjects to whom they are responsible is pitched against the threat of their villages being swallowed by rapidly expanding urban centres.

Farmers: It is not only land chiefs who have started to sell land, but also farmers in general who feel that they have some land to spare. Sometimes land is sold where there is a conflict over who is the rightful owner. Farmers are rarely buyers.

Urban buyers: Urban elites represent the biggest land-buying group. It consists mainly of wealthy merchants and bureaucrats. About half of the transactions studied involved merchants as buyers. Despite other professional commitments, however, the motivation for land purchases by members of this group is generally to engage in farming.

Middlemen: In about a third of the land transactions studied in Koutiala there was an intermediary involved. These middlemen are known locally for having detailed knowledge of the peri-urban land market. In Sikasso, there is an estate agent who is also a speculator in land. In an interview, he stated that he represented 'a new race' which was expected to grow.

Urban communes: Urban communes are major actors in the land markets in the Malian cotton zone. Through the expropriation of customary holdings and their subsequent subdivision into residential plots, urban communes represent the main driving force in the expansion of urban centres. Besides obtaining parts of the revenue from sales of residential plots, urban communes also realise tax revenues from building and occupancy permits.

District and regional authorities: District and regional authorities represent the state as the landowner. The district awards provisional titles, while the region allocates full titles. Taxes are collected from owners with provisional titles, while full titles are sold for a one-time fee. State authorities also realise revenues from expropriation.[8]

IV. LAND TRANSACTIONS AND RENT APPROPRIATION

Erosion of Customary Norms

A feature of the transition from inalienable customary land to alienable and exclusive holdings is the rapid and apparently smooth manner in which it takes place. Three underlying forces can be identified in this transition [*Coulibaly and Joldersma, 1991*]. First, Islam has been spreading in the area, particularly during the last decades and at the expense of local animistic practices. Because customary norms and their sanctioning are strongly linked to such animistic beliefs and practices, an erosion of traditional authority inevitably attends this transition. Because Islam, in contrast to customary belief systems, does not militate against trade in land, the idea of land as a communal inheritance with deep spiritual significance has gradually lost currency.

A second challenge to customary norms is posed by commercialisation, which spreads outward from the expanding urban centres like ripples in a pond. As observed by Bohannan and Dalton [*1962*], it is money, in providing a universal medium of exchange, that will naturally tend to dissolve the boundaries traditionally existing between different categories of goods and their legitimate modes of exchange. When these 'multicentric spheres' disintegrate, goods such as land that were previously only transferred through succession and reciprocal arrangements may enter the market economy.

Modern legislation and the telescopic reach of local and regional government bodies represent a third force contributing to the erosion of the legitimacy of customary norms in land relations. In rural areas, this force involves mainly state management of forests and village woodlands. In peri-urban areas, however, expropriation exerts increasing influence over how rights to agricultural land are perceived. The effect is straightforward and unilateral: in villages in the immediate vicinity of major urban centres, tenure security is reduced through the risk of losing land to local government.

Initial Sales

To potential buyers of land, land chiefs are attractive business partners. Not only do they possess more land than other villagers, and thus possess a greater variety of holdings from which to choose as well as offering the possibility of making large purchases, but land chiefs also possess more secure land, in so far as they retain some influence over other lineages' land. This latter point is illustrated and formalised through the provision that the land chief must sign any provisional title application. Among the 34 straight sales of land registered by us, 16 (47 per cent) represent sales by land chiefs. In terms of area sold, however, their share is much higher: of 301 hectares traded, 221 hectares (73 per cent) were lands previously held by chiefs. The average size of holdings sold by chiefs was thus 13.8 hectares, compared to an average of 4.4 hectares among other sellers.

While the reasons why chiefs are attractive to buyers may seem straightforward, the reasons chiefs themselves are *attracted* to buyers are more puzzling. To understand these motives, it is necessary to consider the limited options faced by chiefs in peri-urban locations with dwindling authority among their subjects, and the prospect of shrinking land areas over which to rule as land-hungry urban dwellers and urban commune officials threaten to swallow their villages through conversion of loans to permanent ownership or expropriation. It appears that in these conditions chiefs, and the communities to which their variable authority applies, fall into three broad categories: those who resign themselves to the inevitability of town expansion and the complete commoditisation of land; those that take the middle road, accepting limited commercial transactions in land while attempting to maintain some level of social cohesion and traditional values; and those who vehemently resist the process.

The basic strategy of those chiefs completely resigned to the process seems to be to cash in quickly before expropriators arrive, selling untitled customary land indiscriminately in quantity at relatively low prices rather than engaging in traditional lending agreements. This is certainly a fair description of what is going on in many villages around Sikasso and Koutiala today, and it is in these villages that the most rapid transformation from customary to market system takes place. Under these circumstances, chiefs, rather than fulfilling their role as guardians of customary law, are often the first to embrace the new market order and thereby trigger a process of land alienation that rapidly spreads to the rest of the village.

Those taking the middle road will follow a slightly different strategy. Chiefs and complying subjects will here sell land at even lower prices, sometimes approaching in value the symbolic or token gestures associated with loans, but will try to restrict the amount of land made available through time. The discrepancy between demand and supply of land will then be used to ensure that outside buyers are of a preferred type: friends or relatives of existing villagers (who might not afford market-clearing prices), or erstwhile townspeople willing to settle and participate in the social mechanisms of the village.

Finally, there are those who resist. There are still chiefs in the area with enough authority both to summarily reject prospective borrowers or buyers from town and convince their subjects to do the same.

Who then are the initial buyers of customary lands? Expropriation notwithstanding, buyers are generally town dwellers who wish to farm but also possess other comparatively lucrative income-earning opportunities. Of the 34 transactions recorded, 16 involved purchases by merchants and shopowners of various kinds. Most of the remaining transactions involved purchases by government bureaucrats and entrepreneurs. In only one case was land bought by an individual describing himself as a farmer, plain and simple, with no other professional interest. It should be noted, however, that initial buyers of land by and large engage in transactions for the purpose of farming.[9] Only one of the transactions registered involved a resale. Of the 18 parcels of land where no fixed improvements existed at the time of sale, only six had failed to see improvements completed subsequent to the transaction. Moreover, two of these six parcels were purchased within the last three months, and all within the last five years.

The inflation-adjusted per hectare price for initial sales, when aggregating land sales registered by us, was roughly 140,000 CFA or approximately US$200. This can be compared to annual per hectare net revenues from the cultivation of typical crops such as cotton, millet, or maize of some 40,000 to 60,000 CFA when hired labour and machinery is applied, giving present values of 400,000 to 600,000 CFA per hectare at a ten per cent discount rate.[10] Part of the rather substantial discrepancy between land prices and net present values from crop cultivation can be found in the very low prices for land supplied by communities following the middle road. The risk of having land expropriated, discussed later, will further depress prices. And, as pointed out by Shipton [1989], it may be marginal lands which first enter the market, because there would be less hesitation among potential sellers to sell this type of land. The discrepancy must, however, also be considered in the light of cash constraints and limited credit markets. Many farmers in rural and peri-urban areas, though poor, possess more land than they can cultivate meaningfully using family labour alone. Since credit is restricted to farmers with legal title to land or to very wealthy individuals, poorer farmers are able neither to till nor to invest on this 'surplus' land.

An alternative that might seem available to sellers is to put their land up for rent. However, rental arrangements, for which the market is limited even in central urban areas, are very uncommon in rural and peri-urban communities.[11] This is due in part to the aforementioned cash constraints within these communities. In addition, urban dwellers without such constraints, though increasingly willing to buy land outside the town perimeter, seem unwilling to rent because land improvements are unfeasible or unattractive. The classic distribution of wealth between landlord and potential tenant is here reversed, with the landlords generally being poor and the potential tenants comparatively wealthy. On the one hand, potential tenants with ability to invest will often be prohibited from doing so, since such behaviour is seen as an attempt to claim permanent possession; on the other hand, they will be unwilling to do so because of the obvious risk of having the rental agreement terminated without compensation for improvements.

Some sellers will, however, attempt to increase their share of the spoils by dubious means. We were told of many instances where the same parcel of land had been sold to more than one buyer. In one such case the buyers took the seller, a chief, to court. The owner with the oldest dated letter of sale was in this case given possession of the land.[12] Further, rather than instructing the chief to return received moneys to the two other buyers, he was told to provide land of equivalent value for these too. Another adaptation is seen whereby sellers alienate land that does not belong to them. A particularly crafty individual in Koutiala had sold, by virtue of his position as chief, vast tracts of land belonging to other lineages. In some cases, these lineages were able to reclaim their land; in others, notably when the buyer was a wealthy individual, they were not.[13] When successful, swindles such as these may increase rent appropriated by sellers, who may or may not be landowners, but may thus also serve the interests of wealthy and powerful buyers.

As far as buyers are concerned, at this stage their rent appropriation is still an unknown quantity, depending on the fate of their land in the future. Clearly, as evidenced by the discrepancy between sales price and obtainable net present value from agriculture, they may gain from cheap purchases of rural or peri-urban land simply by being prudent farmers. They may lose, however, if their land is expropriated, or they may gain considerably more if they manage to acquire legal title to their land. Before we turn our attention to the latter process, however, we must briefly consider the role of middlemen.

The Role of Middlemen

As noted earlier, middlemen were involved in roughly a third of transactions recorded by us. The role of middlemen is, at least for now, one that is mostly enacted in the initial sales described above, and their share of the spoils is therefore constrained by the comparatively modest prices typical of these transactions. At the low end, we find individuals who have, for various reasons, a multitude of contacts among both buyers and sellers, for instance, people whose business makes them familiar with both rural and urban communities. In the process of socialising with these contacts, they register the desires of potential transactors and, if a suitable match is found, bring them together. Their fees, around five per cent of price, is attuned to their modest involvement. More professional agents, who carry out their business in a more systematic fashion at established premises and who probably involve themselves to a greater degree in their clients' hunt for land, require a fee of ten to 15 per cent of the price.

It is possible that a third and more speculative group of middlemen should be distinguished. It is by no means an uncommon practice for middlemen to quote different prices to seller and buyer. This is, of course, a strictly illegal practice in states where the role of real estate agents is more established. In Mali, however, the distinction between fraud and honest speculation with respect to untitled land seems more obscure.

A slightly different type of racket is also in operation. Instead of quoting different prices, middlemen may keep part of the land for themselves, presenting buyers with a plot reduced in size from that which the seller has supplied. The advantage of this arrangement is that it is not jeopardised by face-to-face confrontations between the clients, as long as these do not take place in the field or are unaccompanied by maps of the field in question.[14]

Middlemen are, however, a desirable feature of the land market menagerie in so far as the market itself is seen as desirable. They act as lubricants in a highly imperfect market machinery characterised by vast information asymmetries and differing access to capital. However, despite their often inventive efforts to secure a larger portion of the rent, their share, at least in aggregate, remains modest. Ten or 15 per cent of an already limited per hectare price does not amount to much. In order to become important competitors in the race for the value of land in the Malian cotton zone, middlemen would have to recognise and exploit the potential provided by legal titles. Such middlemen are, as yet, a very rare breed.

Titling

Widespread acquisition of individual titles by chiefs and other original owners of village farmland would be an apparently viable way for peri-urban communities to resist town expansion. This would not only ensure tenure security for original land holders – titled land cannot be expropriated except under extraordinary circumstances[15] – but would mean that those who eventually did decide to sell their land would receive prices for it that vastly exceeded those attained for customary holdings.[16] Such a strategy may, however, backfire, as evidenced in one of the villages we visited, located 17 kilometres outside Sikasso. Here, villagers stated frankly, with the chief in attendance, that sales became legitimate at the precise point when the chief acquired title to his land, an act perceived as doing away with customary restrictions. Thus, titling, even when it can be afforded, may instead trigger and accelerate the process of rapid land alienation in rural areas.[17] Moreover, the fact remains that the cost of legal titles to land is beyond the means of most villagers.

The only cost, officially, of acquiring a provisional title is the 15,000 CFA or so needed to obtain a sketch map. After a provisional title is secured, annual taxes to the district of 4,700 CFA per hectare should be paid. A provisional title, however, is only an intermediary stage on the way to a full title. Unless specified investments are completed within five years, the provisional title will be revoked; a full title will require a further one-time payment of 197,000 CFA per hectare.

These costs appear prohibitive for customary farmers who realise net revenues of some 40,000 to 60,000 CFA per hectare per year. Even when ignoring the costs of maps and investments, farmers would have to save net revenues from around four years of cultivation to pay for every hectare of titled land.[18] In view of this, the lack of titles among original holders is hardly surprising. Apparently, however, these costs do not deter urban dwellers from seeking titles to purchased land to the same extent. If the official cost of a title is high compared to the incomes of peri-urban farmers, it is also low compared to the potential value of possessing such a title. More than 40 per cent of recorded parcels of land without full titles were currently in the application process for provisional or full titles.

In fact, however, obtaining legal titles to land is also for urban dwellers an exceedingly expensive and painfully slow process. First, the very attraction of possessing legal title means that the demand for such titles is huge. Second, for various reasons such as general elections and the introduction of the new ordinance, the titling process has been halted at both district and regional levels in recent years. Third, and more importantly, the discrepancy between demand for and supply of titles, arising from a similar discrepancy between official cost and value, has created a queue. Within this queue, it is primarily individuals with an inside track to government or those capable of affording substantial 'extra-invoice' payments who are given service.[19]

The necessity of bribes in title acquisition has the effect of slowing down the application process. The backlog that accumulates will raise the price in what is, in effect, a monopoly situation. Perhaps importantly, this procrastination is fully in line with the economic objectives of both the state and local government: because awarding titles is financially inferior to expropriation, there is no fundamental bureaucratic incentive at any level to speed up the titling process.

Expropriation

Expropriation, which is the responsibility of the communes, comes about mainly for one reason – the creation of residential plots – but in two different ways. The first is through *lotissement*, involving the expropriation of relatively large areas for which the urban commune subsequently purchases titles from the regional office in Sikasso. Compensation for land expropriated in this manner follows a fixed schedule,[20] the important stipulation being that plots above the size of 3.5 hectares are all compensated for identically, regardless of exact size. Expropriation by *lotissement* occurred twice in Koutiala over the last decade, both times in 1994. According to information supplied by one commune topographer, these expropriations involved some 600 hectares of land; according to another, the area expropriated, based on number of plots, amounted to barely 200 hectares.[21]

The other form of expropriation is through *raccordement*. This involves, officially, the piecemeal 'joining together' of residential areas separated by customary holdings. Large tracts have been expropriated this way.[22] Here, lands are not provided with full title by regional authorities who, instead, simply provide the commune with permission to develop the land for residential purposes. The distinction does not apparently serve any practical purpose other than presumably allowing a faster and more flexible process. In terms of compensation, however, there is an important distinction: compensation does not follow a fixed scale but is determined through negotiations between commune and landowners.

The disinclination, on the part of customary landholders, to simply wait for expropriation now seems obvious. First, if expropriation is through *lotissement*, compensation will be the same whether your land is 3.5 hectares or 50 hectares, investments notwithstanding, and the rational thing to do is thus to sell all land on consolidated plots exceeding 3.5 hectares. Fragmentation through sales will have the effect, among other things, of exacting greater aggregate compensation from expropriation, and thus creating a market. Second, if expropriation is through *raccordement*, even the meagre compensation stipulated for *lotissement* expropriation is uncertain.[23]

It is in the conversion of farmland into residential plots that the big money lies. The arithmetic is quite simple. Of the land seized by the urban commune, 30 per cent is deducted for roads, pathways and other public areas. The remaining 70 per cent is converted into residential plots of 15 by 20 metres, giving roughly 23 plots per hectare. For expropriations up to four hectares, one of these plots (or three per cent of land now greatly enhanced in value), plus occasional cash compensation for any improvements undertaken, is returned to the 'expropriatee'.[24]

Each plot sells for between 200,000 and 400,000 CFA in Koutiala and between 300,000 and 500,000 CFA in Sikasso, depending on location. This provides revenues of between 4.4 and 11 million CFA per hectare, with subsequent revenues from building and occupation levies not included.

With regard to areas expropriated and partitioned by the commune, it is the state that initially receives these revenues, but up to 40 per cent is returned to the commune providing appropriate investment projects can be identified. Taxes paid subsequently by residents for building and occupancy permits add a further 1.35 million CFA per hectare to commune coffers. Again, however, there are various ways in which to extract a share of the rent for shrewd officials. First, it is possible to fiddle with compensation numbers; official documents may indicate greater compensation to expropriatees than was actually given, leaving plots available for sale by individual government officials. Second, areas assigned as public spaces on the official plans may in fact be sold as residential plots on the sly by the same officials. Third, in the past, plots have been sold at official prices as low as one-third of the going market rate, leaving ample room for 'extra-invoice' payments.

Sharing in this bonanza are also some of those individuals wealthy or crafty enough to obtain legal titles to land in areas earmarked for residential development. Among these we find the single, genuine land speculator in Sikasso, who purchases land around the town from chiefs and other customary holders, obtains titles to these areas, then resells the land as residential plots for a per hectare price that is 20 to 100 times greater than that paid for it.[25] It is possible that other urban dwellers are able to take advantage of the opportunity to convert titled land to residential plots but we found little evidence of this; the four farmers we met who had succeeded in obtaining legal titles to their land all used it for farming.[26]

One final strategy does, however, require examination: the direct conversion of customary holdings to residential plots. In the early 1990s, a powerful chief in Koutiala sold large tracts of his land as residential plots without having obtained a title.[27] A few years ago, the commune deemed these sales to be legal. The power and pull wielded by the chief in question is certainly a consideration here, but the practical difficulties of expropriating and selling land on which residents and dwellings are already established should not be ignored. Similar developments were observed, albeit on a smaller scale, outside Sikasso. Here again, a chief sold land as residential plots directly to urban dwellers wishing to settle outside the town centre. The prices obtained, given the absence of security engendered by legal title and occupancy and building permits, were considerably lower than those obtained for residential plots on titled land, but they were also considerably higher than the modest prices obtained when customary holdings were sold wholesale to urban dwellers. It is thus possible that the superior strategy for customary holders, as far as rent appropriation is concerned, is to ignore entirely formal procedures and to effect the process of conversion from customary holdings to residential plots themselves. Strictly speaking, such a strategy is not legal. As should be evident now, however, *de jure* and *de facto* considerations are often immaterial in the Malian cotton zone.

Rent Appropriation

Rent generated by urban expansion in the Malian cotton zone cannot, of course, be attributed to 'the original and indestructible powers of the soil' in the classical sense; it is in the main a location rent.[28] Regardless of source, however, the rent formation that attends the conversion of customary holdings to residential plots is substantial. If we are primarily interested in the rent formation caused by increasing land scarcity as cities expand, then it matters how we regard the value of land prior to such expansion. Qualifications with respect to credit market failures and the attendant notion of 'surplus land' notwithstanding, the net present value of tillable land averages roughly 500,000 CFA per hectare. The total value of land partitioned into residential plots reaches an average of around 9.4 million CFA per hectare, with building and occupation levies included. Rent formation is the difference between these figures, around 8.9 million CFA per hectare.

Who receives this bounty? Consider the typical sequence of land alienation that accompanies urban expansion (Figure 2). In this scenario, a plot of land held under customary tenure is first sold to an urban dweller who, unable to obtain a title, has it expropriated by the urban commune which, in turn, sells the land as residential plots. In this sequence of events, given average figures observed by us, the original holder of land will be left worse off by some 360,000 CFA per hectare – the net present value of tillable land minus the average price of 140,000 CFA per hectare for initial sales – thus 'capturing' a negative four per cent of total rent formation. The urban dweller who pays 140,000 CFA per hectare will in turn receive residential plots worth the equivalent of 160,000 CFA per hectare upon expropriation (he will receive 0.43 plots per hectare, given an average land size of 8.8 hectares per transaction), and thus realise a gain of 20,000 CFA per hectare, or 0.2 per cent of rent formation. The commune and the state will share the 'remaining' 104 per cent, depending on how much of the revenues from sales of plots the commune is able to recoup through public projects. If the maximum 40 per cent is retrieved, then the commune will capture just over 4.5 million CFA (or 50.6 per cent) – 1.35 million from building and occupation fees and the remainder from sales. The state will capture 4.73 million (53.2 per cent), all of it from sales.[29]

The inclusion of a middleman would distort these figures by, at most, 0.2 per cent of the total rent formation, at the expense of customary holders and urban dwellers. If, as an alternative, one chose to regard the initial sales price as representative of the true value of land prior to urban expansion, customary holders would be indifferent to this expansion. The urban commune and state would still capture 99.8 per cent of the rent between them. The basic picture would also change little when one considers the purchase of a customary holding by a speculator who succeeds in obtaining a full title, thus enabling the

FIGURE 2
RENT APPROPRIATION BY VARIOUS TYPICAL SALES SEQUENCE

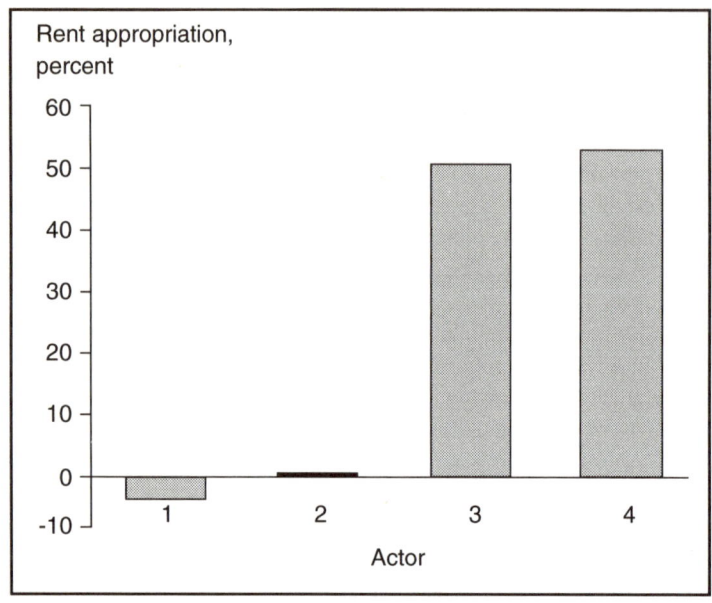

Actor	CFA	Percent
1. Customary holder	-360,000	-4.0
2. Urban dweller	20,000	0.2
3. Urban commune	4,506,000	50.6
4. State	4,734,000	53.2
Total	8,900,000	100.0

private development of residential plots. The question here is how much of the rent the speculator and individual bureaucrats will be able to capture at the expense of the state and the urban commune, and this will depend on the size of taxes and bribes.

It may seem audacious to draw radical conclusions on the basis of such a limited sample of transactions, but the most important points made are insensitive to large variations in sample size and observed variables. For example, even if the true price paid for customary holdings is double what our data indicate, or if true discount rates are twice our estimate, land prices paid to customary holders would still fall short of net present values from agriculture. Note also that any substantial underestimation of initial sales prices is implausible, since negative rent would then be realised by urban dwellers whose untitled land is subsequently expropriated.

V. CONCLUSIONS

Problems of land rent appropriation as towns expand are not confined to the Malian cotton zone, nor are they of recent origin. Suret-Canale [*1971*] describes a 1935 decree for French West Africa allowing the French administration to ignore the claims of 'certain speculators' to uncultivated land in the following manner:

> The 'speculators' here are clearly Africans claiming their rights over lands that had gained in value through town building, or road or railway construction, and which the colonial companies or the settlers had arranged to have 'conceded' to themselves, so that they could 'speculate', in a perfectly legal manner, by parcelling the land out with enormously enhanced values. In effect, the difficulty which the Africans encountered in having their land rights acknowledged was only equalled by the ease with which the companies or individual Europeans arranged to obtain 'concessions' often of immense portions of land claimed by the state [*Suret-Canale, 1971: 257–8*].

According to a popular theory, the source of increased agricultural land market activity in Africa is to be found in population growth and agricultural commercialisation. In short, these give rise to increased land values, creating a demand for more secure and specific rights granted by full titles, which in turn permit redistribution of holdings from less to more efficient farmers [*Platteau, 1996*]. In the Malian cotton zone, both population growth and agricultural commercialisation are prominent features of the overall dynamics, and aspects of the above process can be observed in some rural areas. Around the urban centres, however, there is a sense in which this process is reversed. In what we consider to be a typical sequence, sales take place prior, rather than subsequent, to the acquisition of titles, and it is the acquisition of titles that in turn causes the steep rise in the value of land. There is, of course, nothing organic or evolutionary about this reversal: land market activity is urged on by the fear of losing customary holdings to expanding urban centres, and a title is frequently established only after land has been expropriated. Indeed, it is the lack of protection against expropriation, as well as the meagre compensation that attends it, that depresses the value of untitled land.

We have described the competition for land rent in the Malian cotton zone as a race. As such, the participants involved compete both against time and each other. In order to minimise their losses, chiefs and other customary holders must sell their land before expropriators arrive on their doorsteps;

urban buyers of land must obtain titles before the same expropriators seize their land; the state and the commune must expropriate before titles are obtained; and speculators, such as they are, must on the one hand buy ahead of urban buyers, and on the other obtain titles before land is expropriated.

It is a race which disproportionately favours those who are able to exploit asymmetries of information and discrepancies in wealth. The regional government and its servants control the titling process, which is hardly unusual. Through this control, however, they are also able to create a virtual local government monopoly in the development of residential areas. By slowing down the titling process to a crawl, they ensure that urban development and its attendant riches are carried out and realised only by various branches of government or by individuals wealthy enough to buy into the process through bribes. The expropriation tool acts as a price depressant: directly, through the meagre compensation meted out to expropriatees; and indirectly, by engendering a market for land where per hectare prices are but a fraction of those that apply to sales of residential plots.[30]

It is a system that rewards disregard for formal law and procedure. In government, direct monetary bribes linked to purchases of titles and residential plots are but alternatives to more inventive strategies, such as selling multiple titles to the same land and residential development of areas officially designated as public spaces. Institutional problems also affect strategies at other levels. A single customary holding will be sold several times over to different individuals; land held by one individual will be sold by another; middlemen will quote different prices to sellers and buyers, or adjust the area exchanged in the process. The results of disputes seem to depend not on any established procedure, but on the wealth and power of the individuals involved.

The result of this is that customary holders of land, who are generally poor, end up with very little: they will retain but a fraction of their land and they will retain but a fraction of the value of the land they lose through sales or expropriation.[31] The urban dwellers responsible for most of the initial purchases of these customary holdings do not fare much better. Only those few who are able to obtain a legal title will potentially realise the full value of their holdings. It should be noted, however, that the initial transactions between these two groups might be efficient in that they often bring idle land into cultivation, often attended by substantial improvements.

There is also the matter of transaction costs. An institutional environment where justice is something that is auctioned out must, in the long term, be costly. A surfeit of disputes and litigation, contract insecurity, information asymmetry, and bribes are symptoms of struggling economies, and these will be perpetuated if the institutional environment in the Malian cotton zone is allowed to persist. The problem is that those in a position to do something about this environment have substantial economic incentives to maintain the *status quo*.

Nevertheless, policy measures can be instituted at central government levels that will allow for a more just – and ultimately, we believe, more efficient – division of the rent formation that accompanies land on its journey from rural cradle to urban resting place. First, there is a need for a considerable opening up of the titling process. The price paid for the acquisition of full titles must come down to a level affordable by rural farmers with customary holdings. Further, the capacity to award titles must be expanded significantly, either by decentralisation to district level or by increasing capacity at regional level; this will not only make for briefer application periods and a higher volume of awards, but should also bring down the cost of the bribe, currently far beyond the means of most farmers, that attends each separate application.

Second, the compensation provided for expropriated land must be increased. At the very least, owners of customary holdings should receive compensation equal to the potential net present values realisable through farming. At present, owners of large holdings will receive but a fraction of this. Third, customary holdings should be granted greater security through a more formal recognition of rights, providing greater protection against expropriation and thus higher value in the market. The 2000 land ordinance, not yet implemented at the time of our fieldwork, goes some way towards addressing this problem; but issues regarding the precise nature of group membership through time need to be resolved.

Finally, there is a need for further research into these matters, in particular, information regarding the social dynamics that compel some chiefs and subjects to sell land, while others resist, is required. Studies of rent appropriation from other regions where urban centres are expanding rapidly would also provide valuable comparisons.

NOTES

1. Transactors were identified with the help of middlemen and researchers. In face-to-face interviews, sellers and buyers of land were asked to provide details regarding the transacted land (date, price, size and location), livelihoods, use of middlemen, reasons for selling or buying, relationship to the other transactor, land use (prior, current and planned), existing and planned investments (pre- and post-sale; type, quantity and cost), current and intended legal status (pre- and post-sale; incurred costs), and problems encountered in connection with transactions and title applications. Interviews were also made with residents whose land had been expropriated, and details regarding land size, location, investments and compensation obtained. More general aspects of land use, land transactions and registration were also discussed with respondents.
2. These population figures are taken from the preliminary results of the 1998 census.
3. The *Compagnie Malienne pour le Développement des Textiles* (CMDT) is a parastatal of which 60 per cent is owned by the Malian State and 40 per cent by the *Compagnie Francaise pour le Développement des Textiles* (CFDT) (in which the French State holds 64 per cent). In addition to its main activities related to cotton production (purchase of cotton from the peasants, sale of farm inputs, export of cotton, etc.), it has also been given the responsibility of implementing and co-ordinating an integrated rural development programme in southern Mali.

4. In French legislative terms, a *loi* is a piece of legislation enacted by vote of the National Assembly, an *ordonnance* is enacted by the head of state, a *décret* is an enactement of the executive, often used to clarify a *loi* or *ordonnance* or to provide the guidelines for its application, and an *arrêté* is formulated and promulgated at the ministerial, or even the regional level [*Elbow and Rochegude, 1990*].
5. During fieldwork in February/March 2001, the implementation of this ordinance of 22 March 2000 had not yet started. District and regional authorities were waiting for decrees (*decrêts*) to define the modalities of implementation.
6. Following the decentralisation reform, the administrative levels of the state are *région* (region) and *cercle* (district), each run by appointed state officials. A cercle contains a number of communes administered by an elected mayor and communal council.
7. According to the president of the Koutiala court, it is sufficient for the court that the seller has signed and that the land in question is clearly identified.
8. Most of the expropriated land is formally not subject to expropriation since customary holders do not have full property rights to land. It is said by state officials that the state cannot expropriate something it already owns.
9. Most of these urban dwellers have grown up on farms before moving to the city, and possess knowledge of farming as well as a desire to farm; a desire that no doubt is also fuelled by the general farming boom experienced over the last decade or so.
10. These are average figures, based on statistics collected at CMDT in Sikasso and Bamako, and data collected by one of the authors in connection with previous studies. Net revenues from crop cultivation will, of course, vary between farmers and from year to year, depending on prices, rainfall, soil fertility, management skills, etc.
11. The transactions registered were surprisingly straightforward, free of caveats or complex contractual arrangements. Rental agreements involve mainly swaps of land for use of oxen or machinery, or payment in the form of labour or a fixed amount of grain. Land pledges, though not unknown, are not common in the cotton zone.
12. Such letters of sale were present in 88 per cent of the transactions recorded. In most cases, witnesses were involved, and in many letters were also taken to the local or district authorities for official registration.
13. Victims of the sham felt that taking court action against the interests of these buyers would be of no use. 'The court is for the rich', they said. The chief was, however, dismissed from office by his subjects.
14. These strategies, as well as some of those used by other actors in the cotton zone land market and described elsewhere, are similar to those observed by Sandra Barnes [*1986: 48–9*] in Lagos.
15. This is specified in the 2000 ordinance. Also, topographers for the urban commune in Koutiala informed us that titled holdings were left alone when expropriation for development of residential purposes was undertaken, even when the holding was in the middle of the planning area.
16. Full titles are perpetual and not subject to tax. Their value derives from security against expropriation and the ability to convert titles to residential plots. We did not record any sales of fully, as opposed to provisionally, titled land. One middleman estimated the market price of titled land to be around 1.5 million CFA per hectare. The value of titled land, however, is probably measured more accurately by considering conversion to, and prices of, residential plots.
17. This is in accordance with what Platteau [*1996*] has dubbed the Evolutionary Theory of Land Rights (ETLR), where titling is seen as a prerequisite for land market integration. In the ETLR, however, the link arises simply from the fact that titles are alienable.
18. Although required funds may, perhaps, be accumulated in shorter time when relying solely on family labour.
19. Accurate data on the magnitude of bribes are, for obvious reasons, elusive. Most applicants agreed that receipt payments constituted only a fraction of the total. A figure that often cropped up in our conversations with applicants was two million CFA for parcels ranging in size from two to 50 hectares; it is thus possible that bribes, in contrast to official fees, do not vary proportionally with size of land. Another form of blatant abuse of office is illustrated in the case of one Koutiala landowner, who has held a provisional title to his land since 1998. He discovered that the Sikasso office had sold parts of his land, with full titles, to three separate buyers and

pocketed the money themselves. A bizarre situation thus obtains, where different individuals hold different titles to the same plots of land; the legal tangle has not yet been unravelled.

20. Land expropriated is compensated through the allotment of the resulting residential plots, which today generally measure 15 by 20 metres, permitting the commune to seize land while suffering monetary expenditures only with regard to improvements. For land up to 1.5 hectares, one residential plot is awarded; for land between 1.5 and 2.5 hectares, two plots are awarded; for land between 2.5 and 3.5 hectares, three plots are given; and for land greater than 3.5 hectares, four plots are given. Thus, for land up to four hectares, owners retain 0.03 hectares of land from every hectare they are forced to give up and for bigger pieces of land they receive even less, albeit land greatly enhanced in value through the creation of residential plots. Trees planted by the owner are priced between 500 and 3,750 CFA, depending on species, but the commune will occasionally deflect these costs onto buyers of residential plots by instructing them to pay for any trees cut during the building process.

21. Given the town's population, the former figure seems excessive, since it would involve at least some 6,000 plots accommodating at least 30,000 people.

22. Exact figures were not made available to us at the communal headquarters. A topographer with CMDT, however, estimates that *raccordement* expropriations in Koutiala exceed *lotissement* expropriations in area over the last decade.

23. We recorded eight cases of expropriation; in half of these, expropriatees had received, more or less, the compensation stipulated for *lotissement* procedures; the remaining four cases had received less, and in two cases much less. One respondent was currently in the process of having land expropriated, and had teamed up with seven other landowners in an attempt to build a stronger negotiating platform. The legal position of these landowners, however, seems uncertain to put it mildly; neither expropriators nor expropriatees gave the impression that the latter retain vetoing rights if unsatisfied with the compensation offered.

24. The highest cash compensation received by any expropriatee interviewed by us was 11,250 CFA per hectare.

25. The nature of the investments required of this speculator for him to obtain title deeds was not revealed.

26. Development of urban residential areas by individual urban dwellers, speculators notwithstanding, would happen on a rather limited scale. Whereas land purchased more than five kilometres from the town perimeter averaged 16.5 hectares in size, parcels within five kilometres averaged only 4.1 hectares; and few buyers had purchased more than one parcel.

27. See Bertrand [*1994*] for more information on this particular chief.

28. Beyond noting the lack of public investment that attends the development of residential areas, we will pass over the discussion of the degree to which rent formation can be attributed to 'community' as such or to prior public investments in infrastructure and public services. An investigation of these questions may, however, be important in determining the extent to which the state legitimately can lay claim to an earned, rather than an unearned, surplus.

29. Other assumptions here are: a discount rate of ten per cent; the average price of a residential plot is 350,000 CFA; compensation for investments is ignored (these would anyway not significantly affect the result); the absence of public investment in infrastructure (generally accurate); costs of planning incurred by the urban commune are ignored.

30. One would also expect fear of expropriation to discourage investment. The desire to obtain titles, which require investment, will tend to work in the other direction.

31. Note, though, that it is those customary holders with the largest holdings that have the most to lose through expropriation. The discrepancy between compensation and agricultural land value will be lower for smaller holdings.

REFERENCES

Barnes, S.T., 1986, *Patrons and Power: Creating a Political Community in Metropolitan Lagos*, Manchester: Manchester University Press.

Benjaminsen, T.A., 2001, 'The Population–Agriculture–Environment Nexus in the Malian Cotton Zone', *Global Environmental Change*, Vol.11, No.4, pp.27–39.

Benjaminsen, T.A., 2002, 'Enclosing the Land: Cotton, Population Growth and Tenure in Mali', *Norwegian Journal of Geography*, Vol.56, No.1, pp.1–9.

Bertrand, M., 1994, *La question foncière dans les villes du Mali*, Paris: Karthala & Orstom.

Bohannan, P. and G. Dalton, 1962 'Introduction', in P. Bohannan and G. Dalton (eds.), *Markets in Africa*, Evanston, IL: Northwestern University Press, pp.1–28.

Colleyn, J.P., 1988, *Les chemins de Nya. Culte de possession au Mali*, Paris: Editions de l'Ecole des Hautes Etudes en Sciences Sociales.

Colleyn, J.P. and D. Jonckers, 1983, 'Ceux qui refusent le maître: La conception du pouvoir chez les minyanka du Mali', *Africa*, Vol.53, No.4, pp.43–58.

Coulibaly, N. and R. Joldersma, 1991, 'Réglementation de l'utilisation des ressources naturelles. Cas des 6 villages de la zone Siwaa de Koutiala', Sikasso: Ministère du Développement Rural et de l'Environnement.

Crowley, E.L., 1991, 'Resource Tenure in Mali: An Anthopological Analysis of Local Institutions', The Hague: OECD/CILSS/Club du Sahel.

Dioné, J., 1989, 'Informing Food Security Policy in Mali: Interactions between Technology, Institutions and Market Reforms', doctoral dissertation, Massachusets State University.

Elbow, K. and A. Rochegude, 1990, 'A Layperson's Guide to the Forest Codes of Mali, Niger, and Senegal', LTC Paper 139, Land Tenure Center, University of Wisconsin-Madison.

Gruenais, M.E., 1986, 'Territoires autochtones et mise en valeur des terres', in B. Crousse, E. Le Bris and E. Le Roy (eds.), *Espaces disputés en Afrique noire*, Paris: Karthala.

Jonckers, D., 1987, *La société minyanka du Mali*, Paris: L'Harmattan.

Mathieu, P., 2001, 'Transactions informelles et marchés fonciers émergents en Afrique', in T.A. Benjaminsen and Chr. Lund (eds.), *Politics, Property and Production in the West African Sahel: Understanding Natural Resources Management*, Uppsala: Nordic Africa Institute.

Platteau, J. Ph., 1993, 'The Free Market is Not Readily Transferable: Reflections on the Links Between Market, Social Relations, and Moral Norms', in J. Martinussen (ed), *New Institutional Economics and Development Theory*, Occasional Paper No.6. Roskilde: International Development Studies, Roskilde University.

Platteau, J. Ph., 1996, 'The Evolutionary Theory of Land Rights as Applied to Sub-Saharan Africa: A Critical Assessment', *Development and Change*, Vol.27, No.1, pp.29–85.

Raymond, G. and M. Fok., 1995, 'Relations entre coton et vivriers en Afrique de l'Ouest et du Centre. Le coton affame les populations: une fausse affirmation?', *Economies et sociétés. Série Développement agro-alimentaire*, Vol.22, No.3–4, pp.221–34.

Rochegude, A., 1977, 'Tendances récentes du droit de la terre en République du Mali', *Revue International de Droit Comparé*, Vol.29, No.1, pp 721–46.

Rondeau, Ch., 1980, 'La société sénoufo du Mali Sud (1870–1950): "De la "tradition" à la dépendance"', doctoral dissertation, Université de Paris VII, Département d'Histoire.

Sanogo, B., 1989, 'Le rôle des cultures commerciales dans l'évolution de la société sénoufo (sud du Mali)', Collection "Pays enclaves"', no 2. Bordeaux: CRET, Université de Bordeaux III.

Shipton, P., 1989, 'Land and the Limits of Individualism: Population Growth and Tenure Reforms South of the Sahara', Development Discussion Paper No.320, Cambridge, MA: Harvard Institute for International Development.

Suret-Canale, J., 1971, *French Colonialism in Tropical Africa, 1900–1945*, London: C. Hurst & Co.

Zongo, M., 1999, 'Transactions foncières et usage de l'écrit dans la zone cotonnière du Burkina Faso; exemples à partir de la région des Banwa', in Ph. Lavigne Delville and P. Mathieu (eds.), *Formalisation des contrats et des transactions. Repérage des pratiques populaires d'usage de l'écrit dans les transactions foncières en Afrique rurale*, Working Paper, Institut des Etudes du Développement, Université Catholique de Louvain.

Custom, Contracts and *Cadastres* in North-West Rwanda

CATHERINE ANDRÉ

I. INTRODUCTION

This study examines the data compiled within the framework of two successive surveys: the first conducted in 1988 and spread over five months; the second took place over a period of 14 months between the end of 1992 and the beginning of 1994.[1] Both successive surveys were conducted on the same hill in north-west Rwanda, in a densely populated region, located near commercial and administrative centres. Here, the land 'market' is very active and land purchases and sales multiplied between 1988 and 1993: the proportion of land purchased in relation to those inherited increased relatively quickly within both comparable samples [*André and Platteau, 1998: 19*].

Land appropriation and management are conducted according to 'custom', which is evolving under pressure from individualistic and exclusive tensions as well as that of the market. The former customary system, *ubukonde*, is characterised by a patrilineal management and succession of lands with concessions to leasers or land tenants in exchange for fees and services. During the years of Belgian rule, several factors contributed to a certain individualisation of land rights and the proliferation of land sales and purchases in this region [*Reidsdorff, 1952; Adriaenssens, 1962*]: the *ubukonde* system which was influenced by an individual system of land tenure governing lands in the central and southern parts of the country, through the introduction of property rights for the missions;[2] the increase of land purchases following the eviction of occupants of mission lands; and emigration policies towards Kivu.

This movement towards the individualisation and monetarisation of land occurred in a context of increased demographic pressure in densely populated areas, and the monetarisation of the economy (through the imposition of taxes, introduction of cash crops, increased salaried employment outside the lineages

Catherine André, IED, Louvain-La-Neuve (Belgium).

and taxes on missions and enterprises in the region as well as the introduction of new formal institutions – authorities and systems of rights). Furthermore, a high level of social tension between landowners and tenants throughout the country at the end of the 1950s caused a system of land clientelism to be legally suppressed and prohibited by a decree in 1960 at the birth of the first republic. This decree promulgated a dual pattern of land legislation: on the one hand, rural lands governed by local and customary practices and, on the other, urban lands subject to written legislation recognising the right to private property. A statutory order was adopted in 1976 prohibiting the sale and purchase of land in order to guarantee farmers (who formed 95 per cent of the Rwandan population) a minimum of cultivable land area [*Ruhashyankiko, 1985*]. However, this regulation was not respected in rural areas and, as a result, distress land sales have increased at an exponential rate since the beginning of the 1990s, as is illustrated below in the samples from the hill area studied.

Follwing a description of the context within which monetary and non-monetary land transactions have proliferated, I deal with the introduction and analysis of 129 land contracts (mainly sales contracts), before describing the first *cadastres* and analysing the emergence of informal formalisation of the contracts, the security they offer in a context of population pressure, and the increasing impoverishment and unequal redistribution of lands linked to the development of the monetarisation of land transactions.

II. WRITTEN LAND TRANSACTION CONTRACTS

Samples

The starting point is the detailed analysis of 129 land transaction contracts (mainly sales contracts) of which only approximately 20 households agreed to have photocopied. Some complementary information is introduced into the analysis of these contracts using, as a basis, the results of two other surveys conducted on land transactions. The first survey of 85 households was conducted in 1988, and provided information on the number of plots purchased, land under cultivation, price and year it was purchased as well as surface area. With the exception of some plots of land purchased during the 1930s and 1940s, the households surveyed agreed to retrieve the land contracts in order to answer questions. Hence, the oldest contract on paper which an inhabitant showed me dated from 1934, the exact date of the coin he had kept in the same little plastic bag, so that the piece of paper, which had become almost illegible and as flimsy as a piece of fabric by dint of being folded, was proof of purchase of a plot of land on the hill.

The second systematic survey was conducted in 1993 and gives complete information on 243 sales transactions with regard to the contracting parties (their names), year and price of the transaction, size of plot with a sketch in cases where the contract included one, use of the plot of land (field, banana plantation, woods ...) as well as the reasons that impelled the purchaser to acquire the particular piece of land and the seller's reasons for selling it. The samples relating to the inhabitants of the same hill are not completely dissimilar with regard to the persons in the survey: identical land transactions are to be found in the different selections of samples.

The table below confirms the growing number of land sales and purchases and the increase in land transactions from the second half of the 1980s.

TABLE 1
DATES OF LAND TRANSACTIONS

Samples	Land contracts	Survey of 85 households in 1988	Summary of 243 sales – purchases
< 1950	0	5	0
1950–1959	0	1	2
1960–1969	17	9	17
1970–1979	34	40	62
1980–1989	43	87	84
80–84	19	26	35
85–89	25	61	49
1990–1993	34	–	78
Total	128*	141	243
# of persons	22	85	

*One contract is not dated.

The surveys conducted with regard to the hill population show that the lineages occupying lands of the administrative cell acquired these lands as a result of matrimonial relations with three massive land-clearer lineages. The first monetary transactions date back to the 1930s, years during which inhabitants of the valley were evicted from their lands after construction work on the Nyundo bishopric. The Nyundo mission compensated the households in service, and tenants – *abagererwa* – by re-purchasing plots of land for them in the adjoining hills, while other households lost their lands and became either land tenants of other households or, in exchange for livestock, obtained land cultivation rights with related lineages, and then 'purchased definitively' the land in exchange for money or livestock in the 1930s and 1940s. During the 1950s, money gradually replaced livestock in sales transactions and, from the 1960s, money was used in all land transactions recorded during various surveys.

Of 129 contracts, 119 pertained to land sales transactions; three were gifts (either inheritance or between friends); two contracts concerned plot exchanges; three were rentals; while two others were land pledges. The first contract citing a plot of land as collateral for the loan of a sum of money dated from 1972, and the second from 1989; pledges increased during the second half of the 1980s.

In order to describe land contracts (retained by the purchaser), various systematic elements to be found in nearly all the contracts will be examined, followed in a subsequent section, by an examination of the additional elements of a contract. Below is an example of a standard model sales contract:

> Ishusho, 29/5/85
> I, Majambere Marcel, sell a field to Munyakazi Alphonse for Frw 5.000 (five thousand). This is a permanent sale. He gives me a hoe and I will plant trees for him.
> Both parties are in agreement:
> Signature or fingerprint of the seller
> Signature of the purchaser
> Present and witnesses:
> Name and signature of the witnesses on both sides
> Signature of the secretary

A sales contract was retained by the purchaser.

Standard Elements of Land Contracts

Standard elements observed in land contracts were the names of the contracting parties, the date and place, type of transaction, use of land, price, demarcation and names and signatures of the witnesses.

Generally speaking, all contracts were drafted on paper (usually some pages or half-pages of A5 format and taken from exercise books). The first line of the contract gave the date (with one exception) and, in general, the location where the transaction was conducted. Next, the names of the contracting parties were mentioned, as well as the type of transaction (purchase, sale, exchange, etc.), use of land (field, banana plantation, woods, etc.) price, expression used with regard to the transfer of the property (transfer of the rights of usage and plot demarcation), the signatures of the contracting parties and those of the witnesses. As the person drafting the contract was seldom one of the transacting parties, because of illiteracy, the parties would consequently choose a 'secretary' to draft the contract.

From their introduction until the mid-1970s, each contract began with the date (except for one contract out of the 129 photocopied) and, in the majority of cases, where the transaction was conducted, that is to say, the name of the hill, the exact location, or even the name of the administrative entity (the name of the cell or the sector). In 79 per cent of the cases, land transaction contracts were drawn up in the name of the person relinquishing or granting the plot of land to another person (seller, the person renting, pledging or giving the plot of land). In only 21 per cent of all cases was the contract drafted by the person acquiring the plot of land. However, this practice, though popular in the 1960s and 1970s (half of the contracts were drawn up by individuals acquiring the plot of land), greatly decreased at the beginning of the 1980s and subsequently disappeared, probably as a result of the risks involved whereby a seller might protest or there were accusations of forgery. In all cases where a land contract was elaborated, the person acquiring the land retained the contract, although the assignor might draw up a copy or a note.

All contracts were obtained from persons acquiring a plot of land. The type of land transaction was clearly stipulated, often even more precisely by a second sentence. Thus, out of 129 sales contracts, 95 added a sentence specifying that it effectively concerned the 'definitive' transfer (or purchase) of a plot of land. In fact, this expression demonstrated perfectly the difference between this sort of transaction and the type of transfer prevalent under the previous system of lineage *ubukonde* land tenure. This system gave the one granting the plot of land the right to withdraw the plot of land or to retain a section of the land for his own use.

During the 1930s, 1940s and 1950s, there was an increasing number of abuses throughout Rwanda, particularly in the north of the country: landowners abused their right to retain land and would evict their land tenants, although the latter would contest these practices. Furthermore, during the 1960s, numerous conflicts were linked to the kind of transactions conducted: was this a gift, a transfer or a purchase? Was the compensation (livestock) that an individual gave in exchange for a plot of land, the purchase price for the land or, rather, a fee for the concession of a plot of land under the old clientelist system? Was it a temporary or permanent transfer? Was it a grant valid for only one individual or was it for him/herself and descendants? Several conflicts dating from this period were related to the contest of access rights linked to the ambiguity concerning the real nature of a transaction. They demonstrated attempts to reintroduce old transactions in a context that had changed completely, where not only the relations of power, but also the stakes, were different. The phrase 'definitive purchase' clearly indicated the distinction between a grant to a tenant and a definitive transfer. However, this specification reduced the uncertainties and the risks of future conflicts regarding the exact nature of the transaction. In the case of gifts, the stipulation was also made that it concerned a 'definitive' gift.

In the case of a loan, a sentence stipulated that 'it concerns a loan and not a sale', and the duration of the loan was specified. A grant was temporary (rarely exceeding one or two cultivation seasons) in exchange for a certain sum of money. In cases of pledging, the contract duration and, thus, the cultivation of the plot of land by the person accepting the land as collateral, depended on how the loan was reimbursed as demonstrated in the following example:

Ishusho, 20/8/89

I, Majambere Marcel, give a field as collateral for monetary loan of three thousand Rwandan francs (Frw 3,000). When I have reimbursed this sum, I will recover my field.

In the first contract dated 1972, the use of the land as collateral was set forth as follows:

Majambere gives one thousand (Frw 1,000) to Munyakasi in exchange for a field that the latter has been cultivating. He lends this money to Munyakasi. When Munyakasi is able, he will reimburse Majambere. Majambere will then free up this field.

The reimbursement date was not specified in the initial contract. This type of contract allowed the contracting party to benefit from increased income from the plot of land (usually a banana plantation) over a relatively long period of time, often spanning several years. When the loan had not been reimbursed (which was usually the case), the person who accepted the land as collateral proposed purchasing it. The plot of land was then valued, and the purchaser paid the difference between the estimated value of the plot of land and the sum loaned. In this way, the definitive sales contract stipulated that the debt had been cancelled in these terms: 'there is no longer any collateral or debt.'

Finally, with regard to the extent of succession, the contract relating to a gift of the inheritance of a site on which to construct a toilet and a compost, clearly stipulated that it was a gift of land and not the trees growing on it: 'On this site there are two eucalyptus trees belonging to Sebazungu. The child owns the land.'

In the sample, two-thirds of all plots of land comprised fields for crops or fields which had a few banana trees. The remaining one-third comprised banana plantations except for two woods and one tea plantation. Stipulating how the plot of land was to be used not only allowed witnesses to identify the plot of land but also established its price: a banana plantation was more valuable than a field for subsistence farming, as the revenue obtained from banana beer brewing was markedly more significant than that obtained from a field. The price was stated in words and then in figures.

Based on systematic surveys of land sales transactions conducted between 1988 and 1993, I have attempted to determine the evolution of land prices since the 1950s. The table shows there was indeed an increase in land prices over a period of 40 years, particularly noticeable since the beginning of the 1990s. The table also highlights the disparity in sales prices *vis-à-vis* the average over a decade, resulting from the fact that a large number of factors determine the price of a plot of land. In fact, the price of a plot of land depends, in the first place, on the land value. The criteria influencing this price are productivity, the kind of crop (field, banana plantation), and use (arable land, construction, clay extraction, etc.). Several external factors also determine the price: the period in which the transaction is conducted (the month, a drought period or not), reasons for the land purchase or sale, and also the sort of contracting parties and power relations that could affect the negotiation, whether the request originated with the buyer or seller (mainly the latter), or the need for urgent cash.[3] Knowledge of the land market, negotiation skills and manipulation abilities also played an important role in price determination. External economic elements also had a noticeable influence on the price of the land. The type of relationship (family or other) sometimes influenced the price downward[4] (because the person disposing of the land may have hopes of recuperating it later) as well as the payment mode (in instalments or immediately).

In fact, several sales contracts have been drawn up in different stages (two or three times at maximum). On each payment of the instalment, a sentence by the buyer would denote the payment of this sum. The purchaser and the seller, as well as one or two witnesses for each of them, would then affix their signatures, and it was only when the entire sum of money had been paid to the seller that the property was demarcated and transferred to the purchaser.

This stage is set forth in all contracts using an expression such as: 'He [the purchaser] gives me the hoe and I [seller] plant the trees'. The purchaser would then give the 'hoe used for cultivation' to the one who was selling and who had transferred his cultivation rights. The seller would take the hoe and plant the 'trees', the *imihati*, dracena saplings which are used to indicate the limits of a plot of land or for the construction of fences and boarding. The person acquiring the land would symbolically hand over the cultivation tool par excellence, the symbol of the seller's cultivation rights, who would establish the boundaries of the plot of land that had been transferred. The property is then effectively transferred when the hoe is handed over and when the boundaries of the plot of land sold are determined by the planting of 'trees' on the property. These saplings are planted at five- or ten-metre intervals, sometimes even more. Returning the hoe to the former proprietor and the demarcation of the land would take place before witnesses, who would be offered beer by the seller.

In contracts, the expression also indicated the transfer of property when a sale had taken place. As long as the sale was in progress (while the entire sum of money had not been transferred), this expression did not appear: it was only mentioned when the sale was complete. Over time, however, it was no longer the hoe that was given, but its monetary equivalent. In some contracts, the monetary equivalent of the hoe was stipulated and added to the sales price of the plot of land as follows: 'He (the purchaser) gives a hoe worth Frw 100 and we plant the tree'. In reality, the purchaser would give the monetary equivalent of the price of the plot of land to which would be added the price of the hoe (Frw 100 in this case). The monetary equivalent has increased over the decades as seen in the contracts: in the 1970s, the seller demanded a hoe worth Frw 100, in the 1980s it was Frw 200, while in the 1990s it was Frw 300, illustrating the inflated hoe price. In other cases, the hoe was included in the land sales price.

When payments were made in instalments, the contracts generally did not include this phrase. In actual fact, the property was only transferred when all payments had been made. The phrase then appeared, but not always, at the bottom of the contract when the final payment was made.

In exceptional cases, when the plot of land sold had already been demarcated, only the transfer of the hoe was mentioned. However, generally speaking, it was the seller who demarcated the plot of land as he retained a part of it. In fact, the average land area of plots of land transferred was smaller than those plots of land which were inherited [*André and Platteau, 1998: 19–20*].

The number of witnesses varied between two and 20 in the 129 contracts examined, but there were, on average, ten witnesses. To these witnesses was sometimes added the 'secretary' who drafted the contract on behalf of the seller (very few inhabitants being literate), hence the name, the signature and the capacity of the secretary were also seen below the names and signatures (or fingerprints) at the bottom of the contract.

The contracting parties chose witnesses from among their friends, neighbours and elders, those who 'have a good memory' and who, in cases of conflict, could say where the boundaries of the plot of land were, attest to the history of the plot of land and its transfer and defend them. Generally speaking, the witnesses were usually men, but sometimes, women were also called upon to be witnesses, notably when the seller or buyer was a woman. The head of a lineage or the *mukuru w'umuryango* often assisted in the transfer of property, notably concerning lands belonging to the lineage but sold outside it, or when it concerned a sale which had repercussions for other members of the lineage (when the inheritors were not definitive, or the sale of a widow, etc.): it was then necessary to have the agreement of the family and that of the head of the lineage in order to sell plots of land whose origins lay within the lineage. When the latter was called on as head of the lineage, he would place his signature in that capacity below the list of witnesses.

Some members of the cell administration would help in the transfer of property and sign in their capacity as 'cell members' and representatives of that administration at the level of the hill. In the case of a land transfer as the result of a court verdict (following a dispute and its resolution by a court), it was a member of the sector administration who would assist in the property transfer and who would sign in his capacity as representative of the communal administration.

New Elements Meeting the Needs of Security and Memory in a Context of Rapidly Increasing Land Sales

Over time, various elements have been added to the type of contract described above, in response to the need to remember and identify witnesses in cases of conflicts, in a context of rapidly increasing sales.[5] In fact, both the surveys conducted within a five-year interval, the first in 1988 and the second in 1993, show that the proportion of lands acquired through the market (purchase, possessory mortgages and land rentals) increased in relation to the total of lands transferred, even if inherited (and to a lesser extent, as gifts and loans) and remained the principal way of acquiring hillside lands: in 1988, out of a sample of 56 households disposing of 579 plots of land, 36 per cent of the plots were acquired through monetary transactions and 64 per cent through non-monetary transactions; in 1993, the proportion of lands acquired through monetary transfers increased to 43 per cent (376 plots of land out of a total of 871) from a sample of 87 households. Monetary transfers increased while the land situation became increasingly complex, and the degree of land division was significant with about ten plots on average per household. The various elements thus added throughout the years included plot size, sketch, location of the plot of land and reason for the sale.

During the 1960s, only six of the 15 contracts bore measurements of the plot of land; in the 1970s, measurements of the plots of land were mentioned in two-thirds of the contracts; in the 1980s in 80 per cent of the contracts and at the beginning of the 1990s, only two of the 18 contracts did not state the measurements (undoubtedly because they concerned payments in instalments and the demarcation and measuring of the plot of land had not yet been done). It is obvious that measuring a plot of land allowed one to avoid and prevent some shifting of boundaries and markers (dracena plants were easy to move), and disputes regarding the overstepping of boundaries were not infrequent: land boundary conflicts concerned one-third of the total of land disputes [*André and Plateau, 1998: 30*]. A sketch usually denoted the measurements stated in the text of a contract. Generally speaking, it was a very elementary sketch and often comprised a diamond-shape on which measurements were indicated 'at the top', 'at the bottom', 'on the right' and 'on the left'. Sometimes, the sketch was more detailed, but gave a rather schematic representation of the actual shape of the land: such an outline was sufficient in cases of contests regarding the sale and measurements, but not in cases when the boundaries were surpassed or moved.

The addition of measurements and a sketch were further elements of specification that reduced the risks of certain conflicts. These elements appeared to be sufficient for a hill area where it should be remembered transfers took place between inhabitants of the same location.[6]

During the 1970s, the location of a plot of land was specified and during the 1980s, mention of the location became widespread practice, and at the beginning of the 1990s, the location was indicated in 80 per cent of the contracts. There was also the tendency to be more specific and precise over moving from the hill on which the plot was located (a geographic entity comprising several land clearers' lineages), to the administrative entity of the hill (124 households within the framework of my survey and the regrouping of households having acquired lands from two land clearers' lineages), or more specifically, the name of lands of the land-clearer lineage on which the plot was found, or even the locality.

This additional specification was directly related to the growing number of land transfers and the uncertainty regarding their origin which this increase engendered. If, in fact, in the 1960s and 1970s, land was still strongly linked to the family of the person who possessed it but was selling it, the growing number of land transfers created a stock of increasingly large number of plots of land which had changed owners and lineages once or several times, and whose genealogy no longer followed that of the person who held and cultivated it. From then onwards, it became useful to mention the location of the plot of land in a contract, even among inhabitants who knew each other very well. From the second half of the 1980s, the reason for the sale was increasingly included in contracts.

The contract type was one that seemed rather effectively to meet the needs of the contractors. The additions (such as measurements of the field, a sketch, location, etc.) were elements that allowed one to respond to the uncertainties linked to an increasingly complex land situation during the 1980s. The various evolutions of the paper contract perfectly met the specific need not only to make land transactions more secure, but also ensure access to and occupation of lands in a context where the proportion of lands purchased was generally increasing in relation to other methods of acquisition (inheritance, rental and so on), where land sales were rapidly growing as well as disputes directly or indirectly linked to the land.

Special Contracts: Women Selling and Purchasing Plots of Land

Women conducting land transactions were rather special cases in the sense that, under the old customary system, only men of the lineage had the right to manage and transfer land to their sons or other descendants or to grant it to land tenants. Women worked on their husbands' lands: ensuring lands were cultivated, managing the harvests and overseeing the daily needs of the household. In principle, women did not inherit land from their parents and only had the right to use lands inherited or purchased by their husband. In cases where a woman was widowed, lands would revert to her sons, but the widow would retain exploitation rights, as long as the sons were not adults (that is, married).

Our sample only contained one purchase out of 16 sales by women. Of the 16 sales, 14 related to widows who were selling in order to guarantee their survival during old age, as specified in the following contracts: 'this old lady is selling her field because she is old. She is asking her sons for some assistance to age better. Her children have given her this banana plantation to sell', or even 'I have just sold him land in order to ensure my old age in tranquillity and my children [sons] are in agreement'. In another contract, the reason given by a widow selling was in order to pay school fees for secondary school.

As the expression used in the contract indicated, widows were only usufructuaries of lands which reverted to their sons on their death; they could not sell land without their sons' agreement. Thus, in all the contracts concerning widows' sales of lineage lands, the agreement of the sons was required and stipulated ('with the agreement of my four sons' or, 'my fours sons are taking care of the sale', with even the sons signing below the signature of their mother. Land was always deemed to belong to a lineage and the right to exploit lineage lands was granted by the son or, as seen in one contract, by the head of the lineage (thus indicating that the plot of land was transferred to an individual who did not belong to the lineage of the husband). In six of the 16 cases, permission from other members of the lineage (sons or head of the lineage) for the sales by women was not stipulated in the contract, the reason simply being that this authorisation was not required in cases where the plots of land had been bought 'by his own efforts'. The very nature of the sale thus implied the management of the plots purchased reverted to the purchaser (the couple or his wife) who was free to dispose of it as he/she wished.

It was rare for women to purchase land. However, while in the sample of contracts only one was found, our field surveys revealed several. Which women would purchase land? Similar to the example of recording land purchases, women's purchases of land represented a way of guaranteeing their rights to cultivate and occupy land. But in which cases? These were when women felt their access to their husbands' lands (as well as that of their children) was not certain or barely secure, the main reason being that women were considered illegitimate under customary practices. Consequently, in cases of separation or divorce, these women (and their children) would lose access rights to the lands of their husband (and father). In the same way, in cases of death, their rights would be contested and the lands of their husbands plundered by brothers-in-law or uncles who would view them as being illegitimate. However, once they had the means, these women would purchase land in their name to guarantee their access rights to the land and a means of subsistence for them and their children.

The Written Land Contract: A Local Innovation
Written land contracts were a local innovation which became widespread

throughout the region, meeting the need to secure monetary land transactions. Land contracts had come about in the context of an emerging land market to ensure transfer and individual land appropriation.

Written contracts clearly stipulated the status of the land purchased: the rights to land management and exploitation were transferred on an individual basis (to the purchaser) and these rights were definitive. In fact, the purchased plot of land had a special status when compared to lands inherited from and granted by lineage: it was personally managed by the purchaser and was free from the control of other members of the lineage. In fact, sons could not pressure the purchaser (father) to share it with them, with the father retaining these purchased lands and using them as a pension fund; nor could this land be subject to a transfer linked to a social obligation such as the loan of land to a divorced sister which would then revert to the lineage. The proprietor viewed the purchased land as the fruit of external remunerated work, and having been acquired thanks to 'his own efforts', thus implying an individual, exclusive and private right of access and management. These lands, acquired through purchases, were also used as pension funds and fell outside sons' claims for division and the control of other lineage members. The purchased lands also escaped all kinds of social obligations that remained valid for inherited lineage lands.

These sales took place within a specific context: that of a region dominated by the clientilist, *ubukonde* land tenure system. The example of this hill illustrates perfectly that the emergence of monetary land transactions meets the need to ensure the rights of appropriation and access threatened by the clientelist *ubukonde* system. Initial contracts belong either to former land tenants or members of land-clearers' lineages evicted from their lands and who, due to off-farm income, have been able to purchase lands in neighbouring hills and establish individual rights outside of the control of the lineage which had granted them lands. Even today, monetary transactions allow certain categories of persons who have traditionally had no land rights, such as women, the possibility of acquiring individual and exclusive land rights.

As seen above, land is being transferred to certain categories of persons who traditionally did not have the right to transfer or acquire land. This land evolution is linked to the very nature of land purchases: a personal acquisition, 'thanks to his/her own efforts'.

III. LOCAL *CADASTRES* AND CONTRACTS

Some persons are frequently called upon to attend as witnesses, secretaries or lineage heads (*mukuru w'umuryango*) and be 'responsible for ten households' (*nymba cumi*) in land transactions, as they have been chosen for their ability to judge and 'resolve conflicts'. These people who know how to write often keep a small exercise book in which the main elements of a transaction or conflict are noted. These notes are reminders in cases of disputes or conflicts. This custom of recording the contents of a land conflict or a transaction in a notebook is a result, first, of directives given to members of the administration who are part of the cell committee. They are instructed to write down on paper the contents of a discussion – for instance, during a conflict – and how it was dealt with at the local level in order to form the basis at a higher level (judicial or administrative). However, this practice has been taken over by other inhabitants who frequently assist in disputes or palavers, using their notes as a guide. These informal notes on transactions thus constitute the first '*cadastres*' of transferred plots of land. They serve as a reminder and provide some security when there are numerous and frequent land transactions and conflicts; about 45 per cent of all conflicts are directly related to land [*André and Platteau, 1998: 30*].

The first '*cadastres*' detail systematically all monetary and non-monetary permanent land transfers, of which inheritances alone accounted for 53 per cent of land acquisitions in 1993. Only a few written records are in existence which retrace successions and shares attributed to children, even if some households have taken care to measure the plots of land they have inherited and written down plot measurements. This is not a widespread practice and the conflicts regarding land boundaries remain considerable.

Initial purchases sought to guarantee those rights threatened under the *ubukonde* land system, and the first *cadastres* were elaborated to allow for, in cases of conflict, the introduction of elements facilitating conflict resolution or to reduce the uncertainties associated with land transfer. These innovations, however, do not always prevent land disputes. An analysis nevertheless shows that land disputes fall mainly into three categories: over successions, the type of former land transactions and land boundaries. Conflicts do not *per se* relate to land contracts themselves or the notes made in *cadastres*, but rather the shortcomings of these innovations or uncertainties linked to the complexity of the land situation and resulting social tensions.

Land boundary disputes (between 29 and 33 per cent of land conflicts) highlight the defects of land contracts and the absence of a systematic and precise measurement system for transferred lands. In fact, the measurements and boundaries of plots of land are only sketched and approximate in a majority of land transactions, compared with the complexity of shape of the plots of land. The plots of land subject to temporary transactions are never measured (for the person holding the definitive rights to the plot of land retains measurements and sketches), while inherited lands are neither systematically measured nor measurements systematically written down. Moreover, succession disputes remain extremely significant due to the divisions themselves and the difficulties experienced when conducting successions in a context of growing pressure on and scarcity of land (succession disputes account for between 40 and 45 per cent of all land disputes). Finally, even if land contracts almost systematically detail market sales transactions, other transactions are not written down, thus forming the basis for disputes. Hence, on the contrary, one can confirm that the land contracts and the initial *cadastres* reduce uncertainties linked to a series of contracts. However, these innovations only cover the totality of land transactions in an imperfect and non-systematic manner.

IV. INFORMAL FORMALISATION OF THE CONTRACT: AN ADMINISTRATIVE CUSTOM

There were an increasing number of land transactions. The land situation on a hill was increasingly complex and conflicts were becoming harder to settle by customary land authorities at the local level [*André, 1996*]. Communal records were a complementary means of security *vis-à-vis* local procedures, but on the other hand, some persons who frequently served as witnesses, as well as the lineage chiefs, preferred systematically to record transfers and land disputes.

Thirteen contracts mentioned that a 'receipt' from the commune was attached, or one out of ten contracts on average. Three households in the sample recorded their land purchases with the commune and had a 'receipt' for this. For those individuals who had taken this step of recording their sales transaction, this receipt represented an additional security for their land rights. Legally speaking, however, the receipt is of little value.

In order to understand this, let us look once again at the current land legislation. As noted in the introduction, the customary land system (non-coded and unwritten, in complete evolution and under pressure from strong individualistic and exclusive tensions) governed rural lands and coexisted with a system of written law that recognised private property of lands registered and located in urban areas.

In order to escape from this dualism, the 1960 decree made provision for land registration procedures that offered everyone the possibility of the right to private property, but without imposing it. However, measures to implement this decree, thus allowing the conversion of customary occupation rights into property rights have never been taken and have remained at the level of draft [*Ruhashyankiko, 1985: 10–17*].[7] Hence, the 'recording' procedure has never been adopted. Thus, at the local level, the 'receipts' issued by communes are not based on a legal (registration) procedure but seem rather an 'administrative custom' [*Gasasira, 1993: 58*] developed at the level of communal administration. These communes meet a need at the local level to grant an administrative authority some competence in the area of management and transfer of communal lands, and a ministerial directive sets out the procedure to be followed. However, this directive is not legally recognised but 'as a result of its impact, individuals view it as being equivalent to a given custom, recognised by everyone' [*Gasasira, 1993:60*]. An affidavit issued by communal authority looks as follows:

FIGURE 1

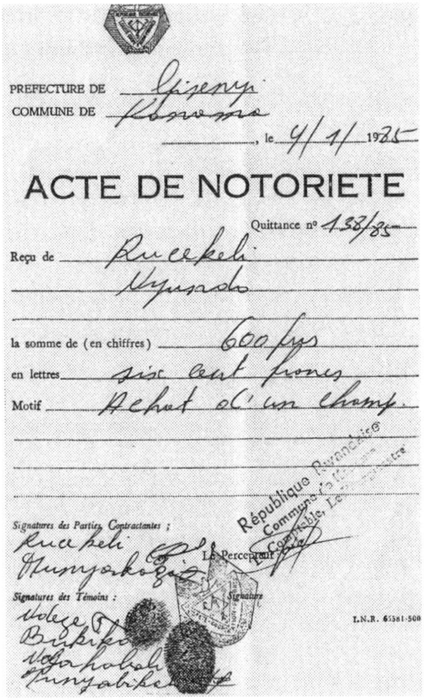

PREFECTURE DE Gisenyi

COMMUNE DE

, le 4/1/1985

ACTE DE NOTORIETE

Quittance nº 138/85

Reçu de

la somme de (en chiffres) 600 frs

en lettres six cent francs

Motif Achat d'un champ.

République Rwandaise

Signatures des Parties Contractantes :

Le Percepteur

Signatures des Témoins :

Signature

I.N.R. 65561-500

As emphasised, this affidavit has no legal status or impact. Moreover, the information it contains is too vague to be legally defended to third parties. Finally, this administrative custom contradicts the law: despite the legal interdiction to purchase or sell land (except in very specific cases set out in the statutory order of 1976), the communal administration 'records' purchases and, above all, communal land transactions which are legally inalienable! Is this an administrative contradiction or the informal formalisation of sales contracts [*Mathieu, 1999: 26–7; 2001*]? As highlighted by Mathieu and Gasasira, it is effectively a local administrative custom and procedure that offers a means of informally formalising the sales contracts (and other transfers) as attested to by the effects produced at the local level. In fact, individuals view the affidavit as a 'registration' at the communal level that gives them additional guarantee or security *vis-à-vis* their land rights for the plot of land purchased.

In which cases do households 'register' their purchase at the commune? First, as foreseen in the ministerial directive, when it concerns a plot of communal land (for example, a plot where tea is planted or another 'empty' communal plot of land managed and allocated by the commune).[8] Next, when

it concerns a plot of land which was the subject of a conflict at the communal
level (court of the canton) or when the verdict of the tribunal implied a land
redistribution in the presence of a communal authority as seen in the following
case:

> Yvette, the legitimate and legally married wife did not accept her
> husband's polygamy. Following the advice and with the support of the
> advisor of the sector, she demands divorce and the separation of goods
> according to the due process of written law. She was granted some of her
> husband's fields as 'alimony'. Subsequent to the verdict passed by the
> tribunal, the commune began measuring some of the husband's lands and
> recorded them in Yvette's name. Since then, she holds personal/
> individual rights to the plots of land recorded in her name and recognised
> by the commune.

Some individuals resort to the administrative procedure either because the
rights with regard to the plot of land are being or could be disputed, or because
these individuals feel they are in a weak position socially, aware of being so
and thus cannot resort to social protection at the local level. For these persons,
the affidavit represents complementary security for their rights and an
alternative to the local means of security (namely through contracts, relations,
networks, etc.) as seen in the following example:

> Vénuste came 'on his mother's back'. His rights to land have been
> contested by his maternal uncles. They had welcomed his mother back
> when she was separated, had given her a plot of land, and, consequently
> had welcomed the child into the lineage. However, on the death of
> Vénuste's mother at the beginning of the 1960s, the head of the lineage,
> a direct relative, sought to take back two plots of land that had been
> accorded to the daughter of the lineage. The latter cited reasons
> regarding this kind of old transaction made with a girl of the lineage and
> the recognised rights that her son possessed: was this a grant which the
> head of the lineage had the right to recall (*ubukonde* principle of the land
> system)?

Was this a grant or a 'definitive' transfer over which the successors had rights?
To which rights could Vénuste lay claim with regard to these plots of land? As
an illegitimate child or recognised as having been raised in the lineage, is he
entitled to land from the maternal lineage?

Today, he can only guarantee his rights to the disputed plots of land by re-
purchasing them and 'registering' them at the commune; this would provide
some kind of legal proof, a way of ensuring his access and occupation rights,
contested by certain 'ancient' customary principles also within his social
group. The re-purchase of these lands would enable him to record his rights in

a transaction register recognised by custom, while their registration at the commune would provide complementary security outside the networks of local land management.

This, however, is a costly procedure (1,000 Rwandan francs in 1990), or one-seventh the monthly average salary. Consequently, only those persons with a relatively high salary would have the possibility of 'registering' their lands. Furthermore, it would also seem that individuals who record their plots of land are 'informed' and up-to-date regarding the procedure, and have links with persons working in the administration. These three criteria (uncertainties linked to their land rights, the ability to assume the cost of the procedure and links with the administrative network) all seem to be present in the cases of those households for which we are in possession of a copy of the affidavit. For the other households which we know have recorded their plots of land at the commune, one of the criteria is seen to be more important than the other.

V. CONCLUSIONS: LOCAL INNOVATIONS AND ADMINISTRATIVE CUSTOM TO SECURE LAND TRANSFERS

Local and institutional changes are endogenous, originate at grass-roots level, are unsupervised but consistent in form. Such solutions are born out of the need for security of monetary land transactions. At the local level, land contracts cover mainly land sales (92 per cent of land contracts) while contracts are rarely drawn up for non-monetary transactions (four per cent concerning gifts and exchanges). There is not a single contract covering successions.

Purchases have multiplied in order to meet the increasing demand for more secure individual rights in a context where off-farm employment has developed very rapidly between the 1970s and the 1990s, and the *ubukonde* land tenure system has generated increasing uncertainty with regard to access to land, notably for land tenants (through the abuse of land retention rights of lineage heads over their land tenants and so on) and at a time when missions expelled the occupants from their lands. Only those households which had sufficient monetary income were able to purchase lands and impose individual rights. Private, exclusive and individual rights were clearly applicable to purchased lands, and this is confirmed in the land contracts. Purchased lands were exempt not only from lineage control but also the claims of other lineage members (obligation to divide up among the sons, grants and redistribution linked to social obligations and so forth.)

Lands have a special status because they are deemed to be the fruit of external remunerated employment acquired through 'one's own efforts'. The share of lands purchased out of the total land patrimony may be used as a 'pension fund' and re-sold little by little to cope with the 'old age' needs. Likewise, in the event of a husband's death, these purchased lands may revert to the widow, who is then free to use them without having to consult her sons or other lineage members, in contrast to inherited lineage lands over which the sons retain control. Thus, the women who traditionally only had usufructuary rights on lineage lands, now have individual and exclusive exploitation rights. Women may acquire lands in their own name once they have sources of income and sufficient monetary means to purchase them.

Monetary transactions are developing very rapidly even if inheritance remains the principal mode of land acquisition. Land contracts comprise a series of old elements, to which other new features have been added to meet the needs of specification and that of remembering, which is linked to the complexity of the land situation and increasing land division. The first local *cadastres* made their appearance during the 1970s, systematically recording monetary and non-monetary land transactions as well as disputes, which were retained not only by administrative authorities but also, informally, by lineage ones. One can henceforth confirm that local innovations appeared in response to local needs, to reduce some uncertainties, contribute specifications and ensure land transfers.

Monetary transactions, particularly purchases, were introduced to secure access rights that were threatened under the old system, and to offer individual rights to persons who acquired land. Written land contracts were used to secure rights resulting from these new transactions. Monetary transactions also played the role of allowing emerging individual rights, while written land contracts secured land transactions.

Monetary transactions were also born in 'the shadow of the law' [*Hesseling, 1992*]. While the state partially supported the claims of individuals in the 1960s and granted individual exploitation rights to a group of occupants of rural lands in conformity with the claims for individual rights for some categories of persons (mainly land tenants), from 1976 it prohibited sales and failed to impose land registration and the conversion of customary land rights and rights to private property. However, in the case of Rwanda, there was such a pressing need for secure land transfers at the administrative level, that the administrative authorities invested a custom facilitating 'the informal formalisation' [*Mathieu, 1999; 26–7, 2001*] of land transfers.

In fact, if the market had developed to secure the rights of some categories of persons excluded from land, it had also caused the exclusion and marginalisation of some categories, via the process of distress sales. The market induced unequal division which benefited a class of peasants having regular off-farm income to the detriment of those with none [*André and Platteau, 1998: 21–7*]. The market also led to more inequality. In fact, 67 per cent of all land sales were distress sales. The rapid loss of lands via this pauperisation engendered the creation of a 'landless' class. Within the space of five years, the proportion of landless or near landless households increased from 29 per cent in 1988 to 37 per cent in 1993.

These processes of individualisation and monetarisation of land rights engendered inequalities, resulting in marginalised access to land and the increased and rapid impoverishment of the population, consequently jeopardising their very existence. The scarcity and inequality of steady off-farm income gave rise to unequal land accumulation and helped to fuel the 'distress sales' process. Rwanda is characterised by the lack of economic alternatives outside agriculture, while the technological and institutional responses of agrarian systems in the light of this strong and rapid demographic growth are inadequate. André and Platteau [*1998*] examine this idea in great detail and describe the 'Malthusian trap' which, in the case of Rwanda, is translated into conflict, violence and the erosion of 'social capital'. Changes in the wealth structure as well as that of non-legitimised social relations engender extremely significant social tensions.

If these innovations were able to prevent certain types of conflicts and substantially reduce existing uncertainty on some types of rights, they have effectively failed to reduce, in the long term, the conflicts and socio-economic tensions caused by monetarisation, the increasing land shortage (due mainly to the strong population growth which reached 3.7 per cent in 1993) and individualistic pressures on inherited lands. In other words, local and institutional innovations help to prevent and resolve some kinds of conflict linked mainly to land sales, but not those linked to the widespread impoverishment process, increasing individualisation of, and exclusion from, land, rapid socio-economic changes and the destruction of the social fabric.

NOTES

1. The first field study carried out during the year 1988 and the processing of data collected in 1988 were financed by the University of Namur. The second field study (in 1993) was financed by the Musée Royal de l'Afrique Centrale (MRAC) of Tervuren, Belgium within the framework of a co-operation project between the Institut de Recherche Scientifique et Technique (IRST), Butare, Rwanda, and the MRAC (coordinator: Danielle de Lame).
2. In 1907, a mission of white priests settled in the region surveyed and appropriated lineage lands by eviction. The dispossessed were forced either to acquire land under the clientele system or from relatives, or to purchase surrounding lands.
3. As 65 per cent of all sales are distress sales, one can confirm that the urgency of cash need will be a determining factor in setting the price [*André and Platteau, 1998: 25*].
4. Sometimes family ties may influence the price of a plot of land downward. However, land scarcity and the need for land are so important that this criteria may be, but not always, a factor. So great is the demand for land that some family norms are no longer respected or valid. Furthermore, it is extremely unusual that a seller will have the financial means to repurchase the land from the relative to whom he had sold it.
5. To give an idea of the 'need to remember' which is representative of the multiplication and acceleration of land transfers, here are some illustrations: in 1993 I conducted a survey of 87 households in an administrative unit comprising 124 households. I noted 341 plots of land purchased out of a total of 871 plots owned whether definitively or temporarily (about ten per household). See André and Platteau [*1998: 20*].
6. Purchases and sales exceeding a certain area pose problems in respect of controlling the plot of land (with the accrued risk of stolen harvests, etc.). Henceforth, land transfers were restricted to certain geographic and social areas.

7. And this, for several reasons, given the complexity and stakes that land represents in Rwanda, of a political, social and economic nature.
8. An important contraction also appears here with regard to the recording of the purchase of a tea plantation: as with all state plots of land, it could be allocated by the competent communal authority, but the lands managed by the communal administration, including the swampy lands reserved for tea cultivation, are the property of the state, the cultivation of which is transferred to individuals but are inalienable. In our sample, we have an affidavit certifying the transfer and purchase of a tea plot.

REFERENCES

Adriaenssens J., 1962, *Le droit foncier au Rwanda* (publisher unknown).

André, C., 1996, 'Accès et occupation des terres dans le nord-ouest du Rwanda', in P. Mathieu, P.-J. Laurent and J.-C. Willame, 'Démocratie, enjeux fonciers et pratiques locales en Afrique. Conflits, gouvernance et turbulences en Afrique de l'Ouest et centrale', *Cahiers africains*, no.23–24, pp.202–13.

André C. and J.-P. Platteau, 1998, 'Land Relations under Unbearable Stress: Rwanda Caught in the Malthusian Trap', *Journal of Economic Behaviour and Organization*, Vol.34, Feb., pp.1–47.

André, C. and P. Lavigne Delville, 1998, 'Changements fonciers et dynamiques agraires. Le Rwanda, 1900–1990', in P. Lavigne Delville *Quelles politiques foncières pour l'Afrique rurale? Réconcilier pratiques, légitimité et légalité*, Paris: Karthala, pp.157–62.

Gasasira, E., 1993, 'Droits des biens et droit agraire', *Manuel de droit rwandais*, no.5, Kigali: Pinterset.

Hesseling, G., 1992, *Pratiques foncières à l'ombre du droit. L'application du droit foncier urbain à Ziguinchor, Sénégal*, Leiden: African Studies Center.

Mathieu, P., 1999, 'Les paysans, la terre, l'Etat et le marché: sécurisation et formalisation endogène des transactions foncières en Afrique', in P. Lavigne Delville and P. Mathueu (eds.), *Formalisation des contrats et des transactions. Repérage des pratiques populaires d'usage de l'écrit dans les transactions foncières en Afrique rurale*, Paris: Louvain-La-Neuve, GRET, IED, pp.14–31.

Mathieu, P., 2001, 'Transactions informelles et marchés fonciers émergents en Afrique', in T. Benjaminsen and C. Lund (eds.), *Politics, Property and Production in the West African Sahel: Understanding Natural Resources Management*, Uppsala: Nordic Africa Institute, pp.22–39.

Reidsdorff, I., 1952, *Enquêtes foncières au Rwanda*, s.l., s.e., cartes, multigraph.

Ruhashyankiko, N., 1985, 'Réflexions de quelques aspects du problème foncier au Rwanda', *Revue juridique du Rwanda*, no.1, Jan.

Index

André, C. 171
accompanying transactions 121
administrative certificate 100
administrative custom 166, 169
adversarial principles 66ff.
ambiguous transactions 115ff., 157
arbitration authority 92
arrêté d'attribution 120
articulation of norms 17
attestation de notoriété 98
attêté d'attribution 120
autochtonous peasants 109

Bambara 132
Banwa district 113
Basserie, V. 103
Bena 72
Bentzon, A. 54ff.
Berry, S. 28, 71
Blundo, G. 102
Bohannan, P. 137
borrowed land 75
bricoleurs 16
British Common Law 34
bureaucratic institutions 13, 19
Burkina Faso 97ff.

Cadastres 164–5
cash-based land transactions 91
Catchment Councils 37ff.
cattle militia, *see Sungusungu*
Centre for Applied Social Sciences (CASS) 37
certificates 91, 95 (*see also* paper)
certificats de notoriété 95
certificats de palabre 97, 102
Charnley, S. 58ff.
Chauveau, J.-P. 103
Cleaver, F. 53, 60, 66
CMDT (Companie Malienne pour le Développement des Textiles) 130
Code Civil 134
Code domanial et foncier 134
Code forestier 134–5
commercial transactions 76, 93, 99, 109, 114
Committees for the Defence of the Revolution (Burkina Faso) 123
commoditisation 126
conditional long-term grant 117

conflict avoidance 25 *see also* disputes over land
conflict mitigation 67
contracts 95, 96ff., 154 *see also* paper
Convention of the Rights of the Child 31
cotton cultivation 112, 122, 129ff.
cotton provinces (Burkina Faso) 109ff.
cotton strike 131
cotton zone (Mali) 129
Cousins, B. 53ff., 66
Covenant on Social, Economic and Cultural Rights 31
crafting institutions, 12
crop-share contracts 93
customary land rights 74, 78, 89
customary land transactions 133

Dalton, G. 137
decentralisation 134
deeds 52
Department of Water Development (Zimbabwe) 40
derived rights 93
disputes over land 115 *see also* conflict avoidance, conflict mitigation
District Development Funds (Zimbabwe) 37, 40
District Irrigation Officer 68
District Land Officer 68
documentation, 91
double safeguards 77ff.
Douglas, M. 15ff
Dublin Principles 32

Edja, H. 101
embedded institutions 14
enforcement 53
erosion of customary norms 137
ethnic groups 58
euphemism 93–4
Evolutionary Theory of Land Rights 9, 89, 126, 147
exclusion 19, 80ff.
expropriation as price depressant 148
expropriation 142

forest code 134–5
formal law 134
formal rights 52, 53ff., 77

Titles of Related Interest

Economic Mobility and Poverty Dynamics in Developing Countries

Bob Baulch, *Institute of Development Studies at the University of Sussex* and **John Hoddinott,** *International Food Policy Research Institute* (Eds)

This book takes issue with the popular perception that poverty in developing countries is a structural long-term phenomenon. It demonstrates that evidence from the relatively small number of longitudinal household surveys conducted in these and other countries shows that considerable numbers of households move in and out of poverty from one year to the next. It also shows there is considerable economic mobility elsewhere in the income distribution.

This collection assembles six country studies which use household panel data to examine these issues. One set of these analyses – based on panel data from China, Ethiopia, Pakistan and South Africa – looks at short-run poverty dynamics. A second set, drawing on household panel data from Chile and Zimbabwe, examines determinants of long-term economic mobility over periods of 14 years or more.

192 pages 2000
0 7146 5131 1 cloth
0 7146 8154 7 paper
A special issue of The Journal of Development Studies

FRANK CASS PUBLISHERS
Crown House, 47 Chase Side, Southgate, London N14 5BP
Tel: +44 (0)20 8920 2100 Fax: +44 (0)20 8447 8548 E-mail: info@frankcass.com
NORTH AMERICA
5824 NE Hassalo Street, Portland, OR 97213 3644, USA
Tel: 800 944 6190 Fax: 503 280 8832 E-mail: cass@isbs.com
Website: www.frankcass.com

Labour Mobility and Rural Society

Arjan de Haan, *Department for International Development* and
Ben Rogaly, *University of East Anglia* (Eds)

Most books about migration are concerned with a long-term or permanent
rival to urban mobility. In contrast, this study illustrates the dynamics behind
the much more common movements made by poor people in South and
Southeast Asia and Africa. Consisting of seven pieces of detailed analyses
drawn from recent research carried out by the contributors, it focuses
specifically on the idea of migration for short-term employment, often in
rural areas, showing how labour migration is a social process, structured by
such issues as gender, class and ethnicity.

208 pages 2002
0 7146 5334 9 cloth
A special issue of The Journal of Development Studies

FRANK CASS PUBLISHERS
Crown House, 47 Chase Side, Southgate, London N14 5BP
Tel: +44 (0)20 8920 2100 Fax: +44 (0)20 8447 8548 E-mail: info@frankcass.com
NORTH AMERICA
5824 NE Hassalo Street, Portland, OR 97213 3644, USA
Tel: 800 944 6190 Fax: 503 280 8832 E-mail: cass@isbs.com
Website: www.frankcass.com

Globalisation and Trade
Implications for Exports from Marginalised Economies

Oliver Morrissey, *University of Nottingham* and
Igor Filatotchev, *Birkbeck College, University of London* (Eds)

Many countries, mostly poor developing or transitional economies, appear not to be benefiting from the expansion in the international trade associated with globalisation. Most of these economies have been implementing the economic policy reforms, especially trade liberalisation, predicted to help them share in globalisation. Nevertheless, the growth response of exports has been slow. A four-year 'Trade and Enterprise Research Programme' financed by DfID examined possible explanations for this slow export supply response. The various projects explored some of the obstacles and opportunities to increasing exports from countries in sub-Saharan Africa (SSA) and the former Soviet Union (FSU). Important findings have emphasised the need to invest in labour productivity and improved infrastructure, the importance of ownership and management structures, and the role of global buyers and distribution networks. The papers collected in this volume report the results of research on these issues.

224 pages 2001
0 7146 5159 1 cloth
A special issue of The Journal of Development Studies

FRANK CASS PUBLISHERS
Crown House, 47 Chase Side, Southgate, London N14 5BP
Tel: +44 (0)20 8920 2100 Fax: +44 (0)20 8447 8548 E-mail: info@frankcass.com
NORTH AMERICA
5824 NE Hassalo Street, Portland, OR 97213 3644, USA
Tel: 800 944 6190 Fax: 503 280 8832 E-mail: cass@isbs.com
Website: www.frankcass.com

Changing the Conditions for Development Aid

A New Paradigm?

Niels Hermes and **Robert Lensink,** *both at the University of* Groningen (Eds)

> 'Recommended to all involved in the debate on aid allocation and aid effectiveness.'
>
> **Development Policy Review**

In 1998 the World Bank published a report entitled 'Assessing Aid: What Works, What Doesn't, and Why'. This report has led to heated debates, both among academics and policy-makers, about development aid and aid policies. Many have questioned the methodology used, the results and the policy conclusions of the report. This book contributes to the ongoing discussion about the future of development aid. In particular, it re-examines a number of issues that are crucial to the analysis and to the conclusions of the World Bank report.

160 pages 2001
0 7146 5241 5 cloth
A special issue of The Journal of Development Studies

FRANK CASS PUBLISHERS
Crown House, 47 Chase Side, Southgate, London N14 5BP
Tel: +44 (0)20 8920 2100 Fax: +44 (0)20 8447 8548 E-mail: info@frankcass.com
NORTH AMERICA
5824 NE Hassalo Street, Portland, OR 97213 3644, USA
Tel: 800 944 6190 Fax: 503 280 8832 E-mail: cass@isbs.com
Website: www.frankcass.com